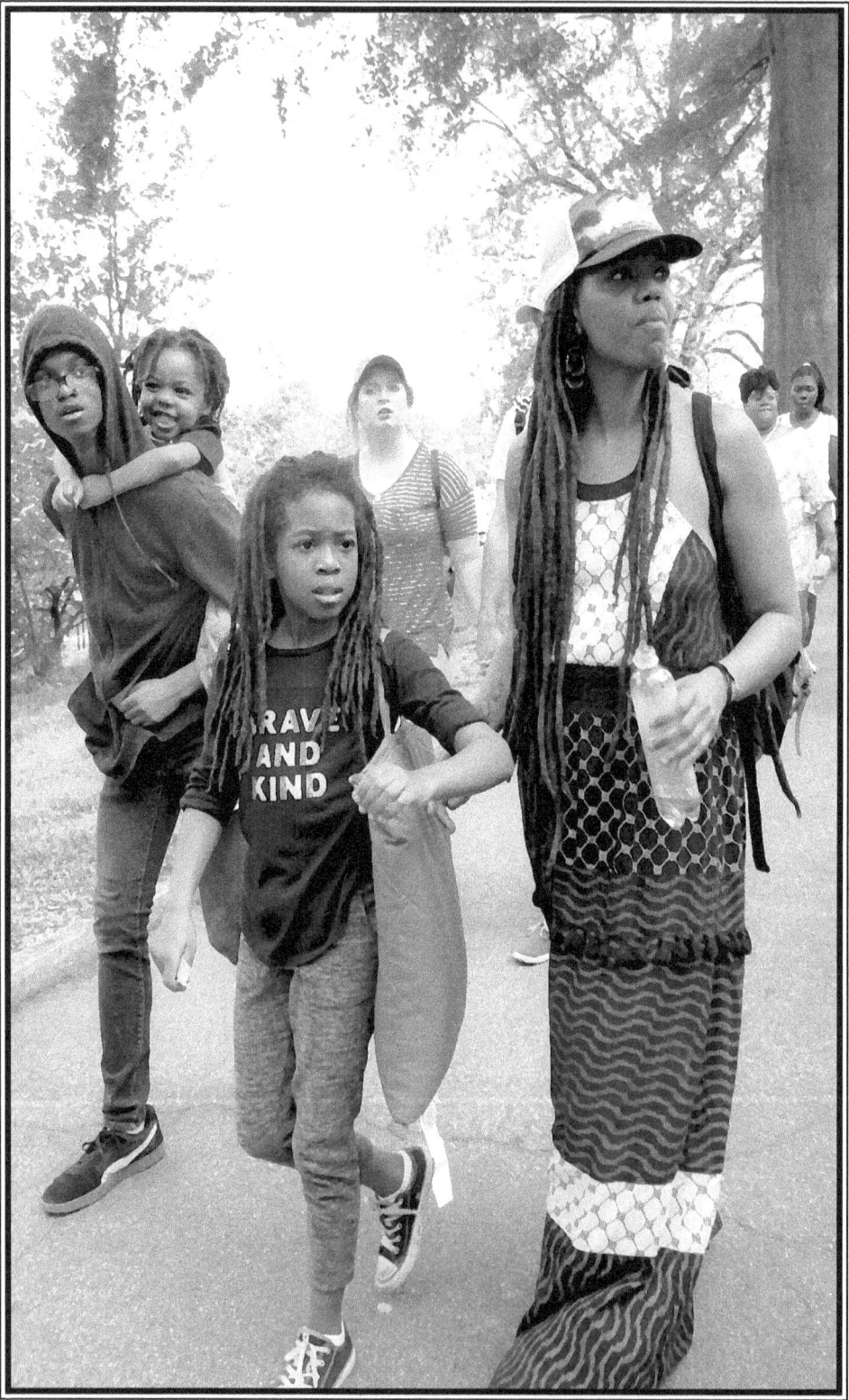

RE-CREATING
OUR COMMON CHORD

WISING UP ANTHOLOGIES

ILLNESS & GRACE, TERROR & TRANSFORMATION

FAMILIES: *The Frontline of Pluralism*

LOVE AFTER 70

DOUBLE LIVES, REINVENTION & THOSE WE
LEAVE BEHIND

VIEW FROM THE BED: VIEW FROM THE BEDSIDE

SHIFTING BALANCE SHEETS:
Women's Stories of Naturalized Citizenship & Cultural Attachment

COMPLEX ALLEGIANCES:
Constellations of Immigration, Citizenship, & Belonging

DARING TO REPAIR:
What Is It, Who Does It & Why?

CONNECTED:
What Remains As We All Change

CREATIVITY & CONSTRAINT

SIBLINGS: *Our First Macrocosm*

THE KINDNESS OF STRANGERS

SURPRISED BY JOY

CROSSING CLASS: *The Invisible Wall*

RE-CREATING
OUR COMMON CHORD

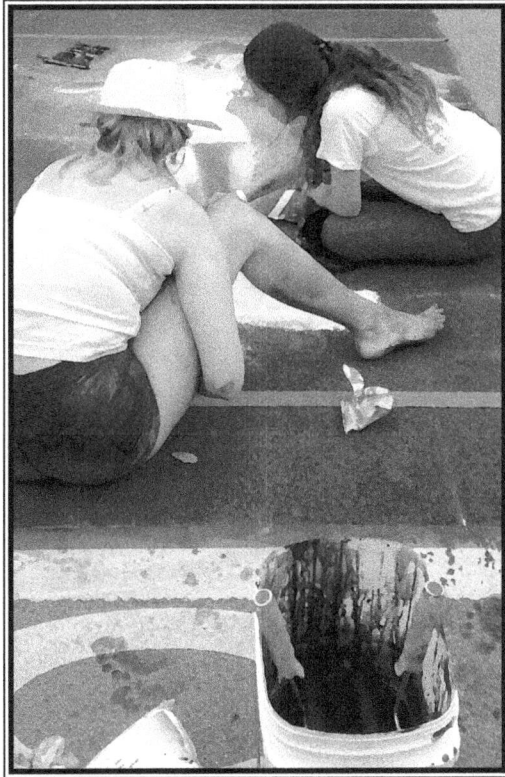

Heather Tosteson & Charles D. Brockett
Editors

Wising Up Press

Wising Up Press
P.O. Box 2122
Decatur, GA 30031-2122
www.universaltable.org

Catalogue-in-Publication data is on file with the Library of Congress.
LCCN: 2019949023

Wising Up ISBN: 978-1-7324514-4-5

For each—and all—of *US*

and our capacity to create and recreate

a common chord,

whose many distinct notes

sounded together

form the basis of harmony

and can lift all our souls

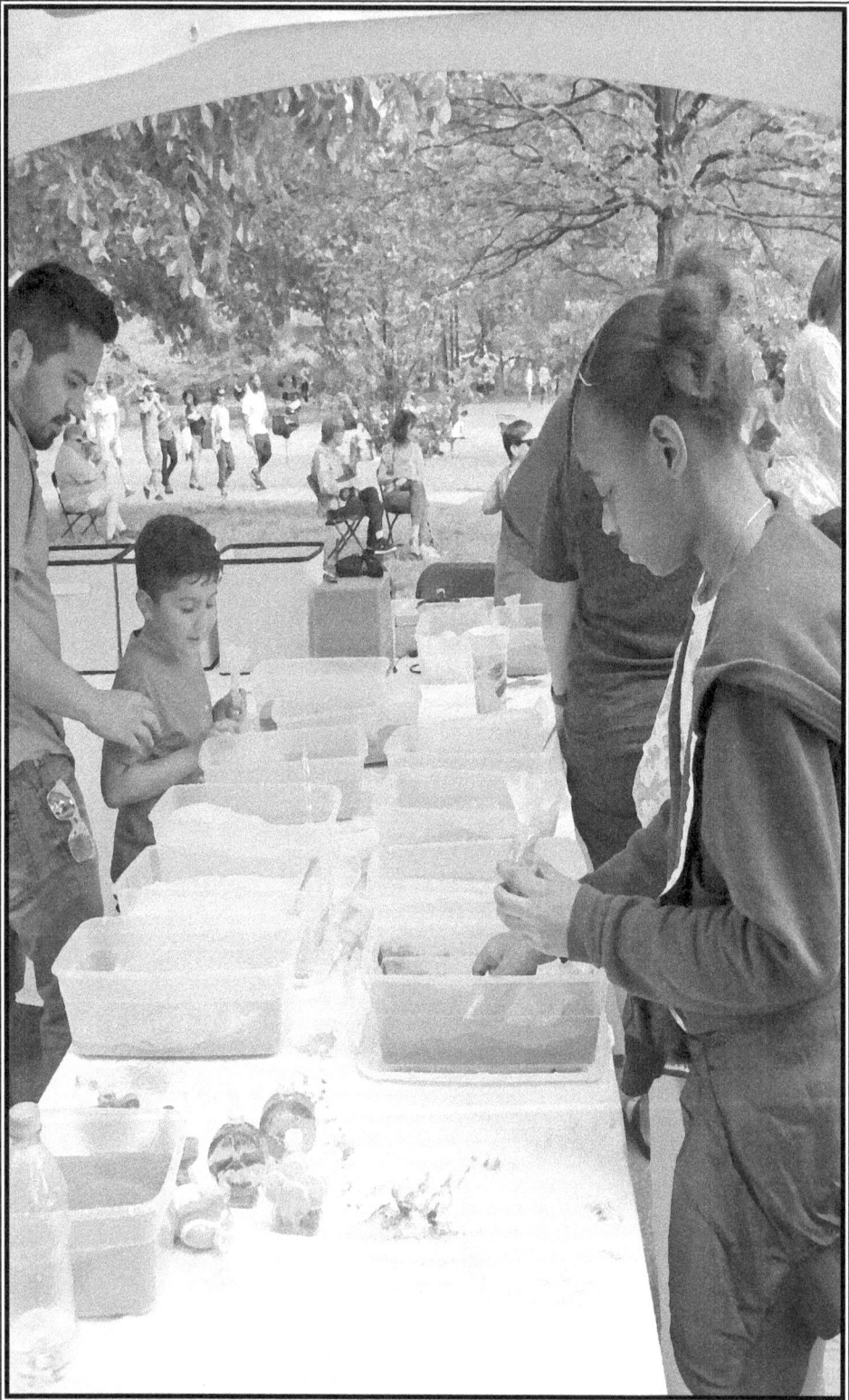

CONTENTS

INTRODUCTION

HEATHER TOSTESON

I. CULTURE/NATIONS

JUDITH GILLE

J.O. HASELHOEF

MARYAH CONVERSE

EVE MILLS ALLEN

THOMAS ABAKAH

LORETTA DIANE WALKER

II. CLASS

BONNI CHALKIN

MIMI JENNINGS

SHARON LASK MUNSON

LAURIE KLEIN

TYREE WILSON

III. CRIMINAL JUSTICE

HEATHER TOSTESON

IV. RELIGION

V. RACE

VI. POLITICS

INTRODUCTION

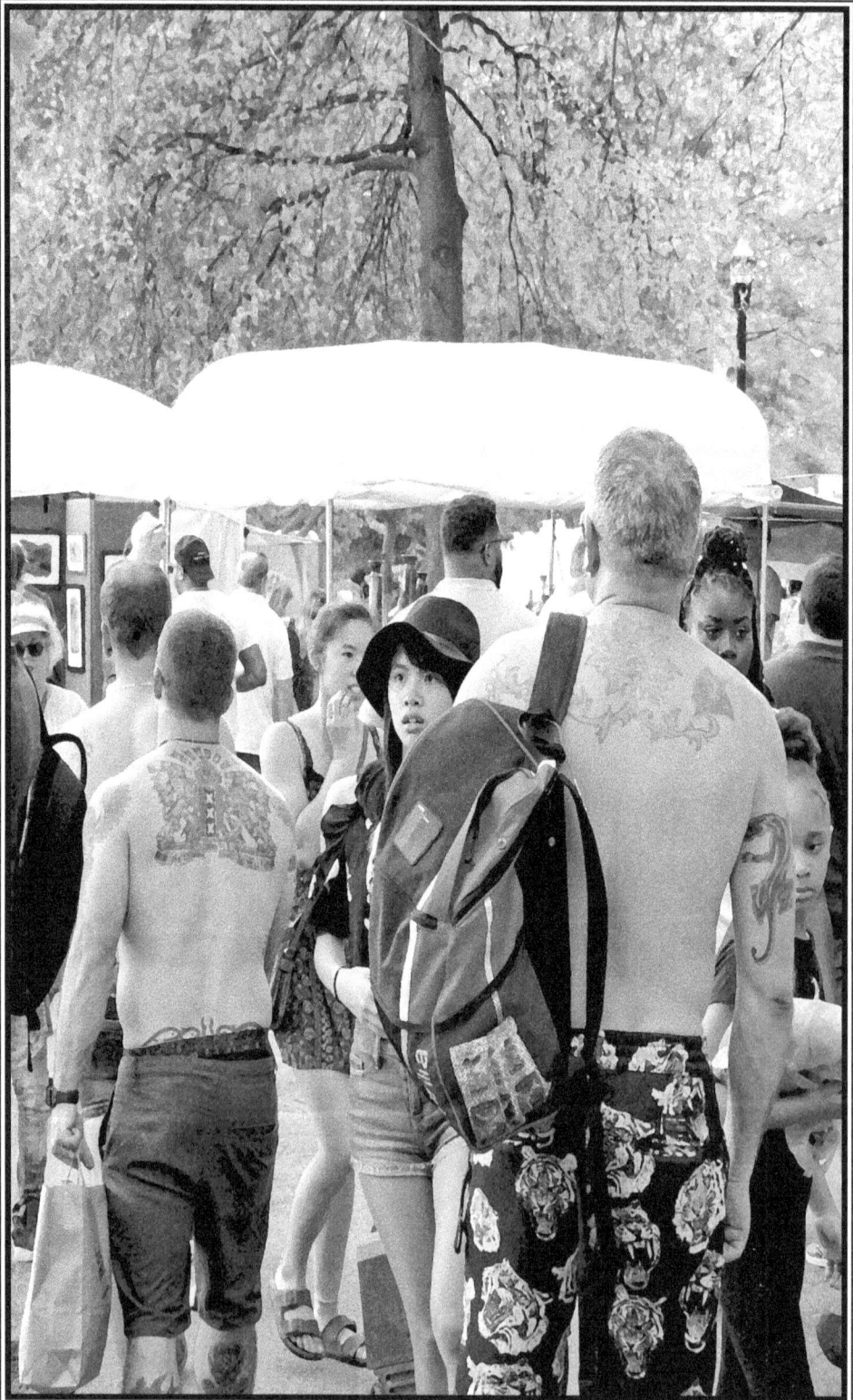

HEATHER TOSTESON

RE-CREATING OUR COMMON CHORD
What It Requires of Each of Us

Some claim that not since the Civil War has our country been as polarized and divided as it is now. It's certainly true that, as fellow citizens, we are in great need of finding a way back to a fundamental respect for each other and a way forward that makes us feel that belonging to this country—with all its competing visions, loyalties, and priorities—holds enough good for us and for people like us that we genuinely want to be part of it and to do what is needed to sustain its promise.

I don't know about you, but there are many days I wonder whether it's possible. But I can't contemplate the alternatives either. As someone who has a commitment to diversity that is over-determined by temperament, repeated experiences as an outsider, and raw yearning, I am horrified by how deeply I am part of the problem. I hate it, but more days than I like to admit, I can't stop myself from joining, at least internally, in what is clearly a vicious cycle.

Which is why I've asked for help in the form of this anthology so that we can together identify ways in which we are already participating in more virtuous cycles. What are the small steps we're discovering—despite inner turbulence and reactivity—that can draw us back together, help us start building social trust instead of tearing it down? I'm very concrete about this. This isn't about vague intentions. I want to identify ideas, words, gestures, sustained attitudes and actions we can put into practice right now to help us.

This essay begins with various ideas that have helped me in the last few years keep my feelings in check—and ends in story, the real testing ground, where the heart evaluates the mind's sufficiency by opening or closing. If the ideas feel too ponderous, skip to the story, which is the emotional landscape in which I believe many of us find ourselves these days. Then, if you're so inclined, revisit some of the ideas I share here and see if any of them serve for you as they have for me—much needed, but momentary, stays against confusion.

WHY WE'RE SO POLARIZED

It's not as if this happened all at once. The election of an intentionally polarizing president certainly has accelerated—or made indisputable—the reality. But he's a manifestation, an exacerbation, not the cause. Even if he serves only one term, the polarization will remain. The polarization is *US*.

There are many reasons why we have come to such adamant differences of belief, many centrifugal forces that perpetuate and intensify them. The social psychologist Jonathan Haidt, in his article "The Age of Outrage," begins his explanation with our species, that as tribal primates we are "exquisitely designed and adapted by evolution for life in small societies . . . and violent intergroup conflict over territory." In other words, *not* for large, diverse democracies. He lists additional, more proximal causes for the polarization: currently having no external common enemies, the divisive impact of media, immigration and diversity, Republicans in Washington (in 2017), and the left on university campuses. Other people identify geographic divisions as a major contributor, not just the divide between the economic conditions of the rust belt and coastal cities, but the great voluntary sort that has people all over the country choosing to live among those who share their perspectives and values. As we segregate—by world view or party affiliation or class as much as by race or culture—many of our presumptions and prejudices go unchallenged by direct face to face daily contact with different people and values. Unchallenged, our assumptions about each other abstract, intensify, harden. We forget we are *all* so much more complex—and interesting—than our *ideas* about each other.

My husband and I have participated in that great sort, since we live on the outskirts of a small town, Clarkston, that is described as the most culturally diverse square mile in the U.S. Its population is as different as you can imagine from the mansions in the northwest of Atlanta, the all-white suburbs farther to the north of us, the all-black ones to our south, the militia who gather in small towns to our east to protest a Muslim mosque. *My people,* I think driving to the library at the hour when the sidewalks are filled with school children returning home escorted by mothers in hijab or sarongs, men leaving the mosque in their long white tunics.

That *my* is a mixed blessing because group identity is distressingly tightly linked with group hostility. Think about sports fans, political rallies, social protests. This is the dark underside of belonging. The strength of our identification with a party or group will determine how *angry* we are at other groups, independent of the level of agreement we have with our party's positions, Thomas Edsall notes in an article exploring various explanations for the rise of authoritarianism in our country. That anger has an absolutizing quality to it, an unwillingness to tolerate difference or debate. The innate primate tribalism at its heart is stoked constantly by the polarizing and inciting quality of social media and journalism.

Polarization becomes pernicious when we begin to see other groups as essentially different from us, evaluating their motives in ways that bear no resemblance to our own. Arthur Brooks describes the motive attribution asymmetry in which we all seem to be engaging now in this way: "Each side thinks it is driven by benevolence, while the other is evil and motivated by hatred—and is therefore an enemy with whom one cannot negotiate or compromise." Most concerningly, he argues, these asymmetric attributions lead to contempt, "the feeling that a person or a thing is beneath consideration, worthless, or deserving scorn." That contempt has profound emotional, moral, social, and political consequences—to the one who feels it and to the one who is its object. Too often now, too many of us are both.

WHY POLARIZATION MATTERS:
THE FRAGILITY OF DEMOCRACY

The American experiment, which now seems so natural to us, is a thoroughly artificial device designed to counterbalance the natural impulses of group suspicions and hatreds.
E.D. Hirsch, *The Making of Americans*

Our innate tribalism can lead us to be ferocious and inequitable. Haidt notes that this danger was taken into account by our founders when creating a representative rather than a direct democracy. This is a form of democracy that must constantly be fine-tuned, and involves a conception of citizenship that isn't innate, it must be modeled, taught. In her book *Talking with Strangers: Anxieties of Citizenship Since Brown vs. Board of Education,* the political philosopher Danielle Allen echoes this idea, insisting that it is the main responsibility of democracy to promote the allegiance of all its citizens *in spite of* majority rule.

Published in 2004, Allen's book is both painfully relevant—and painfully dated in terms of the intensity of the dynamics of polarization she explores. She is specifically interested in how the rights and sacrifices of minorities, particularly the black minority, are acknowledged and incorporated into a healthy democracy. The reality is that with the intensification of identity politics in the last fifteen years, everyone feels like a maligned and helpless minority, and her observations about the disaffection of minorities have even broader relevance today. As does her emphasis on the critical role that social trust between citizens plays as a necessary counter-balance to group suspicions:

> *Trust in one's fellow citizens consists of the belief, simply, that one is safe with them. . . . When an election rolls round, citizens will cast a doubting eye on prospective representatives, but they can vote—that is, they can think it is reasonable to participate in public institutions—only if they trust that the effects of the votes of other citizens, combined with their own, will not produce their political oppression. . . . Citizens' distrust not of government but of each other leads the way to democratic disintegration.*

VICIOUS CYCLES: THE DYNAMICS OF EXCLUSION

Identity Politics: Identity politics, the growing tendency to create political allegiances out of group characteristics such as religion or race or class, has both positive and negative aspects. It can help people identify and join forces to combat powerful structural injustices that contradict the essential commitment of our democracy to equal dignity and opportunity. It can speak to the need to keep the allegiance of all, minorities as well as majorities, by acknowledging the costs of those injustices. On the other hand, it can also lead to asymmetric motive attribution, imputing malicious conscious intent on the part of people who benefit differentially. Haidt describes this distortion, which he attributes especially to the academic left, as "Anything that a group has that is good or valued is seen as a kind of privilege, which causes a kind of oppression in those who don't have it. . . . Every situation is to be analyzed in terms of the bad people acting to preserve their power and privilege over the good people."

Competing Definitions: Often large political and social conflicts come from very different definitions of the situations: Is this a climate crisis or variable weather? Structural injustice or a failure of individual initiative? About the essential vulnerability of fetuses or the physical autonomy of women?

How we define a situation is hypothetical, but it changes things concretely. As the sociologist W. I. Thomas, who advanced the concept years ago, referring in particular to our social need to have a shared definition in order to act coherently, emphasizes, if we "define situations as real, they are real in their consequences." If we define a situation as a crisis, we make it one.

The shifting demographics of our country mean that everyone at present is feeling vulnerable, unable to find a common definition of *our* situation. No one has the power to dominate, to unilaterally define the situation, but that is exactly what hyper-polarization and the contempt it inspires push us towards. When our norms are challenged, we all become more absolute, authoritarian. We *all* feel deeply misrepresented, misunderstood, anxious, alienated, angry, *retributive*. We want not only to preserve but to *impose* our norms—whether those norms are located in a more just future or more just past. Would we trust someone with a one-dimensional, negative, threat-based interpretation of our motives to define *our* situation, determine *our* future? Hell no!

One definition of the situation that *is* shared by hyper-partisans of both the right and the left now, I fear, is the belief that *their* interests as citizens will not be respected should anyone else become a majority. The real consequences of that belief are what we're seeing now. The norm they are both appealing to now is winner-take-all, no-holds-barred conflict. And it isn't pretty. And it feeds on itself, creating more contempt, more fear, more anger.

Threat and Affiliation: As a species we are very social. We attune with one another consciously and unconsciously through mirror neurons, synchronization of movements, theory of mind. We attach emotionally. We identify. We reciprocate. Affiliation is often a silent, tactile, sensory experience, one that exchanges proximity, shared gaze and shared focus for words. We pay more attention to what people do than what they say. We see ourselves in them and feel they do the same with us. We develop layers and layers of social trust, a deepening sense of belonging, using all of these dimensions of intimacy.

Unfortunately, we are profoundly retributive as well. How do we notice when, in any difference of opinion, we have slipped from a trust cycle to a *distrust/disdain/retribution* cycle? When and how and why do we otherize and dehumanize each other? When will we begin to see this shift as *our* deepest threat, individually and communally?

Threat-based Thought: When we become primed for threat, we rely on different parts of our brains. In some ways those differences map to the different sides of our brains, the different forms of our thought. Threatened, our brain flips into abstract, categorical thought. Even people's names become shorthand for categories: Obamite. Trumpian. Because it is the nature of categorical thought to *be* divisive, it is a very useful form of thought when we *feel* divisive. Categories are *meant* to be distinct. A fruit cannot be a vegetable. A friend cannot be a foe. Every concept has an opposite, an antonym, at every level. And when you activate one, you activate its opposite as well because that is what gives it meaning. Risk/Safety. Right/Left. Mine/Yours. Right/Wrong. Democracy/Authoritarianism. These divisions are rarely neutral. Threatened, we define *them* as not only different but also worse than *us*, we define *our* territory, *our* beliefs, we presume conflict, we make plans to defend ourselves. We define people by whether they will fight for us or against us.

Abstract thought is also innately hierarchical. Our concepts build on each other, and our systems of thought can quickly become self-referential, divorced from the life conditions that inspired them. Our lives are reduced to being exemplum for our ideas. It is also the nature of reasoning abstractly that ultimately you are arguing for *one* right, predictive answer. The mode of thought itself invites the autocratic.

Categories are more rigid when they are imposed rather than experientially derived, in other words when they are used as labels. If induced from experience, they have a provisional quality, a fluidity because they are accountable to experience rather than to a system of thought. For example, defining yourself as a Republican because you are like your mother or a Democrat because you are like your father is a much more interesting and mutable definition than defining yourself by your allegiance to a fixed ideological structure. Your real-life parents can change . . . so can you.

Threat-based Imagination: We *imagine* differently when we imagine threatening situations. Social media incites and feeds threat-based imagining. The stories we tell when in these states are qualitatively different. We see it in thrillers and action films. Survival, not understanding, is the goal. Our opponents have no redeeming qualities, no complexity of motives, no good intentions. When we shift into this mode, we become *like* the bad guys. Our motives become one-dimensional, often retributive. Our thinking becomes rigid. Reconciliation isn't possible in that state, only victory. Unfortunately, fear and anger and the stories they lead to are a dopamine high, a rush, and quickly become addictive.

ENCOURAGING VIRTUOUS CYCLES:
HOW WE CAN CHALLENGE POLARIZATION

Reconceptualizing Democracy

To reconceptualize how we think of our country and our government and our roles in them may help us find new ways to respond to each other. I share two ways of reconceptualizing our form of government that I've found helpful when I'm feeling beleaguered or bleak: one involves telling a different story, the other involves understanding our value preferences differently.

Sacrificial Democracy: Whole as Our Goal

Danielle Allen suggests that if we change our idea of the goal of country from being *One* to being *Whole,* our definiton of our situation as a democracy might change from one that defines homogeneity as success to one that considers what might be healthy for a "complex, intricate, and differentiated body." She also encourages us to think rather differently about how that complex, intricate body works.

Her ideas about the role of sacrifice in a democracy are particularly evocative and promising. The reality of political sacrifice is difficult to reconcile with an *idea* of democracy that claims its role is to permanently secure the good of all its people. She proposes instead an image of democracy as a constant rebalancing, a *sacrificial* rebalancing, in the service of the whole:

> *Democracy is not a static end state that achieves the common good by assuring the same benefits or the same level of benefits to everyone, but rather a political practice by which the diverse negative effects of collective political action, and even of just decisions, can be distributed equally, and constantly redistributed over time, on the basis of consensual interactions. The hard truth of democracy is that some citizens are always giving things up for others.*

How we as a country consciously incorporate this hard truth is core to our continuity and cohesion as a whole. The key step, she suggests is to honor sacrifice as a *gift to the whole,* thus starting a virtuous cycle of reciprocity:

> *Properly undertaken—with foreknowledge, consent, and the prospect of honor—a democratic sacrifice opens a covenant so those who benefit from the sacrifice see themselves as the recipients of a gift that they must not only honor but reciprocate. . . . Sacrifices draw people into networks of mutual obligation and in so doing have the capacity to rejuvenate political relationships.*

Our core role as *citizens* is to honor this oscillating sacrifice by each other, for each other. Part of that responsibility involves asking, "Who is sacrificing for whom? Is the sacrifice voluntary? Is it honored? Will the sacrifice be reciprocated?"

Allen suggests that the way we as citizens take responsibility for rebuilding social trust after sacrifice is by practicing political friendship with strangers—a rather shocking, but useful, idea in this polarizing time. It invites back to humanizing each other.

> One doesn't even have to like one's fellow citizen in order to act toward them as a political friend. There is a very easy way of transforming one's relations to strangers. We might simply ask about all our encounters with others . . . "Would I treat a friend this way?" When we can answer "yes," we are on the way to developing a citizenship that is neither domination or acquiescence. When the answer is no, we have not escaped our old bad habits.

Allen uses friendship as the model for the relationship, because we don't expect our friends to be exactly like us. Our bond comes not from likeness but from shared conditions and experiences. Friends have equal standing, equal interpretive power. What they add to the situation is their unique viewpoint, which helps us all to enlarge our understanding, our ability to be able caretakers of the whole.

I would add to Allen's statement that we need to listen in such a way that we actively seek to see the *good* in very different views of the world. One of the most painful experiences for all of us is not to have the good in us recognized, to have our motives and values depreciated, maligned.

Sharing the Wisdom in Our Moral Emotions:

Another way of reconceptualizing democracy is to take the moral emotions that Haidt and his colleagues have associated with various political preferences—and see the social value in each of them *for* democracy.

These moral emotions are powerful, alogical, almost instinctual in us, but speak to something precious and crucial. There is social wisdom in each of them. They play crucial roles in how we order our societies. The emotions include care/harm, fairness/reciprocity, authority, purity, loyalty, and possibly liberty. Our individual visions of a just society usually evoke several of these emotions. Haidt would argue that conservatives incorporate more of these emotions in their conceptualization of a just government than liberals, who rely almost exclusively on care/harm and fairness/reciprocity. (Allen's vision of a functioning democracy depends heavily on care, reciprocity and loyalty.)

However, all societies need some level of each of these qualities and it is interesting to see what level of each value we call on in different situations.

When someone else is sharing their vision of a just and good society with you, it can help to notice—especially if you are having trouble with that vision—which of these moral emotions is salient for them and to respond in terms of that emotion. For example, when someone talks about being invaded, that often is a purity/violation emotion, not a fairness or authority emotion. If so, it calls for a different response, one that explores what purity consists of for them and what it means to lose it.

Changing Our Practices: Bearing Otherness

What is often most challenging when trying to create virtuous cycles is the management of our own emotions in the service of the whole. Crucial at the individual, interpersonal, and group levels, I call it the ability to bear because it has so much to do with holding steady, hopefully enduring.

Daring to Cross-Identify: Bearing otherness applies to ourselves first. We each contain multitudes, not all of them chosen. The interesting thing about identity politics is that although it increases our sense of belonging, it narrows our sense of personal identity as it expands our sense of group identity. We feel more socially fluid, more socially validated within our chosen group. But the more partisan we are, the more heavily we invest in creating an antithesis, a NOT-I, NOT-US to define ourselves against. If we are going to be heroes, someone else needs to be a villain.

If we are interested in reducing polarization, however, we need to be secure enough to see what we might share emotionally even more than intellectually with people with very different views. Some of that shared range of emotion doesn't fit tidily under the category heroic. Threatened, we don't *want* to know our own range of negative emotions, rancors, fears, or our own authoritarian impulses. We don't *want* to know our inner Trump, for example. Or, our inner Hillary. Or our inner Putin. Dutarte. See what I mean . . . it's not easy. Paradoxically, accepting these difficult negative emotions in ourselves, we are often more open to acknowledging more positive and complex ones in others.

Bearing the Gaze: When world views vary radically, as they do in a hyperpolarized society, one of the most difficult things to do is to be able to bear being seen by others in ways that are so different from how we understand ourselves that they make us dizzy. We want to fight back, make someone see us the way we see ourselves. Most significantly, we want the flow of good in us recognized. But there is no *real* rapprochement possible if we can't absorb how someone else sees us and people like us. The ability to stay in there, to bear the gaze is a powerful contributor to social trust. It enlarges the world for both people.

In our several listening projects, I've been struck by what happens to me when, because of the structure of the interaction, I am *committed* to listening in good faith to people very different from me. My job for several hours is "only" to listen with the intention to identify, to understand as well as I can how someone else experiences and understands their own life. I'm not there to judge, to reconcile, to compare, or to defend my own self-concept. I'm there to join them in an attempt to understand their own experience and share that understanding in good faith. One of the most surprising results of this practice is that I *like* almost everyone I talk to in this way—and they like me for that way of listening as well.

But the process is not always easy. The challenge in these situations is being able to stay physiologically connected even when our mind is having to dramatically shift perceptions and interpretations, especially if someone is expressing hostility for groups that we identify with. Sometimes I use a simple exercise I call breathing with your enemy. It's fascinating to match breaths with someone, you learn something crucial about them—and about your-self—that you can't learn in other ways. Ways that implicate and complicate and remind you of what you share: The rhythm of breath. The miracle of it.

Staying intellectually connected can also be a challenge when someone is voicing beliefs that you disagree with, often strongly. One way to enter a more accepting space together is to ask a simple question: "*How* did you come to believe . . . ?" Just asking that question moves you into a mutable reality. *How* did you come to believe that abortion was unacceptable? *How* did you come to believe that it is crucial for women's dignity and freedom that they have the right to choose whether to give birth or not? *How* did you come to believe that anyone who isn't Christian will go to hell? *How* did you come to believe that immigrants are taking jobs away from Americans? *How* did you come to believe that African Americans are creating most of their own problems? *How* did you come to believe that white people are holding you back in your job?

Under One Roof—Relinquishing the Hidden Transcripts: A significant step in building broader social trust is to bring the stories we tell about each other in private into the public sphere, to bring them all under one roof. A crucial dimension of social trust is feeling that someone will say to your face what they say behind your back. There are many situations when this is not the case—but the social cost is great. The social cost of *believing* that is the case is also great.

James C. Scott in *Domination and the Arts of Resistance* explores the idea of hidden transcripts, the ways that one group talks about another group publicly and the way they talk about them privately. These hidden transcripts are, in other words, part of how we otherize each other. They are how we talk *about* people not *with* them. They include the ways employees talk among themselves about bosses, bosses among themselves about employees, Democrats about Republicans, Republicans about Democrats. One result of the intersection of our hyper-polarization and social media is that there are very few hidden transcripts any more. All the bile is right out there. Sadly, our more conciliatory comments about each other may now have become our hidden transcripts.

Having all that bile out there may be for the best. There is no real "whole" in Allen's terms unless the truths at the heart of those hidden transcripts can be voiced openly and absorbed by all. Unshared, they are where contempt breeds and amplifies. These hidden transcripts are about the ways and the reasons that we distrust each other. The most difficult part of absorbing the hidden transcript of another group is accepting the possibility that there may be some justice in it. Another is to accept that our preconceptions about another group's hidden transcript may be very distorted—that we are presuming a level of hate and malevolence that don't actually exist. A major question when returning from intense polarization is how do we *undo* the stories we have been telling about each other. The light of day helps.

An important test of whether we are engaging in hidden transcripts is whether or not we feel free to voice the same thoughts and beliefs that we express in private spaces among people who share our views when in direct conversation with others who do *not* share those views. Whether we can accept the social consequences *to the whole* if we were to do so is a crucial measure of social resilience and trust. It means that we feel safe enough to show up, really show up. That is the beginning of commitment to a larger whole. The second step is recognizing when someone else is showing the same measure of social trust and commitment. When both those occur, we have the beginning of a reciprocity cycle. We are beginning to speak *with*, not about, each other.

CREATING THE CHORD: VOICING THE VISION

Affiliative Thought and Imagination: The modes of thought associated with affiliative states seem more associated with qualities of the right brain, which favors image, sensory impression, direct experience, emotion, and whose natural form of abstraction is narrative, a profoundly social, sensorially and affectively rich form of thought. I've written often about the role of narrative in developing social trust. The stories that do this best are those that draw more heavily on these right brain characteristics. They invite affiliation, cross-identification. We relax into them. Stories help encapsulate our experience of what it *feels* like to live life, help give meaning and shape to often overwhelming experience.

Stories also invite us safely into a world of multiple interpretations. In a good story people are complex, their motives shifting, their situations shifting as well. We see ourselves in them. We recognize the situations they are in as ones we could find ourselves in, that feel *emotionally* real. Chance is present—so are unexpected consequences as well as intended ones. Characters, especially our protagonists, get tossed around by circumstances; they are far from prescient, they make mistakes, they learn from them. We learn vicariously from them too, but what we learn varies depending on our own experience of life. Even the teller of a story can't impose a unitary meaning. The interesting thing is that when we are in narrative mode, we don't mind that. The mode itself invites a kind of modesty. We usually want to share a story. We don't go berserk if someone understands it differently.

Assuming Responsibility: Who is most responsible for moving our country in a less polarized direction? I would say those who have a mental framework for diversity, those who have benefitted most from the overall demographic and economic changes of recent decades, and those who like change. Above all, those who *like* expanding circles of affiliation, those who *want* to get along.

Sharing Your Flexibility: A current idea about authoritarian attitudes is that they are based on a single psychological trait, aversion to change. This seems to be an innate characteristic which is surprisingly well correlated with later political attitudes. In other words, those of us with a natural taste and tolerance for diversity have no reason to think highly of ourselves for it. It requires less of us to get there. That means we can use that resilience for the general benefit, expand our understanding of diversity to include those who baulk at or fight it. Adopt a bigot! Adopt a totalitarian of the right or the left! Don't reason with them, just befriend.

Speak Up for the Whole: The concept of the active bystander is useful when thinking about how to reduce polarization. In polarized situations, the extremes take over the conversation and intensify the polarization even more. For some reason, the center is often silent. In part because there's no point in trying to find points of conciliation when people *want* to see the worst in each other. You just become grist for their hate mill! But there is a role for the active bystander, the political friend who keeps reminding us that we *share* a condition, a country, a hope, a *whole.* The political friend who names the cost of that virulence and intolerance, the very real harm done by failing to see the essential dignity in each other. The political friend who keeps asking, how would *you* feel if someone treated you this way? The political friend who names and lifts up the loss and sacrifice that community requires—whether that gift to the whole is finding the patience to let long lasting injustices change at a rate that feels far too slow, or accepting the very real costs of a more just redistribution of resources and opportunities at a rate that feels far too fast. The political friend who honors the promissory note of democracy *and* the good that already exists.

Expanding Vision into Story: An important part of helping voice the vision of the whole is to honor all of our needs for inclusion. Often, when we are listening to someone else's vision of the social good, one that ignores what *we* feel is essential, we are wondering, where is the reciprocity, what is in this definition of our society that benefits me and people like me? Sometimes the most important thing is just to claim this fear and concern directly and engage around it. It helps to think in narrative, not categorical, terms—for these are concerns of the heart. *We never argue ourselves into consensus, we reassure each other into consensus.*

It is interesting to ask someone what their *vision* of a just and healthy country is and where they personally fit into that vision. To respond to it as a *story*, which means to test it against what we know of real life. If this vision were to come to pass, what would *their* daily life be like? What would change from their current real life situation? What would they gain? What might they lose? What would make those changes worthwhile? And then to ask where someone whose views are diametrically opposed to theirs—along religious, racial, cultural lines—fits in as well. What would *their* daily life look like? What might they gain? What might they lose? What would make it worthwhile for them? And, finally, the essential question: If they changed places with that person, lived their life, their circumstances, would they truly feel that the society was equally just, equally beneficent?

Building Our Life Raft: Singing Our Chord: Some days, I see all these ideas and observations I've shared here as small flotation devices tossed into a turbulent sea. I don't believe any of them alone, or together, are enough to build the life raft we need. But they *are* a beginning. As you read the stories, poems, memoirs and essays in this collection, I invite you to see them as more contributions to that life raft. I also invite us all to return to the metaphor used for this project, our common chord, and see how that image changes the definition of the situation. Maybe there is a song here already and we're finding a way to sing it together, creating a harmony that depends on difference, grows in strength and beauty with every voice that joins in.

THE IDEAL AND THE REAL

To close, I share here the story of a close friendship of mine that has been buffeted by all these forces. I think that it describes what it means to have friendship be at the heart of citizenship—and I do believe it is possible . . . with more than a little help from our friends.

Since the latest presidential election, I have struggled with the challenges increasing social and political polarization has posed for me in one of my closest friendships. My friend, I will call her Val, has been close to me since I first moved to Atlanta twenty-six years ago. We have always been a rather improbable pair. I am ten years older, but that is the least of our differences. She is a conservative Catholic, a Republican, a lifetime civil servant, an environmental engineer, and I am a mystic, a life-long Democrat, a writer and artist who works most often independently. She has raised four sons inside a conventional marriage. I raised one child primarily as a single parent. But we meet in many ways—in our ideas of public service, the importance of family and friendship, in what it means to use your God-given gifts to their full potential, in our inclusiveness. I have written letters to each of her sons before their adolescent spiritual retreats, recommended them for Eagles Scouts, for the Air Force Academy (writing as a pacifist). Our friendship has weathered the Clinton years, the Bush years, and the Obama ones. She volunteers every Wednesday at a pregnancy center whose purpose is to encourage a mother to decide that giving birth and rearing a child is both preferable and feasible. I understand and respect her position, and she understands the reasons that I am pro-choice. We understand, in other words, how each of us has come to believe what we do.

The F-word between us refers to feminism although Val is, in practice, one of the most formidable feminists I know. Once early in our friendship she gathered up her two young sons and took them home when I teasingly suggested that feminist might be a better description of her than conservative since all her closest friends were liberal feminists and she had much in common with them. "My husband is conservative," she said as she quickly buckled the boys in the stroller. Around the same time, my son, dropping by her house with me, said as we were pulling out of her driveway, "Mom, we've never known people with bumper stickers like that." Since then, we both have avoided labels, ignored bumper stickers, and focused on how we are likely to respond in specific situations. In all crisis situations we have faced, our responses are remarkably similar. We take care of the children. We act quickly and we act decisively. We help out. We believe in making, not taking. We believe in moving as best we can into deeper alignment with our best selves. In practice, she is steadier at this than I am.

But with this last election, politics entered our relationship. The day after the election when she called about something else, I said, "We never talk about politics, but I need to tell you I am profoundly depressed about this." She said, "It may not be so bad." She went on to share her oldest son's wisdom. He had told her, as she worried during the election returns, "Remember four years ago how you were so sure it was going to be the end of the world if Romney lost—and nothing really terrible happened."

"So you might discover the same," she said.

I listened to her in disbelief. There was no similarity. Surely she could see this. This was a completely different order of experience.

"I feel this defies everything I stand for, everything I have believed about this country," I said.

"I understand. I feel the same way about abortion," she said.

This wasn't about one issue. This was about *every* issue. "Fine. Just so you understand, whatever happens, this is on you," I said.

Life intervened, and we welcomed the distraction, so we didn't meet again until late January, after the inauguration, after the marches. We walked through town and she brought me up to date on her family as if nothing had happened. But when we sat down in a restaurant for tea, I asked her how she, a lifelong employee of EPA and the environmental agencies at CDC, was handling the repercussions of the election for her and her colleagues. She told me that after the election colleagues at work had come up and verbally attacked her. I wondered if these included her closest friends there, one of whom was a Muslim and an immigrant from Turkey, the other an immigrant from Cuba. I wondered if in the face of their questions and concerns, she could still "justify" her vote. Members of her own family had attacked her as well, she added. Most likely her two gay siblings, I decided.

"What did you say?" I asked.

For her, this was just a normal election. It was worth a try to change things. This is what we all had the right to decide every four years. This was what it meant to be an American. She didn't understand why people treated her as if *she* was different. Hadn't she survived the Obama years without making a big issue of it? Government *was* too big. The problem is that it would be the good employees who would be leaving, the deadbeats who would stay.

"This is *different*," I told her. "Is this what you stand for? Religious exclusion? Hate mongering? Is *this* how you want your sons to behave? Is *this* the model you want to provide them? *I cannot reconcile this with anything, with everything, I know and treasure about you.*"

She sat there, holding my gaze, as I described what it felt like to see someone boast of sexual assault as if that was what *merited* their vote. I could see her begin to tear, for me, for what she knew it activated in me. I talked about what I saw on the faces of people at the rallies. "It is the hatred, the *ecstatic* hatred on peoples' faces that I can't get over. *That* is what I am most afraid of. This opens the floodgate to such animosity, such intolerance, such cruelty." I looked at her. She was still holding in there. I finished, "But what I'm most determined about is that this will *not* destroy a friendship of such duration."

Her neck had flushed a deep red, but her eyes were still fixed on me when *she* spoke. Her voice was steady. "I didn't see that in the rallies I attended," she said. "In any case, it's not all there is. People will go on being people. They will go on doing good, being kind. Because they're people, and that's what people do. That's not going to stop because of an election."

In the years that have followed, as we continue to take our walks, share news of our families and our work as honestly but less copiously, more cautiously than before, I have had to come to terms with my own intolerance.

If I'm not careful, in my inner dialogues, she still becomes the object of my most authoritarian, totalitarian, either/or fury. All of those areas where our differences were once fields of encounter, exploration and surprising affinities, have been narrowed, solidified, hammered into weapons. *This* is on you. Another Muslim ban. *This* is on you. Pulling out of the climate accords. *This* is on you. Decimation of the EPA. *This* is on you. Charlottesville. *This* is on you. Kavanaugh. *This* is on you. The recent six-weeks abortion law in Georgia. *This* is on you. The children in cages at the border. *This* is on you. The last and the next mass shooting. *This* is on you—

What pulls me out of this destructive litany is remembering how she listened to me that afternoon, the expression on her face as I described the pain I felt, how *she* didn't blink, didn't bolt, how *she* continued to hear the flow of good in me. And how I also saw the hurt on her face when she said, "*I* haven't changed. *My* values haven't changed. *I* have never treated anyone the way people are now treating me."

What pulls me out of my own polarization are all our years together, all the challenges we have faced. How in the dark years of a sustained depression, every day she would *ask* something of me, remind me that I had something to give, to contribute. How, moving into a new home, when the bank beside our stream began to collapse, she was out there within an hour with a truckload of dirt. I know she remembers how involved we were with her sons on her husband's tours in Iraq. We both remember what a powerful dyad we were when we worked together bringing social construction—as story—into the daily practice of environmental scientists, how we wanted to make sure *our* government remained responsive, worked for all of us.

The fact is that in a crisis I know without any doubt that she will be there for me, and I know that I will be there for her as well. I know that, despite my fury, my intolerance, our friendship remains a faith story, one in which we are still able to honor the flow of good in each other, to allow it to move through us and between us in unexpected ways, that we are both committed to feeling the gracious, constantly changing sense of it.

REFERENCES

Allen, Danielle S., *Talking to Strangers: Anxieties of Citizenship Since Brown v. Board of Education.* Chicago: University of Chicago, 2004.

Baumeister, Roy F. and Mark R. Leary, "The Need to Belong: Desire for Interpersonal Attachments as a Fundamental Human Motivation," *Psychological Bulletin:* Vol. 117, No.3, pp. 497-529.

Bishop, B. and R.G. Cushing, *The Big Sort: Why the Clustering of Like-Minded Americans Is Tearing Us Apart.* New York: Houghton Mifflin, 2008.

Brooks, Arthur C., "Our Culture of Contempt," *The New York Times*, March 2, 2019.

Bruner, Jerome. "Explaining and interpreting: Two ways of using the mind" In Gilbert Harman, ed. *Conceptions of the Mind. New York: IEA,* 1992. pp. 123-137.

Edsall, Thomas B., "The Contract with Authoritarianism," *The New York Times*, April 5, 2018.

Edsall, Thomas B., "Integration vs. White Intransigence," *The New York Times*, July 12, 2019.

Haidt, Jonathan, "The Age of Outrage: What the current political climate is doing to our country and our universities," *National Review Online.* December 28, 2017.

Haidt, Jonathan, *The Righteous Mind: Why Good People are Divided by Politics and Religion.* New York: Random House, 2012

Staub, Ervin, *The Roots of Goodness & Resistance to Evil: Inclusive Caring, Moral Courage, Altruism Born of Suffering, Active Bystandership, and Heroism.* New York: Oxford University Press, 2015.

Wikipedia. "Definition of the Situation," "Thomas Theorem"

ADDITIONAL READINGS

CONCEPTUAL:

Berrenby, David, "The Things that Divide Us," *National Geographic*, April 2018. pp. 46-67.

Duhigg, Charles. "Why Is America So Angry?" *The Atlantic*, January 2019. pp. 62-75.

Eberhardt, Jennifer L., *Biased: Uncovering the Hidden Prejudice That Shapes What We See, Think, and Do*. New York: Viking, 2019.

Edwards, Mickey. *The Parties Versus the People: How to Turn Republicans and Democrats into Americans*. New Haven: Yale University Press, 2012.

Gest, Justin *The New Minority: White Working Class Politics in an Age of Immigration and Inequality*. New York: Oxford University Press, 2016.

Hunter, Albert and Carl Milofsky. *Pragmatic Liberalism*. New York: Palgrave, 2007.

Payne, Keith. *The Broken Ladder: How Inequality Affects the Way We Think, Live, and Die*. New York: Viking, 2017.

Sitaraman, Ganesh. *The Crisis of the Middle-Class Constitution: Why Economic Inequality Threatens Our Republic*. New York: Knopf, 2017.

Stenner, Karen, *The Authoritarian Dynamic*. New York: Cambridge University Press, 2005

Williams, Kipling D., Joseph P. Forgas, William von Hippel, editors. *The Social Outcast: Ostracism, Social Exclusion, Rejection, and Bullying* New York: Psychology Press/Hove. 2005

EXPERIENTIAL:

Bailey, Isaac J. *My Brother Moochie: Regaining Dignity in the Face of Crime, Poverty, and Racism in the American South*. Boston: Other Press, 2018.

Hoschschild, Arlie Russell. *Strangers in Their Own Land: Anger and Mourning on the American Right: A Journey to the Heart of Our Political Divide*. New York: The New Press, 2016.

Mason, Nicole C. *Born Bright: A Young Girl's Journey from Nothing to Something in America*. New York: St. Martins, 2016.

Smarsh, Sarah. *Heartland: A Memoir of Working Hard and Being Broke in the Richest Country in the World*. New York: Scribner, 2018.

Vance, J.D. *Hillbilly Elegy*. New York: Harper, 2016

I. CULTURE/NATIONS

JUDITH GILLE

THE TROUBLE WITH WALLS

> *I will build a great wall—and nobody builds walls better than me, believe me—and I'll build them very inexpensively. I will build a great, great wall on our southern border, and I will make Mexico pay for that wall. Mark my words.*
> —Donald Trump, June 2015

In early 2017, as liberal America waged its war against Trump and his inane border wall, I became engaged in my own personal battle with walls. I'm staunchly opposed to Trump's wall, as are all of my Mexican neighbors and ninety-nine percent of my American friends, a few of whom insist I shouldn't be discussing my little wall issue in the same breath as the great border-wall debate. As my daughter would remind me, mine is such a "first world" problem. Still, as Trump's border wall with Mexico became the hot-button issue in American politics, walls simultaneously became a major theme in my personal life. It began when the vacant lot below Casa Chepitos, my home in San Miguel de Allende, was sold.

✗✗✗

Our Fantasy, Crushed

For years my husband Paul and I had fantasized about buying the property below ours, not only to protect our Mexican home's lovely view (for which I named a memoir), but to plant a garden and small orchard of citrus and avocado trees. In 2015, I reached out to the owners through my friend Gracia and her husband, Sebastian, who had known the family since child-hood. However, upon seeing my *gringa* face, the sellers jacked up the asking price to more than twice what adjacent properties of the same size had sold for the very same year. Not having that kind of disposable income, and with a daughter to put through college, I was forced to pass.

A couple of years later, when Gracia informed me that the lot had been sold, I went on a mission to meet the new owner and find out what he had in mind for the property. Since she personally knows everyone who lives within a five mile radius of callejón Chepito (and to bolster my courage), I asked Gracia to come along. Rumor had it the property's new owner was renting a house off callejón Landín, the alley directly below ours. We stopped by the house of a woman who lived in the middle of Landín, and was, of course, also a longtime acquaintance of Gracia's. She told us an older gentleman who spoke Spanish fluently but was not Mexican had bought the property below ours and pointed to the house where he was currently renting. Gracia and I walked over and knocked on the door expecting an older non-Mexican man, but instead a young Mexican man answered the door. After we explained who we were and what we wanted, he asked us to wait outside. Twenty minutes later, a fastidious little man with thinning grey hair and a thick accent arrived. He told us his name was Berny, "spelled with a *Y*." I introduced myself and pointed uphill to show him where I lived and then explained why I was there. He told me that he, indeed, planned to build. I then politely asked if Berny with a *Y* and his architect could take our home and its view into consideration when siting and designing his new house.

"I know exactly what the rules are and how high I can build," he said firmly. He opened the door to his rental wider and invited me in to take a look. A massive brick wall completely blocked the view from a bank of six-foot-tall windows.

"This is what people do here. Everyone wants to take advantage of the views." Then he added: "If you didn't want someone building in front of you, you should have bought the property yourself."

Disheartened, I shuffled back to Casa Chepitos, hoping against hope that I'd made an impression on Berny and that, despite his response, he'd be inspired to build a low-slung, ranch-style house like the Mexican woman to the south of his new property had.

)X()X(

Killing Trees Does Matter

In October of 2017, three young men arrived and began chopping down the trees below our house. Trees that had been home to red-winged blackbirds, vermilion flycatchers, woodpeckers, goldfinches, and kingbirds. Twenty-foot-tall Peruvian pepper, mesquite, and jacaranda trees that had created a feathery green canopy in front of our house for sixteen years. I watched in tears as they hacked away at the trees' branches and ravaged their trunks with anemic chainsaws. When I said to the one guy within hearing range that it was sad to see trees I'd lived with and loved for sixteen years being cut down, his response was *"Ni modo."* But it did matter. To me.

Shortly after all of the trees below my Mexican home were chopped down and hauled away, a crew of *albañiles* showed up to excavate a foundation for a dividing wall between the properties. I freaked out. The hole they were digging abutted my retaining wall and was three feet from my house, which would be illegal most places in the U.S. In Mexico, however, building codes are often nonexistent or not enforced even when they do exist. I had been well aware that the new wall would likely block the view and light from my living room, but each day, as my neighbor's perimeter wall inched higher and higher, I was suddenly worried it was going to block the view from the master bedroom, too.

I consulted Gracia's husband, Sebastian, who informed me that the maximum height limit for walls in San Miguel is 8½ meters. He also said the city would enforce them, especially if there were complaints. I then talked to a couple gringos who'd battled Mexican developers over height restrictions: one had won his case, the other lost. I frantically dropped a fifty-foot tape measure out of my bedroom window to see if I even had a case. From the ground, 8½ meters (27.88 feet) came to just below the master bedroom's window seat. The one that overlooks the steeples and domes of San Miguel's many churches, the steely waters of the Presa de Allende, the grey-green hills of Guanajuato. I breathed a little easier.

✗✗✗

War Zone

Once started, construction on the wall and house dragged on for months. I awoke each morning to a pounding so intense that I felt as if I lived in a war zone. All morning long, it sounded like small bombs were being detonated below my window. Work started at 8 a.m. or earlier and sometimes continued until 8 p.m. Dust from the mixing of concrete covered every horizontal surface inside the house and most of the plants in my garden. The workers trampled my plants, destroyed a ficus tree, filled my small patio with rubble. They smoked dope all day and played the weirdest mix of music—from old Eagles pop tunes to reggaetón to Mexican boleros—at a feverish volume. After six weeks of this, my nerves were completely jangled. The construction ruckus became so unbearable, I began going down to Starbucks on the jardín every day to write. When I arrived home one day to discover that my gardener had butchered the last remaining ficus on my patio because "the new neighbor told him to," I exploded. I later apologized profusely but asked José Luís to please confirm any further pruning projects with *me*.

That night I lay awake—my anger and frustration spinning out of control—imagining all sorts of bad things happening to the man responsible for so negatively impacting my peaceful Mexican life. I imagined him dropping dead of a heart attack. Becoming so disabled by a stroke that he could no longer walk uphill. Being roughed up by the gang of tough boys who live on Landín and deciding the alley was far too dangerous. A little too gleefully, I fantasized about buying a voodoo doll, naming it Berny and sticking pins in it.

Enough already! my better nature shouted, interrupting the downward spiral my ego was on that night. *You sound just like Donald Trump, the other asshole you love to hate.*

)()()(

Stuck in Mexico

In early March, desperate for a break from the dust and the noise and the acrid smell of marijuana mixed with fresh concrete, I booked a flight back to Seattle for ten days. But at the airport in Mexico City, I was blocked from boarding the airplane by an Alaska Airlines clerk who insisted that I report immediately to an immigration official at the INM office downstairs.

In an ironic twist, it turned out I was not allowed to leave because of my immigration status. I'd applied to become a permanent resident of Mexico and, after three months of waiting, still had not received my ID card.

"I could give you a tourist visa, but if I do, your application will be invalidated," the INM officer said.

The woman I'd hired to help me with the application had failed to mention one small detail: I was not allowed to leave or reenter the country without that card. But I was not mad at her; I wasn't even upset. I figured my problems were nothing compared with the way Mexicans and other immigrants were being treated by the United States government. Plus, with all the stupid anti-immigrant shenanigans going on in the United States, I'd rather be stuck on the Mexican side of Trump's wall. The "fun side," as a sign in one San Miguel café says.

XOXOX

My New BFF

Over the next few weeks, while I awaited the card that would permit me to return to the U.S., Berny began stopping by Casa Chepitos for regular visits. If the doorbell rang before 9 a.m., I could pretty much bet it would be him. The man I was prepared to hate (or, at least, dislike intensely) turned out to be pleasant and helpful. When I showed him the mess on my side of the new wall, he ordered his workers to clean it up. When I complained that his roof's design was likely to block the view from the master bedroom, he changed it. When I asked if the workers could play their music at a slightly lower volume, it was quiet the next day. Berny was Colombian-American, multilingual, charming, and funny. He'd led an interesting life as a trauma surgeon, was a great storyteller, and reminded me of my husband's grandfather. By the end of April, we were fast friends and I felt ashamed of the terrible things I'd imagined happening to him. And my new friend also, inadvertently, taught my ego to take a joke.

It happened one day, when on my way down to the jardín with friends, I ran into him on the Cuesta de San José. I'd given him a copy of my memoir *The View from Casa Chepitos* a few days earlier, and he told me he was enjoying it so much that he'd recommended it to his friend Clay, who had also recently bought a property on callejón Landín.

"But his copy is the new edition," Berny said.

"There is no new edition," I replied.

"Oh yes, there is. Clay sent me a photo of it."

He searched his phone and finally pulled up the image he was looking for: it was an image of my book all right, but in lieu of the photo of San Miguel's Parroquia on the cover, there was a photo of a roughly mortared brick wall with the original title and subtitle of my book superimposed on it. Even the award sticker was there. Below the title a line was added in pink letters: *2018 Edition.*

I was outraged. Someone had stolen my book! A minute later it dawned on me: it was a joke. When I Googled him, it turned out Berny's friend was a world-class photographer who, evidently, also had a great command of Photoshop. That Berny and I had both been duped by the parody was a testament to the guy's abilities.

)X()X(

A Blank Slate

I obsessed about what to do with the blank slate that now stretched across the front of my property and was 8 ½ feet tall. I visited the homes of friends and friends of friends to see various artistic treatments they'd done on their walls; I consulted Anado McLauchlin, San Miguel's renowned mosaic artist; I discussed the problem of my blank wall with several friends who suggested everything from planting a green wall to installing a giant horizontal wall fountain. Berny had many suggestions for what I should do on my side of his wall but the idea of a mural was his favorite. Paul also liked the idea of a mural; he thought we should hire an artist to paint a picture of the view we used to have. I wandered around San Miguel's Guadalupe and San Antonio neighborhoods photographing the colorful murals. In barrios outside of the *centro historico*—where there's a prohibition on signs, paint colors, and artistic expression—there's been an explosion of fabulous public wall art in recent years.

In the end I bought two large boxes of colored chalk and invited the kids from the callejón who came to my sixty-fifth birthday party to decorate the wall. Aged three to thirteen, they embraced the art project with zeal. By the end of the evening my slate was no longer blank—it was covered with birthday greetings in Spanish and English, fanciful flowers, colorful birds, smiley faces, stick figures, odd geometric shapes, and horse-like creatures I suspected were unicorns. When Berny arrived an hour later with a box of the finest chocolates from Joffrey's in hand, he gave a gleeful thumbs-up to the young artists and their handiwork.

)X()X(

Good Fences, Good Neighbors?

I don't believe that good fences make good neighbors. That tired old maxim was first introduced into the national zeitgeist by the recalcitrant neighbor in Robert Frost's 1914 poem "Mending Walls," and remains a rallying cry for people mainly interested in protecting their own self-interests.

But I also don't believe walls necessarily make bad neighbors. What makes bad neighbors are people with character traits such as arrogance, insensitivity, and selfishness. Traits on full display in the United States right now. My experience with my new neighbor and his wall helped me see that I can choose to be that kind of person or I can choose to be an ambassador for the character traits I'd prefer to see all Americans, and especially our President, embrace more whole-heartedly: empathy, tolerance, humility, generosity, and fairness.

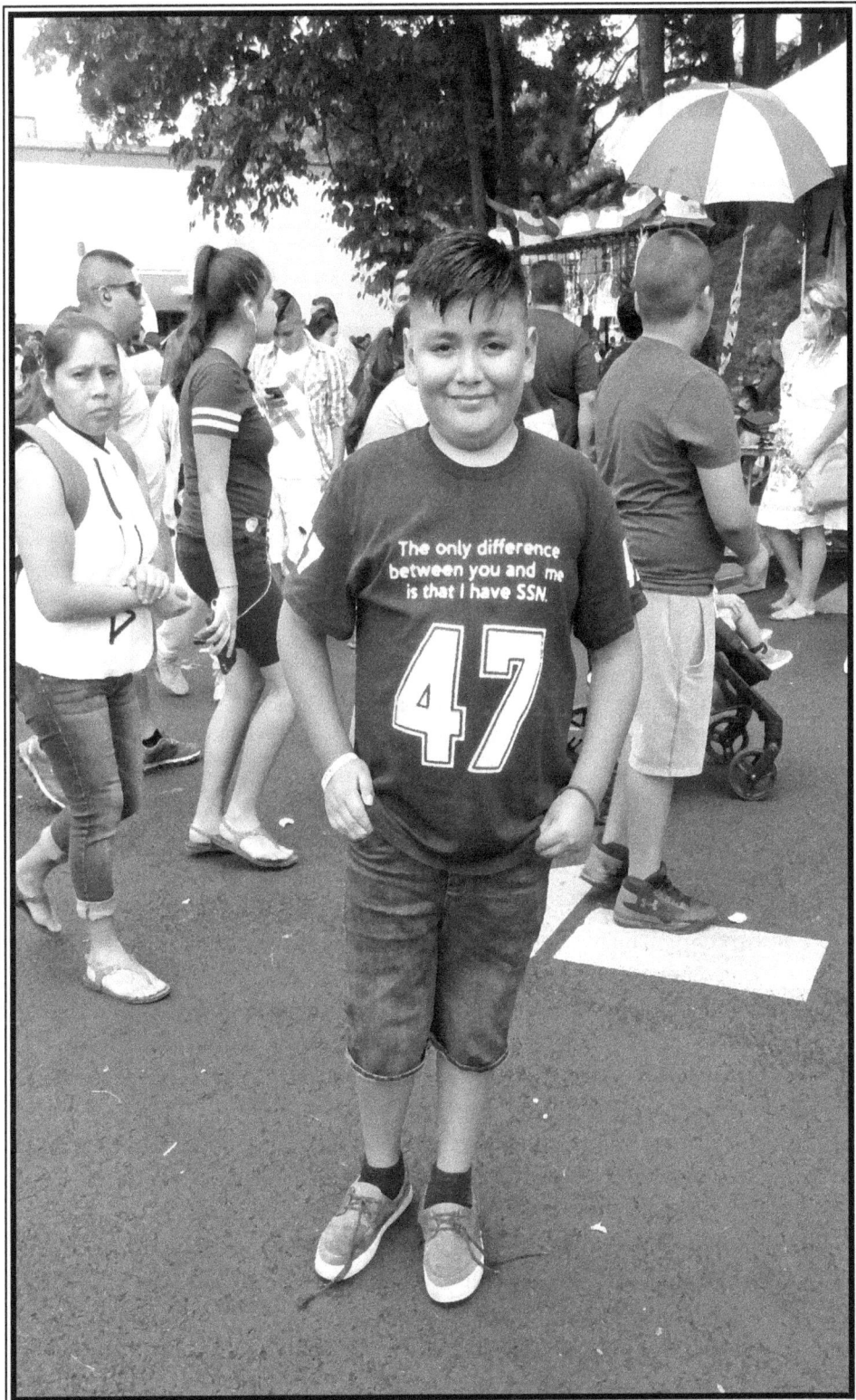

J.O. HASELHOEF

NOT ONE FIT MY IMAGE

The refugee camp in Chios, Greece, looked peaceful. White tents and metal containers stood in neat rows; an occasional line of hand-washed laundry flapped in the breeze. We stood on the drawbridge of a medieval castle, looking into the moat below. Jeanny, our center's manager, announced, "Here is where the Molotov cocktails were thrown onto the refugees last winter."

Her comment served to reinforce my fears of a refugee camp. The stories I heard and images I saw—harsh physical conditions, disagreements between occupants, depressing histories—didn't encourage visits. But already, I met a number of women who lived there—immaculate in their dress, positive in their attitude, well-educated in their conversations. They were not what I expected—the image I carried of refugees was wrong.

Some months before, a friend suggested I volunteer at the refugee camps in Chios. I hesitated. I knew little about the 25 million individuals worldwide fleeing the instability of one country and searching for safety in another. I understood less about individuals from the Middle East whose countries, ethnicities, and religious branches never appeared to line up.

Eventually, I threw out my hesitancies, welcomed the opportunity to volunteer, and knew I would learn more only if I pushed myself beyond the simplicity of my life in Wisconsin, USA. The friend recommended I volunteer at the women's center because it effectively and efficiently filled a need for the refugee women.

The United Nations High Commissioner for Refugees (UNHCR) and the Greek municipality created two camps (Souda and Vial) on the island of Chios to hold those arriving across the sea from Turkey. A total of 2500 individuals and families lived in the camps, and, for those considered at risk, if spaces were available, in small apartments. Most individuals who entered Greece were in the asylum-seeking process.

Of that number, forty percent considered Syria home; twenty percent,

Afghanistan and Iraq; and the rest, Iran, Congo, Ethiopia, and Algeria. The vast majority listed Muslim as their religious background and represented many branches of Islam. Although most spoke Arabic, others spoke Farsi, French, German, Kurdish, Dari, Pashto and English.

The two lines of white tents, stamped with UNHCR, lined the base of the moat. They reminded me of the relief tents used in Haiti after the 2010 earthquake. The material did not breathe; it stayed hot in summer, cold in winter. The refugees occupied the tents for much longer than the short-term relief they were meant for.

Jeanny and I walked to the front end of the camp, the entry where gates and guards and distribution trailers defined its official character. A Greek guard with the muscular build and aviator sunglasses of Arnold Schwarzenegger looked closely at our badges, consulted his mobile, and denied us entry. Jeanny insisted, "The same paperwork provided clearance to me last week!"

He scrolled through a list on his phone and again shook his head. "Check with the people working for the local municipality."

Many Middle Eastern men stood outside the gates, in this area that housed the front desk. They looked like any other group of males, dressed in shorts, T-shirts, and flip-flops. Some played soccer. A few sat on white plastic chairs in the shade of tall eucalyptus trees. Others talked in small groups. To the side, at a picnic table in the sun, two orange-vested relief workers attended to a boy's facial cut. They spoke German to one another and English to their patient. The boy's mother, in jeans, a long-sleeved blouse, and a Muslim headscarf (hijab), watched, while a clutch of small children looked on.

While Jeanny talked with two Greek women in charge, I sat on a low wall outside the door and watched the soccer game. One scored; his teammates cheered.

Jeanny and I visited Souda to do outreach for the women's center. This week, a small number of new asylum seekers arrived in Chios. Most female refugees knew about the organization we represented, told by other women at the camp. We did outreach in case they didn't.

On a sunny day, we could look east and see Turkey. Turkish citizens, with their identifications in hand, often crossed the seven miles of the Aegean Sea in a fast boat and spent a summer's day visiting a Greek village and eating a grilled fish lunch. They paid $20 for a round-trip ride. In contrast, refugees paid up to $1000 each to smugglers to cross that same body of water in the middle of the night.

Initially intent on reaching Europe, these displaced families traveled north through Turkey to Hungary. When Hungary closed its borders in 2016, the entryway to Europe shifted to the nearest European Union country, Greece. Refugees still traveled to Turkey and then crossed the sea to the Greek islands. If the Turkish police came across a refugee-filled rubber raft, they forced its return to Turkey. If the raft passed the halfway mark, then the refugees entered the European Union, landing on a Greek beach or getting pulled from the water by the Greek Coast Guard. In either case, officials met, registered, and eventually interviewed all.

Authorities deemed a refugee "vulnerable" if old, pregnant, shipwrecked, a single parent, with a serious illness, or a victim of rape or human trafficking. In these cases, the individual remained in Greece. If those in charge determined the refugee was not in danger when in Turkey, he or she was deported back—something the refugees wanted to avoid at all costs. Turkey's treatment of refugees was brutal. Greek officials offered asylum to refugees who claimed a need for safety from their originating country and could not live, for a specific reason, in Turkey.

Lots of locations in Chios posted flyers describing a shortened version of this complicated and lengthy process in many languages. The papers also listed the date and time those individuals or families held upcoming meetings with officials. All refugees clung to their relationship (past, present, or future) with those lists.

Our second attempt to enter the refugee camp went well. As Jeanny and I passed the entry guard, he said with a sudden upbeat tone, "Come in, you are welcome to visit."

We walked between rows of temporary structures within the moat. To the left, tents—one after another with no spaces between—sat on a wooden platform above the dirt. A set of tarps protected them from the sun and rain. The white material drooped as the ropes supporting them stretched through the months. To the right, shipping containers, converted into living spaces, offered a hard-shell version of the same camping experience.

As we passed a container, Jeanny said something in Arabic to a woman standing in the doorway and the woman invited us in. We left our shoes outside with many others. Three families lived in the ten by twenty-foot space: six children and six adults. There were no tables, chairs, or beds. Two blankets hung from clotheslines. Now pushed to one end, at night, they provided the only privacy between families.

The two women in their mid-thirties, fully garbed in long dresses with hijabs covering their heads, rushed to find pillows for us to sit on. They joined us on the floor and offered us tea. A cardboard carryout box from the camp distribution center held numerous paper cups, each filled with black tea. The boy to my left drank his out of one cup, with seven or eight stacked below.

The six children found places on their mothers' laps or nearby to sit and listen to Jeanny, who pointed to the center's flyer and showed them a map to our location. I heard the word "hammam" (Arabic for showers) and "English" (for the classes that the center offered), and saw Jeanny do a little dance with her upper body to indicate the center offered Zumba on Wednesdays.

As she and I left, the husband of one of the women arrived, welcomed us to stay, and thanked us for coming. At the camps, fifty percent were male, thirty percent female, and twenty percent children. The men watched, undoubtedly curious, as we walked past. When we smiled or nodded, they responded in kind and greeted us in English.

The refugee camp of Souda housed a different population than Vial, the camp five miles away. Authorities, acknowledging a fiery Middle-Eastern history, separated the Arabic-speaking individuals and families from the Farsi-speakers. For the most part, Syrians and Iraqis lived in Souda; Afghanis and Iranians in Vial.

We continued to the far end of the camp—to an area from which we could see the drawbridge where we stood not long before. Here, there were more tents, as well as men's and women's toilets and shower rooms—one group painted blue, the other, pink. Jeanny said unprompted, "The toilets are not clean." She didn't need to. They smelled badly from where we stood.

As we began our return to the entry of the camp, she spoke about the center to two women outside their container home. They looked nervous and uncomfortable. Later, Jeanny suggested they thought we were camp administrators wanting information about them.

As Jeanny described the women's center, a young man interrupted her. "He's from Iraq and supported our organization on my earlier visits." He wore sunglasses and a beaded necklace made, I guessed, at a craft program offered by one of the charities. Pushing Jeanny aside verbally, he launched into a sales pitch about our services. The women laughed at his gregariousness and relaxed. They took the flyer about the center.

The length of time each individual or family stayed in the camps differed as each case took a unique form and amount of time to process. Those granted asylum went to the Greek mainland. Details for that status—family reunification, economic hardship, the internal political conflicts of a country—complicated an already confusing process, the details of which appeared to change every six months or so.

Within the moat, the high walls provided a sense of both comfort and claustrophobia. The camp gates established a controlled entrance to visitors, but the UNHCR, needing more space, expanded the camp outside. Those shelters felt exposed.

Passing among those tents, we recognized from the center three women in their mid-thirties. One grew up in Spain and spoke Spanish fluently. She returned to Syria as a teen and recently lost her husband in the war. The two others were sisters to each other and a friend to the first woman. They wore black long-sleeved, full-length dresses and headscarves—one maroon, one black, and one hot pink. All used dramatic eye make-up and painted their lips bright red.

The three stood in the entryway of their tent. Different from the white official issue, their green one, like others nearby, looked as if it came from an REI catalogue. The only event that could explain these fashionably well-dressed women at the entrance of a tent might have been a creative photographic shoot for the season's newest fashions—but that couldn't possibly be.

That night, it was said that one group of refugees beat to death a pregnant woman from the other group. Men from one camp marched to the other to seek revenge. Innocents fled both areas, sleeping at friends', in parking lots, alongside the road. The next day, I saw the three women at the center, huddled in a corner, distraught. One cried, the second comforted, and the third showed anger. The bucolic image of the green tent with the three well-dressed women standing at the entrance shattered.

)(()((

The women's center, not much more than 1000 square feet, operated on a side street near Souda, although it served the populations of both camps. It opened its doors six days a week from 11 to 2 and 4 to 7. The small space limited the number of women who could visit to fifteen at a time. Many, many more wanted the opportunity of a quiet, private environment. We encouraged morning visitors not to return on the same day, allowing others to come in the afternoon.

Eleven a.m. at the center, I heard the first knock of the day. Two women

stood outside the front door. They practiced their English—"Good morning," "How are you?"—shook my hand and kissed my cheeks twice. At the
front desk, I wrote down the phonetic spelling of their names and in what
camp they lived.

More women arrived and greeted me in Arabic or Farsi. They too kissed
me on the cheeks twice. They removed their shoes, asked if there was room in
the schedule for a private shower, and then disappeared to English classes or
to make coffee or chai in the kitchen.

One distinctive woman, Uri, came almost every day. A Syrian in her late
forties, Uri stood six-feet tall. Large-boned and strong, she wore a black burka,
a full-length dress with long sleeves and high neckline. She rarely smiled, but
her eyes watched intensely. She spoke no English and did not kiss my cheek.

My job at the center filled simple, cursory functions—welcoming new
refugees, ensuring stocks of tea and toilet paper, vacuuming at the end of
each day. The staff provided a point of stability for the women. Our role was
to reassure, be consistent, and direct the refugees to other non-governmental
organizations in the area that offered legal, psychological, and medical help.

The center offered diversions—from yoga to cooking together during
Ramadan, to Wednesday evening movies, when younger children were al-
lowed to attend. For the four-week period I volunteered, I taught an advanced
English class, encouraging the women to tell or write their stories.

Aalia wrote and then read to our small attentive group, "My boyfriend
and I, we attempted the crossing from Turkey to Greece eight times, always
stopped by Turkish authorities. On the ninth, when our boat began to sink,
I thought we would die." Aalia, a Syrian, described their landing in her new
language, "We swam all the way to shore . . . we were reborn!"

I looked at the nineteen year-old in front of me. She was dressed in
light pink and white with a matching headscarf. She reinforced her upbeat
ending—"My boyfriend and I, we were married the following week."

My own emotions stuck somewhere between horror and happiness. This
last news jolted me to hug her, hold her close.

Forozan, a gynecologist from Kabul, also came regularly to the English
class. She wished to seek asylum in an English-speaking country so she could
utilize her medical expertise as soon as possible. She received a special visa
from Greece to work with a non-profit agency serving the refugees as she
waited.

At thirty-five, Forozan had dark intense eyes and a serious demeanor.

On the weekends, she wore a sleeveless blouse (Muslim women tend to cover their shoulders and upper arms), matching pants, and no *chadri* over her jet-black hair. When I asked why she did not cover her head, she showed me photographs of Kabul in 1999. Muslim women wore clothing similar to what we did in the U.S. at that time— sleeveless dresses with hemlines at the knee. The choice of wearing a head covering was often a familial decision. In this case, Forozan made an informed decision based on her individual life and needs. She chose not to.

After the conservatives overthrew the moderate Afghani government, they required women to cover their hair with small veils. When the Taliban arrived, they demanded women wear burkas—clothing that covered all the body, often with a dark net through which to see and breathe. Forozan too wore this clothing at the time.

During the war, she lost her family to suicide bombings. With nothing but sadness and hardship left, she chose to emigrate. She remained a Muslim as she held dear the beauty and peacefulness described in the writings in the Qur'an. "That's what Islam is really about," she said and referred to, "the equality of all individuals and the kindness expected to all people."

As the days passed, I took on tasks outside the English class and front-desk duties. Often, I drove Salma, a refugee from Afghanistan, from her home to the center.

Salma married at age fifteen and lived in a small Afghani village with her husband's family. "I cleaned and cooked all meals for him and my twenty-eight in-laws. My mother-in-law would not let me watch television or attend school, but insisted I followed the conservative traditions."

Her husband became a drug user and they moved to the city where she worked in a bank to support her family. "I had an important job," Salma said as she handed me photos of herself taken at her office, showing her full-length Muslim dress and veil. The Taliban did not approve of her employment. Threatened, the family fled first to Iran, then to Turkey. In Greece, Salma filed for divorce—something not allowed in her home country. Her husband's violent response sent her and her children into hiding.

We took her kids to the beach where her sons rushed the waves and her daughter drew in the sand. Her mother called on FaceTime, and as it often happened with many of the women I met, Salma thrust the screen in front of me to show a woman my age just as surprised to see me, as I was her. We had no language in common, except for our concern for her daughter.

I enjoyed these women, the refugees. They appeared positive and happy, though I knew many experienced hell in their past. Perhaps they felt they cleared the worst part. Now that they were in Greece, maybe they, too, were reborn.

In the women's center, I re-organized a box from storage, putting crochet hooks in one cup, knitting needles in another, and rewinding donated yarn. Uri, the six-foot tall woman in the burka, watched me. She moved nearer to see the tools. She reached over my arm and jostled the cup of crochet hooks. Finding no number six, she asked through Jeanny if I would buy her one. I obliged. She paid me and spent the next few days crocheting a scarf.

Over the days that Uri added to the scarf, I looked over her shoulder as she crocheted. She demonstrated and then helped me hold the tool and give tension to the yarn, bringing the material over from back to front and grabbing it with the hook. I was touched by the whole experience and kissed her hand in appreciation. She blushed. She flustered. She acted much like a young schoolgirl—her eyes got big, her head bobbing with surprise. I regretted making her feel uncomfortable initially, but eventually, we laughed together.

)()()(

The journeys of these refugees were long and unscripted. Many points along the way offered them sufficient reason for bad memories or fear of the future.

Many Americans and Europeans viewed images of thousands of refugees crossing Hungary's borders, walking through Europe. They wondered why the refugees left their homes and belongings, walked miles, paid thousands of dollars to smugglers, and risked their lives. A friend in Hungary shortsightedly wrote, "They want the German's free money and support—that's all!"

Those weren't the reasons I heard. For the Syrians, escaping war was the primary reason. "They bombarded our house and school." "They wished to conscript my husband to fight." "We couldn't raise our children in Aleppo. It was too dangerous." One female engineer did mention the stipend that the Germans offered, not as an incentive to leave Syria, but an assurance there would be a way to survive until a proper job could be found.

For those not from Syria, reasons for leaving their homeland differed. A man from Africa said he had a traffic accident in his home country. The amount of restitution he would pay was too much for him and he would die in jail. A man from Pakistan had no income in his home country; he needed work. A young woman from the Republic of the Congo fled from the atrocities she witnessed during the twenty-year civil war that left 5.4 million dead.

Consistently, the refugees suffered harrowing experiences with the smugglers who brought them across the Aegean Sea from Turkey to Greece. With sixty people loaded into a single inflatable boat, the smuggler profited well with no guarantees to his passengers for a safe passage. One account described by a refugee was similar to many others:

> *We waited in the forest for the night. The smuggler took a few of the men to help inflate the boat. We had to keep the children quiet so that the Turkish gendarmes wouldn't hear us. Finally, we put on the life vests we bought and went to the beach with what little we owned. When we arrived on the sand, we could see that, though the smugglers, who were armed, promised our group two boats, there was only one. Chaos broke out. Everyone ran to claim a place in the boat and those who hesitated were pushed forward.*
>
> *The smuggler told the women and children to sit in the bottom of the boat on top of the luggage. The men sat around the edges. If someone's bag was too big, or in someone's way, or the owner wasn't watching, it was tossed into the water.*
>
> *The passengers came from many countries. They did not speak the same languages fluently. Many times during our passage, they argued.*
>
> *Sometimes the smuggler did not go and appointed a refugee to drive the boat. In our case, the smuggler went. He shut down the motor five times during our three-hour crossing. I think the motor got too hot and he feared it would stop altogether.*
>
> *Finally, we saw land. It was four in the morning. We were off course. No one met us. When the smuggler dropped us short of the shore, we got wet and cold. We went away in all directions. A woman near me asked if we were in Greece or returned to Turkey. I pointed to a Greek flag in a house window. We made it safely.*

Initially each night, fifteen to twenty rafts filled with refugees landed on Chios. The event repeated on other Greek islands. The Greeks remembered their own history when, persecuted by the Nazis, many fled to Syria whose people accepted them. Now, the situation flipped and the residents of the Greek islands responded. During that first year, there were many stories of Greek fishermen who pulled refugee boats to shore. A local man donated the first shelter for the refugees on Chios. Others provided those first arrivals with food and clothing.

Two years later, the refugees continued to arrive, though it was only a handful each week. The pace slowed to process each case. There were changes in European temperament, international policy, and UNCHR procedures. A bottleneck developed; fewer refugees moved to Athens in a timely fashion. They remained in Chios, waiting.

As time wore on, the local Greeks' attitude toward the refugees re-adjusted. Some took a nationalistic hardline view and threw Molotov cocktails at the refugees' tents. Others held protests and town hall meetings against the proposed building of a permanent detention camp. And still others blamed the downward turn in island tourism on the refugees.

While many wished the refugee problem would go away, individual Greek kindnesses continued, quietly. The owner of the motel where I stayed gave two-nights at one of his apartments to a refugee family who fled the Vial camp the night violence erupted. He said to me, "You came thousands of miles to help the refugees in my country—it's the least I can do."

As much as local shop owners denied it, they made money from the refugees. The women's center supported local shopkeepers by buying the necessities for its programs—books and pens for the English classes, Coca-Cola and potato chips for movie night. Often, the refugees had family members supporting them and bank accounts to draw from. One evening, I ran into two refugee friends shopping for hats, and then a couple treating their children to ice cream. Another three joined us with a bag of fresh apricots purchased from an outdoor stand.

Many European humanitarian organizations filled in the gaps the Greek municipality could not during the first year the refugees arrived. Charities met the specific needs of male refugees, children, those needing clothing, or schooling. Some agencies received funding from the UNCHR. Others, like the women's center, found its own donors. A website listed all the organizations involved and how individuals could help. Scores of Europeans (and a few Americans), from retirees to college graduates, came to help at the camps. They met at 9 a.m. for morning organizational meetings and after work at the Pizza Palace for beers.

Like any set of volunteers responding to a crisis, their individual reasons for involvement and level of dedication varied. Some did it for political reasons, some for humanitarian. For others, the refugee work offered a first job or a second—a place to get experience on the international development track. Some volunteers developed friendships with the refugees; others drew a professional line they did not cross. Some refugees noted a volunteer's arrogance. Others gave blessings to their volunteer lawyers who helped navigate their asylum interviews.

Holes in the support network to the refugees appeared occasionally. On an eighty-degree day, two women stood outside the center, one of them dressed in a full-length wool coat. The sisters lived in one of the camps for a month and went to the distribution centers daily, without finding anything suitably cool or appropriately sized for petite bodies. We talked about their limited clothing options and found some humor in saying, "The spring line of fashion has not yet arrived."

Charities that provided clothing to female refugees forgot the importance of bras and underwear and did not offer them. The women's center fixed that problem with a closet full of donated bras. I became accustomed to sizing up a woman's bust from across the front desk. "You look like a 36B—maybe a C. I'll get both."

The fact that violence occurred in the camps wasn't surprising. It was as if the world heaped all the root causes of disagreement onto the people living in Souda and Vial and expected them to be calm and cheerful. The camps looked like mini United Nations, and, like on the rafts, disagreements ran generations in length.

The camps lacked the stimulus of the workplace, universities, or communities from which the refugees came. UN rules indicated refugees could not be employed. Some found volunteer opportunities to give their lives focus and purpose. But mostly, men, accustomed to providing for their families, felt emasculated. Women, who nurtured their children within a family structure that no longer existed, felt exposed.

Generally, I found each individual I encountered, from Greek Coast Guard member to UNCHR authority and volunteer relief worker, wanted the refugees' process to be better, to be right. Everyone did his or her best. Everyone tried within this unfortunate set of circumstances.

The individuals and families who lived in the camps were surprised by the poor conditions they found, and appalled by the horribleness of the experiences they endured. But the thing that beat them down was the lack of respect they so often encountered.

Still, they continued to arrive. The camps did not provide easy or simple solutions, but they provided something these people did not have in recent past situations—a timeline in which the furthest point on it was "hope."

)O(O(

For Mother's Day, the center's director assigned me the job of creating a celebration. In preparation, I asked many of the women how they wished to acknowledge it. Just its mention drew responses of both sadness and joy— some left their mothers behind; others had their children with them. When I asked the women what made a party for them, most answered Coca-Cola and potato chips. In addition, the center gave attendees flowers, an opportunity to write wishes and memories, and a spice cake baked by Salma for the occasion.

The mood felt festive. Women drew patterns on one another with henna. Jeanny downloaded the songs from YouTube of favorite vocal artists and many of the women, including Aalia and Forozan, sang along. Uri sat at the edge and watched. She seemed unusually quiet. I learned the Greeks rejected her family's application for asylum. Three appeals could follow; but if refused, they would be returned to Turkey.

At the celebration, I did my best impersonation of a dancer from the Middle East. I wasn't very good if you compared me to my partner, a middle-aged Syrian woman who wriggled and twirled to this music all her life. The others smiled and nodded and encouraged my hijinks because they knew I was enjoying something they loved and reminded them of home.

The daily life in Chios—the peacefulness of the camps, the similarity of all Middle-Eastern women, even the directness of the asylum process—differed from its broader reality. Similarly, the images of refugees I was given differed from the women I met.

Here in the center, whatever characteristics might have separated us during our celebration of Mother's Day—ethnicity, culture, religion, skin color or nationality—didn't. Together, we laughed, sang and danced.

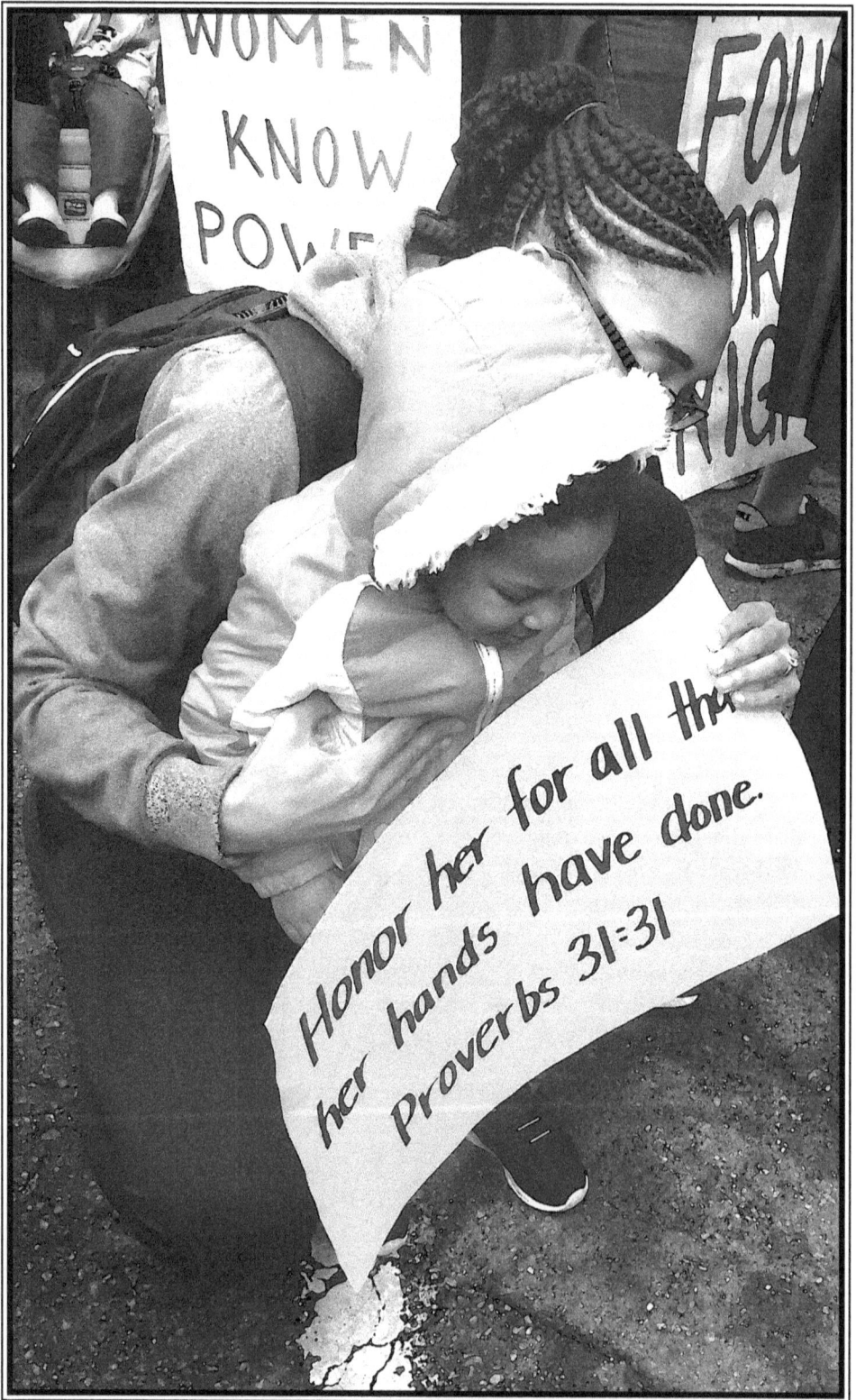

MARYAH CONVERSE

THE PEACE OF IRAQ'S MOTHERS

I moved to Jordan with the Peace Corps in 2004, less than a year after my country invaded Iraq, just before the torture at Abu Ghraib Prison came to light. My fellow Jordanian teachers brought the gruesome images to school, insisting, "You must look at these pictures. These are our brothers." By the end of that year, two devastating battles had been fought in the streets of Fallujah.

Early in my second year, Operation Smile asked if Peace Corps Volunteers could assist their medical mission by staying at an Amman hotel with forty Iraqi children, each with one parent. Most had only rarely left their villages, never stayed in a hotel, certainly never left Iraq. They were asking us, with our Arabic and intercultural fluency, to keep the parents calm and informed, and entertain the children.

I almost didn't do it.

It should have been depressing, living with forty families from the impoverished Iraqi countryside—ravaged by American-made land mines, littered with the remains of radioactive American bomb casings, and now sprayed with insurgent gunfire and IEDs. I was sure I would be so distraught by the deformities of these children that I wouldn't be able to look at them, let alone help them.

I volunteered anyway, because I needed to do something for this country that my country had invaded, for these families in need so close to my new Jordanian home.

My first encounter was in the hotel lobby at check-in with Nour, a chubby little girl, nine months old. Her mother had brought her to Jordan to have a double cleft repaired that divided her upper lip in three. For a moment, she became her deformity. Then she smiled and transformed. "Nour" means light, and a delighted glow radiated from her fat round face and big liquid eyes when she looked up at me and grinned. There was only one thing to do. I grinned back, tickling the bib of her red ruffled dress until we both giggled.

After Nour, it was easy to love them all. I wasn't disgusted or even uncomfortable. They were blithely happy babies, cheerful, playful, and I was instantly charmed. It took me longer to appreciate the quiet strength of their mothers.

✗✗✗

I especially loved two-year-old Serdar. His parents had been given special dispensation to both come with their son, because in addition to his cleft lip and cleft palate, he was blind, deaf and possibly autistic. Then, after he arrived in Amman, the doctors doing his pre-op found a hole in his heart. Despite all that, he energized that whole dim hotel dining room.

After dinner, his parents sat Serdar on top of a big round table. He rolled over onto his belly, pressing his cheek and ear to the navy blue polyester tablecloth. Though deaf, he could feel people talking through the table beneath.

His father tapped lightly on the table's edge. Serdar tapped back, arms and legs splayed out to the four directions. He mimicked flawlessly his father's more and more complex rhythms, keeping perfect time.

Then his father started doing drum rolls, at first softly with his fingertips on the edge of the table, a light crescendo growing faster and louder, until he was pounding the table like thunder with both palms. Serdar's back arched, his hands and feet slapped against the table, and he gave a great, loud peal of laughter.

His delight rang out across the room. Heads lifted and turned. I moved closer, grinning, enchanted. The war was a world away. Caught up in the innocent joy of the moment, it was impossible not to laugh with Serdar.

His father de-crescendoed, bringing the drumroll down to just the light, intermittent tapping of two fingertips on the table edge. Serdar laid down his arms and legs and pressed his ear to the tablecloth again, listening intently to the light tap-tap and chortling softly to himself. Then his father started again, faster and louder, drawing out that peal of uninhibited laughter once more.

Crowding around the table without speaking, we all got involved at the peak of the crescendo, then dropped away one by one as the drumroll came back down again. Serdar entertained a dozen of us for nearly an hour, helping us forget entirely where we were and what was happening back in his homeland.

)(O)(

More than half the children came with their mothers. Some framed their faces in loose *hijab* of navy blue or espresso brown, but most wore black headscarves. They all wore *chador*, a large semicircle of black cloth. The center of the straight edge balanced on the crowns of their heads, trailing to the ground all around, held closed under their chins with one hand. The *chador* rippled and billowed in even the slight wind of a woman's own passing, lending a poetic, ethereal quality to these mothers, petite and demur and preferring the company of other women.

One mother was none of those things. She was tall, with a long, blocky face, lined and leathery from sun and wind. There was a faint patina of sandy dirt permanently ground into the lower edge of her *chador*, made of a thicker material that didn't billow so romantically. I guessed from her thick, coarse hands and her easy manner with the fathers that she must have been a Bedouin shepherd or farmer like my Jordanian neighbors.

She stopped me after dinner one evening, taking my forearm firmly in her big, dark hand, the skin dry and cracked. "Do you know what my name is?" she asked. She had a booming outdoor voice in the dark, low-ceilinged dining room. "My name is Amreeka."

"*W-allah?* Really?" I wasn't sure what to say, or if she was pulling my leg. She had spoken slowly and clearly enough, in a thick Bedouin accent almost identical to my Jordanian neighbors, but *amreeka* means America.

She laughed at my confusion and gestured expansively. "My parents named me Amreeka because you supported us in the war"—this must have been the Iran-Iraq War—"and my parents thought you would bring progress and democracy to Iraq. And now here you are, helping my daughter. Thank God for you!"

Though Operation Smile's doctors hailed from across the Western world, Amreeka would go back to Iraq and say that Americans had fixed her daughter's cleft lip. In the Bedouin tribes, disability may be seen as a family's punishment from God for some sin, tarnishing the reputations of whole extended families. This surgery meant that not only Amreeka's daughter, but her sisters and her girl cousins would have better marriage prospects, that Amreeka and her husband might look forward in their later years to the support of a more successful son-in-law.

That is, if there were enough hale and whole young men remaining for her daughters to marry, and if those young men lived into Amreeka's later years. If Amreeka lived into her own later years. With American soldiers' fingers nervous on the trigger, and desperate Iraqis perpetrating their own violence, Amreeka's future and her daughters' futures were far from certain or rosy.

Still, she remained certain that America held the key. I feared she would be brutally disappointed, but I couldn't make myself contradict her optimism.

※※※

The war in Iraq was the daily reality back home for these families, and a frequent topic of conversation. They kept using a word to refer to American soldiers that sounded like the Arabic word *Hmaar*—donkey. Arabs use it much the way Americans do, as in, "You jackass!"

Yet, it was clear from the Iraqis' tone and body language that they were speaking kindly, even fondly of these *hamar*. Finally, another Volunteer realized that it had nothing to do with donkeys. *Hamar* was an English loan word—from Hummer or Humvee—referring to a patrol of Coalition soldiers in an armored vehicle.

"The Hummer saw my son's harelip when we were on the way to the market," one mother said, tugging her filmy, slippery *chador* back into place on the crown of her head. "We always wave and smile at the Hummers and say thank you for helping us."

These women did not see themselves as I saw them, as victims of my arrogant, angry government. The Hummers had brought war and death. American troops had bombed infrastructure, destroyed their priceless ancient monuments, brought chaos, insurgency and Al Qaeda to their country.

Yet, these women were grateful, and this was not that often-infuriating practice of Arab hospitality where they tell the polite fiction they think their host wants to hear. They were not talking to me. They said these things to each other, and they said them with confident sincerity. So I listened as best I could with my imperfect Arabic, and tried to understand.

The young, pretty mother continued, "Usually, we thank them from a distance. We don't get too near the Hummers. It makes them nervous. But one day, a soldier waved at us to come closer, me and my son." He was a slight boy beside her, about seven, hesitant to meet my gaze.

I listened silently, worried what would come next. I knew the Hummers were harbingers of destruction.

"The soldier smiled at me and my son. He said hello," she said. "He asked him his name. My son is shy. He wouldn't answer." Shy seemed the wrong word. The children at the hotel were more reticent, subjected all of their short lives to shame and ridicule from their neighbors, and then the traumas of war and occupation.

"Then he leaned down from his Hummer and gave me the paper with information about Operation Smile. That's how we got here." Other mothers jumped into the conversation with their own stories about how the Hummers had won their hearts and minds.

)()()(

Every time I hear the news from Iraq, I remember those families. Nour should now be finishing elementary school. Does her smile still glow? Do her big doe eyes still dance? I cannot imagine what she has seen, or how it may have dimmed her light.

Operation Smile arranged for another organization to take Serdar and his parents to London for open heart surgery, and then the facial reconstruction he had come to Jordan for. I remember him as a toddler, but he should be a teenager now. Is he still the happy drummer boy on that dining room table? Is he still strong-limbed and pudgy with a pealing laugh that fills the room? Or have explosions vibrating up through his living room floor tempered his *joie de vivre*?

Amreeka's daughter should be in her twenties, married with at least one baby of her own. Are her children healthy? Maybe Amreeka's village of farmers and shepherds is small enough to have escaped the violence, the bloody conflict, the decimated manhood.

)()()(

In 2014, Iraqi cities fell like dominoes to the fanatics calling themselves "Islamic State." Yezidis who had managed to survive both Saddam and the occupation now starved on mountaintops. Journalists lost their heads trying to plead the Iraqi cause. I clicked through pictures of women walking back into Mosul, after the Iraqi army had retreated and the extremists had taken control.

I see their black *chador* rippling and dancing on the dusty wind. They turn and reach out black-gloved hands for small children just out of frame. I want to grab them by the shoulders and shout, "*W-allahi*—By God, why? Why would you go back there?"

"*W-allahi*," they say, "why not? Now it's the fundamentalists, before them the Hummers, before them Saddam, before him the British, before them the Ottomans. *Ma shaa' allah*—What God hath wrought! All we can do is go back to our homes, where our grandfathers lived and their grandfathers. *Allahu 'alem*—God knows, and His will be done."

Demur but determined, they float away down the streets of Mosul, steadfast pillars of black smoke silhouetted against the pockmarked shells of their whitewashed homes. And I remind myself that Iraq is also the land of Nour's smile, and of Serdar's laughter. When Mosul is liberated, it will be these women, these children and their children who rebuild. If there is to be peace, it will be theirs.

I still struggle for Amreeka's optimism, but I still have hope.
Allahu 'alem.

EVE MILLS ALLEN

MORE THAN A NAME

For many years, I believed my skin must be the wrong color. This feeling of *being different* was glaringly acute when I moved into the First Nations community of Oromocto (*Welamooktook*) in southern New Brunswick, Canada in 1991 with my new Maliseet husband and baby granddaughter, Sasha, who I was raising. I did my best to fit in and that included attending every ceremony or powwow in most of the First Nations communities in the province, especially those held in Woodstock, just over an hour away. It was there that my granddaughter received her *spirit name* and I received something even greater – the gift of acceptance.

Lounging in my lawn chair, as the drummers gathered for the naming ceremony on the wooded property of Maliseet Elder Ervin Polchies, I tried to guess what name would be chosen. I could see Sasha was anxious for the music to begin. Jumping up and down, in her red ribbon dress, her long dark hair shimmering with auburn highlights in the sun, she reminded me of a hummingbird. She loved the beat of the drum and now she was clutching a small drum in her chubby hands. It had been given to her by her Maliseet stepfather.

We were no strangers to the Aboriginal gatherings at the home of Elder Ervin. We'd been coming to them since Sasha's first birthday. Now, she was only a month away from her fourth birthday.

The festival atmosphere was intoxicating. From the fragrance of sweet grass infiltrating each ceremony and the smell of fresh salmon as it fried in large black skillets, to the constant beat of drums, repeatedly joined by strong voices in chants that would go on for hours, I savored every minute. When the drumming stopped, ear-pleasing renditions of Neil Young accompanied by guitars filled the air. Most of all, I loved the stories, and the elders had many to share.

I loved the stories about birds and animals the best. They reminded me of the legends my father told me when I was a child, stories that illustrated how every living creature had a special place in the world and that all were related in spirit. Many opinions competed to dominate how I saw myself as I tried to find my own place in the world. These stories helped me feel connected. I'd been outside the circle on too many occasions. It was a cold, lonely place where I was accused of being either "too white" or "not white enough" by people I loved.

Sasha was a direct descendent of Mohawk blood but today she would be given a Maliseet name by a Passamaquoddy elder. I had no clear lineage that linked me to any one tribe so I was too often treated like an outsider. I was just a "mutt," I'd been told on one occasion.

The name Sasha would receive would help her, give her guidance on how to live her life, and how to protect any areas of vulnerability, I was told by Elder Ervin. I wasn't quite sure how that all came together but I was intrigued. I had already met a number of people with *Indian names*; Snow Goose, White Bear, Eagle Child and Feather were all in attendance. They told me the spirit of the animal or bird (or even, in some cases, plant or tree or water) chosen would be her guide, her totem.

In honor of the day, a couple from the Tobique Reserve presented her with a gift, a T-shirt that read *Freedom from 500 Years of Oppression—At What Price?* I appreciated the gesture but couldn't help but think the message was a bit heavy for a preschooler and it was not hard to detect their coolness toward me as the perceived descendant of the "oppressors."

Elder Ervin and his wife Nadine also presented Sasha with a gift—a poster of a smiling dark-skinned girl dressed in buckskin dress and leggings. The girl was standing beside a wolf and there were birds and flowers all around her. I have always had a special penchant for wolves so I was quick to voice my admiration of the picture.

When the drumming started to mark the beginning of the naming ceremony, Sasha was the first one on her feet. She bobbed to the beat like a buoy gone wild on the ocean. Completely oblivious to any outside cares, she became one with the drumbeat. The elders told me this was the best stress reliever anyone could find, to dance to the drum and forget about everything else. Later, I tried to do that myself, but felt a bit self-conscious at first. However, it didn't take long to let go and follow the soothing tide.

The elder who was giving the names had been fasting for two days and praying for each individual who would be part of today's naming ceremony. I was told that the names would be given to him by the Creator during the fast, either in a dream or perhaps an animal or bird might visit him personally. I was excited as I waited for Sasha's turn. There were two other children ahead of her. I wondered what name had been chosen for her. Maybe it would be a wolf. *That would be so cool*, I thought. Sasha said she wanted to be a grasshopper. I don't think she quite understood what the ceremony was about.

When it was her turn, the elder beckoned her into his circle. I followed. We all smudged with the smoke from the sweet grass and the elder sat and smoked his pipe looking at both of us without a word. Ervin was seated nearby with a few other men I didn't recognize.

It was hard to tell how old this elder might be. His face was almost free of wrinkles but his hair was silver and hung in a braid down his back. He was dressed in buckskin trousers and a vest beaded with fiddlehead symbols hanging loosely over a red shirt with ribbons to represent the four colors of men—traditional regalia for the eastern tribes.

"What's your name, *dus*?" he asked.

I wasn't sure if he were looking at Sasha or me. His gaze seemed to envelope both of us.

"Sasha," my granddaughter responded shyly as he reached for her hand.

"I'm her grandmother, Eve," I whispered when his glance seemed to rest on my face.

He asked Sasha to come closer.

"Don't be afraid, *dus*," he said in a voice so hypnotic and welcoming I felt compelled to move closer also.

Sasha was staring at his face, completely still for the first time all day. The elder pronounced a prayer in Maliseet as the drums beat softly in the background. When he finished, he put his hand on Sasha's head.

"You are a very gifted child," he said. "You will be a messenger someday to this world. That is why you have been given the name of one of the Creator's messengers. You are *oqim*, the loon—*the little loon that floats across the waters*. Respect your name and honor it."

He looked at me as he spoke these last words, and I nodded my head, realizing I would be required to remind Sasha as she grew older.

I thanked the elder, took Sasha's hand and turned to leave.

"Wait, Eva," the elder called out. I was surprised to be called by my birth name. Only my mother and one brother still called me *Eva*.

"Me?" I turned to look at him.

"Don't you want a name?" he asked.

"Well, I didn't really expect . . . "

"You could use a name too," he said as I moved closer.

Again, he began to pray in his Native language. I could barely make out the drums over the beating of my own heart.

"You need to study well the nature of your spirit protector," the elder told me. "It will help you know how to handle situations you haven't handled so well in the past."

I was getting excited. Maybe mine would be a wolf, I hoped.

"I see many flowers around you, flowers of all colors. They attract many things. Not all of them are good. You need to be careful."

Flowers? I tried to figure out what this had to do with a name.

"You are *alamossit*—hummingbird," he said quietly.

Hummingbird! I thought to myself. *Not a wolf or bear?* I was a little disappointed until I heard his next words.

"The hummingbird is a very strong, wise creature," the elder said. "Study it well. It never stays where danger lurks and she knows who she is wherever she goes. All the tribes of man admire her strength and beauty. That is you, Eva. You are a gift from the Creator to all colors and races."

The elder shook my hand Native style and smiled.

As I walked away, my heart was full. I knew I had been given a great treasure, even more than a special name. I'd been given the hand of true acceptance and, for the first time in my life, I no longer felt like an outsider.

THOMAS ABAKAH

DOORWAYS OF MEMORIES

A scattered dream is like a far-off memory. A far-off memory is like a scattered dream.* In the dream, I stood in front of so many doors. They stretched out on both sides of me, and I did not know which to choose. The doors were big, with double handles. I opened the doors one at a time. When I opened the first door, a heavenly light shined out and it let me see my deep past. When I was about five or six years old, I lived with my mother and my little sister. Even though my father did not live with us, he often came to visit us in Sierra Leone where I was born. My father stayed with us a couple weeks, and then he left afterward. I did not understand why he was leaving us. I tried to ask him "Why are you leaving us?" but I could not say it. One of the few memories I had of my dad was when he saved my life. My sister and I were eating yams and soup with fish at lunchtime. Suddenly, I accidently ate a fish bone, and the bone got stuck in my throat. I couldn't breathe. Panicking, I put my hands to my throat and ran to my mom. I fell down and started spinning on the floor like a top. Then, I gasped, "Mom, mom something is in my throat." My mom exclaimed, "What's wrong, what's wrong?" Then my dad showed up, took me to the tub, and filled it up with water. After that, he put his fingers down my throat to make me throw up the bone out of my mouth. The door slammed shut, and it locked. I couldn't open it again. So I opened a new door.

The new door showed me experiences of danger, joy and sorrow. One sunny afternoon, while I was playing with my little sister, my mom popped into the room and yelled, "Hide under the table." I did not understand what was going on. So, my sister and I quickly hid under the table. Then I heard something outside of the window. It was loud and sounded like thunder "boom, boom, boom." We stayed under the table for hours. Then, my mom whispered to me, "Look out the window and see if anyone is outside," so I did but I did not see anyone. My mom knew that the civil war was near our home. The next day, my mom was packing our clothes to leave. When we walked outside, my eyes only saw bombed out buildings and I felt confused by what was going on.

Soon after that, my mom took us to my dad's side of the family in Ghana by boat. My mom, my sister and I stayed at my grandparent's house. After a couple weeks, I went to school there. When my mom took me to kindergarten, I was scared. By the time my mom was about to leave, I was left behind. I tried to run after her but the teacher grabbed me. I screamed, "Mamma, mamma don't leave me." I didn't understand why I was being left alone. I was crying so hard because I did not know anyone in school. After that, my teacher took me to the classroom to meet my classmates. Then some kid I did not know came toward me and gave me a teddy bear to comfort me because my tears would not stop falling. After that, I fell asleep while holding the bear tight.

However, I also experienced brief periods of joy. The family members I had the closest connection to were my little sister, my cousin, my uncle, and my grandpa. My sister was my first friend and we always played games together. However, sometimes at the end of the day we would go our separate ways. My cousin was like an older brother because of the kindness he had towards me. My uncle was like a father figure because he always took my sister and me to his home for a sleepover along with his other nieces and nephews. I didn't like his wife, though, because she was always mean to me and she would hit me every time I did something wrong or saw me drooling. My uncle was nice, though, as was my grandpa. My grandpa would always call me up to buy cookies for him. He gave me money and I would run to the store to buy them. Then I would run back fast and he would share the cookies with me. We would chat a little bit. He was a good old man. A couple of years later he died. Every one of my family members went to the funeral, except my sister and me. My dad even came to Ghana for the funeral, but he left a couple weeks later.

Every day I would go to my friends' house from morning to night to play. I was free like a bird. I could go and come as I pleased. Often, I liked to mess with the old lady who was living under the building of my grandma's house. I always knocked on her window then ran across the street. The old lady would slowly come by her window to see who was knocking but then would leave when she saw no one there. I would go back to her window again to knock and run across the street again before she could see me. However, the third time I knocked she came outside to see who was knocking and I was laughing so hard that my tears were coming out from my eyes. Then I walked into my grandma's house, cracking up. I was jealous of kids who had their parents at their side. Once I was in a school play, and I saw my mom there, but she stayed for only a little bit and then left. However, I never stayed sad because I had my friends.

Although I had happy times, I also felt sorrow. My dad came to visit from time to time. Usually my mom slept with my sister and me, but when my dad came, he and my mom slept in the guest room and my sister and I slept in our own room. My sister wanted to go to my parents' room to sleep with them. I tagged along with her. When my sister got on my parent's bed, I got on too but my dad said "No! Go back to your room," so I went back to my room alone and sad. I thought that I was not part of this family. Deep in my heart, I was jealous of my sister.

One day my sister was sick and went into the hospital. My mother and I went to visit her. I asked, "How are you?" My sister smiled, "I'm fine," and we chatted a little bit. That afternoon my mother and I went back home. Later that night my mom returned to the hospital. In the middle of the night I went downstairs and saw my mom outside talking to a neighbor and crying. I asked, "What's wrong, mom. Why are you crying?" She held me tight and pressed my arm and said, "Your sister has died." And I said, "It's okay." I never cried about my sister's death because I did not understand death. I felt like a robot because I had no emotions.

The door slammed shut, and it locked again, so I opened a new door. When I opened the door, bright light poured in; then later it became dim and I saw a road ahead and I started to walk on it. At first, the road was smooth; then later, it started to crumble. A few years after my sister died, my mom and I went to the U.S. to live with my dad. My dad picked us up at the airport with his two friends. By the time, I saw him, I ran toward him; I jumped on him because I was glad to see him. After that, my dad took us to where he lived. When we reached home, I looked around the house. I saw a tricycle and I rode on it in the house. My aunt came with her daughter. She was so surprised to see me and she hugged me, but I did not know her right away because she was living here with my dad. My aunt's daughter was next to her and looked at me in confusion; in her mind she was saying, "Who is that kid and why is he riding my tricycle?" I came to her and said "Hi." After that, we became friends. In addition, she became like a sister to me. One time my aunt, cousin, and I went to the zoo. I saw different animals and it was my first experience seeing animals besides dogs, goats, and monkeys. It was my first good childhood memory.

Before I could go to school, I needed to get four shots. It hurt so much I felt like my body was being drilled into. I tried to run away from the doctor but my dad held me so tight I could not move. All my life I hated getting shots because I did not like needles in my body. At the time, I was starting to develop significant speech problems. I'd always had some difficulty talking, but suddenly it got a little worse. In third grade, I met a nice speech therapist; she was my first friend that was a teacher. We always played a card game called "Go fish" to improve my speech. One time in fourth grade, she took me to a doctor to check my tonsils. Afterwards, she took me to buy ice cream. Then, she took me back to school. Some disability helpers came to my school and gave me a device where I could type what I wanted to say and it would say it aloud. My speech therapist teacher was going to move, and she told my dad that she would take me to Disney World with her kids in the summer. I was so happy. However, by the time it was summer, she had already moved and I was disappointed. I used the device until sixth grade because for some reason it just stopped working. The disability people came again to give me a new device. It looked like a microphone with a speaker. One time I gave the device to my English teacher to hold it for me so when I came back it would be there. However, when I did come back I asked for the device and she tried to look for it but she could not find it. After that, I stopped using my device.

One day I was in the middle of my eighth grade, my mother told me that my father's brother had died. I said, "Oh." Again, I had no emotions about death.

The bright light became dim. In ninth grade, my English teacher told me I had to use the device again or I would have to transfer to a special aid school. I was so mad at her because she told me I had to go to another school and she forced me to use my device. Then, she contacted the disability people to give me a new device and I told them that I wanted a small one so I could carry it around. Therefore, I used the device until eleventh grade. When I used it, I felt like a robot because I was using a device to talk to other people and I wanted to talk with my mouth so that I could talk to my friends. Also my speech problems made me feel like an outsider inside of my own family. That same year my parents told me that my cousin had died, I asked my parents "What happened?" "How did he die?" My father answered, "He fell off the roof while he was fixing it." After my father finished explaining what happened to my cousin, I was silent for a while. I did not cry for him. Again, again, and again I had no emotions for death. I asked myself "Why, why, whyyyy, why you did not cry for him? He was like your big brother to you. Or maybe you did not want to show your emotions so you kept your emotions deep in your heart."

In my junior year, I tried to commit suicide because I was depressed. I felt like I was in a deep ocean and the water pressure was too much on me because I was sad, alone, and I had no one to connect with. So, my friends and other people tried to talk me out of it. Then, some of my friends came to my house and took me to the church. After that, I did not attempt suicide.

In my senior year of my high school, I had someone to connect with. She was my English teacher. One time she helped me write my essay after class. While she helped me out, we just talked about our private life. She told me that her sister and brother had a disability like me. I would tell her how I did not want to use that device I used before and she told me, "You don't want to use it anymore because you want to talk by yourself." When she said that, it touched my heart. In my mind, I said "Oh my God. She was the first person who understands how I feel." Meanwhile, I often would go to see her to talk after school. I felt comfortable, like I could be myself, but sometimes when I hung out with my friends I felt hurt and sad at the same time. Then the door shut.

I opened the second to last door. I saw a path ahead but it was blocked with no way through. Then it began to clear. After I graduated from high school, I went to college and I thought about the subjects I wanted to study, but I needed to take a placement test before I could take my courses. I failed the college placement test because my score was below average. I went to the counselor, who told me to take an ESL placement test so that I could be placed in the ESL program. After taking ESL classes for a couple of semesters, I took the college placement test again. This time, I passed the test. After that, I took American English One. I passed that class and level two as well, but when I started American English Three, I really struggled. I failed two times in a row. While taking it a third time, I thought that I would stay there forever. I felt that time stood still but the world kept going. I was frustrated and I wanted to give up because my future was too far away from me, and I could not keep up. I told myself, "I give up." In my despair, I realized that I needed help, so I got baptized. After I was baptized, good things began to happen to me. First, I got my driver's permit; then some jobs I applied for called me. I was so happy that they called me, but I did not get the jobs. Then, the third good thing that happened to me was that a wonderful person helped me get out of the English as a Second Language program. I was so grateful that she helped me out. In addition, she knew that I was a hardworking person, so she tried to talk to the department chair. After she finished talking to her boss, they switched me from the ESL program to the regular English track. I was grateful for that because now I could move forward to start my major.

I try to open the last door, but I cannot because it has a chain with a lock on it. Although I try to saw it off, the chain is so powerful that the saw breaks into pieces. Therefore, I stand there looking at the door and thinking to myself "hmmm." I think that this door is my future door. I wonder why it has a chain with a lock on it. I think to myself again, "What is behind this door and what does it hold for my future? How long will it take for the chain to break off?" Then I look at the future door one more time and say, "Well I cannot open the door for a while." So I leave while looking back.

To Be Continued One Day!

*Opening phrase adapted from *Kingdom of Hearts 2*

LORETTA DIANE WALKER

CHRONICLE OF MUATH'S EYES

What flag can we wave? I wave the flag of stone and seed,
table mat stitched in blue.
          —Naomi Shihab Nye

September 6
Muath's arms are invisible when joy propels him
across the threshold of my classroom.
His *Happy Birthday to you* is a proclamation, not song.
In one hand, half dozen roses, in the other,
a giant KitKat bar.

I go to Granbury where my roses drink
from a Sonic Drive-In cup and the memory
of Muath's smile crawls from my suitcase.

December 16
The end of day, fatigue is trapped on my face.
I meet Muath, his mother, in the checkered hall
where thousands of small feet scuff the floor
with the heels of their mischief.

His pride hangs in the air; "This is my mom."
I smile at the origin of his eyes
shrouded in the cocoon of a gold hijab.

"Here. Take. They're for Christmas."
I eat a hoskia; the sweet bread is happiness
on my tongue. They smile, walk away.
Their eyes a pair of luggage
carrying a language I do not understand.

January 11
We sing the *Star-Spangled Banner.*
He is a ten-year-old boat drifting between two countries.

"Now let's sing Palestine's national anthem," he asks.
"I don't know it. We can look for it."
The class crowds around the computer, we search.

The flag of his native tongue is stuffed
in the long arm of a rifle, pointed at a fearful boy
who could be his cousin, curled like a snail.
Tears float around the harbor of his eyes.

He hides shame that does not belong to him.
Silence. We begin to drown in the cold deep
river of shock. When my voice returns, I tell them,
"This is not Palestine."

The lungs of the classroom fill with air.
Sorrow tears through the cuff of my heart
when Muath's head brushes my shoulder.
My words, soft against his ear.
"Go get water. Take a friend."
I watch healing escort two countries out the door.

II. CLASS

BONNI CHALKIN

AN UNFORGETTABLE ACT OF SHARING

When I was thirty years old, I went through what I think of as an early midlife crisis. I was working at the time in a high-powered, high-paying showroom in New York City's fashion industry. But feeling that something was missing in my life, I decided to sign up for a Voyager Outward Bound course in northern Minnesota. For a few weeks, I lived in the woods, canoed the boundary waters, hiked and rock-climbed, and was left alone on an island for three days and three nights—truly enjoying and living life to the fullest with what some consider nothing. While away, I developed a painful infection on my foot, but dared not say anything because I didn't want to be sent home. I felt so free—so *me*. I had discovered a strength within that I didn't know existed.

Once back in New York City, I saw a doctor who treated my foot. While hobbling home with my new bandage, I passed three homeless men sitting on the street who caught my attention. I was drawn to them, wanting to better understand and learn about their circumstances. I always traveled with a notebook and a camera, and I politely asked if I could spend the day writing about them. One man asked if I was a reporter, and I explained I was just a regular girl.

These three men took me into the fold and couldn't wait to tell me all their stories. I am left recalling the sense of camaraderie they not only shared between themselves, but which they extended to me as well. And I will never forget two experiences from that indelible day.

I had wanted to document my new acquaintances, and asked passersby if they would please take our picture together. Everyone ignored or avoided us fearfully. Some even made a half moon circle to prevent coming too close. I remain struck by the sense of isolation that these men had to endure on a daily basis.

I will also never forget the ultimate act of sharing I experienced that afternoon. Donnie, who seemed to be the group's leader, was responsible for collecting the change thrown our way. When a stranger tossed us a handful of coins, Donnie handed one to each of us—including me. I was so taken by that moment. Someone who had so little had the generosity of heart and spirit to share their humble bounty, even though he knew I was not homeless.

Each day, I try to keep this memory close to my heart. I wonder about the many ways we might give to other human beings—not just through money, but through compassion, time, and a shoulder to cry on. Donnie cried his story on mine. Not only did they welcome me—a complete stranger—into their group, they embraced me as if I were one of them. That's an honor I have never forgotten.

MIMI JENNINGS

INCLUSION

I have a real ID a user ID
pins, passwords a passport my name
brings nods
doesn't have to be spelled I got a loan

at the bank. My dentist
appointment's at four on Friday. My phone's
charged full gas tank my dress my skin
doesn't arouse
hate my language
is spoken. I'm not followed
around the store I vote. I have luggage
receipts an adequate
coat. A text
brings a ride and dinner.
I donate.

A desert
isn't a death sentence.
I don't take shaky measures
for passage
a bed I'm not sleeping
under a broken box in a doorway.
Flapping plastic isn't a windborne
treasure.

The waiting line I stand in
is the short
one. But my heart's not
gotten used
to the isolation.

SHARON LASK MUNSON

WHAT COMES AROUND

After the clerk completes my purchase,
he pauses, "I know you."

"You used to come
to the Substance Abuse Car Wash
when it was on West Elm Street.
Your donations paid for candy and movies."

"I want you to know, I'm clean seven years.
The judge was tough. It wasn't easy.
My wife stood by me. I'm back with my kids.
I have two beautiful daughters
and a three month old son."

"Life is pretty darn good.
I've been here five years—
just made manager."

             ✠✠✠

The following Saturday
I'm at the new Substance Abuse Car Wash
across from Greenwood Mall,
scrutinizing my red Jeep Grand Cherokee
being hand washed and showered,

overhearing three young men with hoses and sponges
chatter about the spankings and punishments
they received as children.
They're laughing, cracking up.

"Nice car," one man shouts to me.
"Looks new."
"Eleven years old," I call back.
He nods. "That's what you get
when you take care of business."

LAURIE KLEIN

HUNGER'S PLATE OF SECRETS

Goodwill plates barely contain
wild salmon, asparagus, roasted potatoes—

their feast almost muffles
the serrated scrape of resentment,
like knives on ironstone.

Factor in fear and hurt
with time's slow etch—no wonder
they call it crazing when
porcelain's gleaming surface
breaks down, the inroads graying,
finally immune to suds, and vigor,
propelling the emery sponge.

And then there's the loaf, a tearing
and afterward, the merest
brush of hands:

"You take the heel."
"No, you. I insist."

TYREE WILSON

BEYOND THE PHYSICAL

We grew up on different sides of the tracks.
What do you live for?
The conversations we've had, that's what I've prayed for.
I didn't expect you to embrace me, but in reality you wanted more.

I was down on my luck,
Your were finishing school.
In myself I started to lose trust,
And I started to reject my jewel.

Can we exist together with the paths we take?
How will I be judged by your circle of trust?
Truth or Illusion, which one would you embrace,
If the flesh of your lover was never to be unstuck?

Her reply was a comforting smile,
Unaware that in me these worries exist.
Her nature, and my worries separated by a mile.
Her true beauty becoming known, and my fear of her love extinguished.

CASHIER

I jump out the whip,
I'm usually running behind, so I'm technically late when I clock in. That's a little less change to work with,
but I finished my project.

I'll embrace this pay cut if it means I have a little more time on my hands,
that's a money multiplier depending on what you do with it.
"I remember you, when you were doing well."
That's what some of the haters say to screw with me.

Where the love go?
Sir got a little gas on his hands and he's coming to me to project,
but Ma'am has been kind since she walked in.
And she just lost a kid.

Holding back her tears,
there's only so much you can do when a levee breaks.
She's just taking it a day at a time.
She's apologizing because she knows she's in pain, but doesn't want to ruin my day.

"We need change." Is what the young say.
And then you have the young brains, in old vessels that don't want to change,
because they claim to be stuck in their ways.
Same input means same output, they'll never relate.

At the end of my shift I clock out.
Taking lessons from those that taught me so much.
Lessons about character, and when my name is mentioned, what I want people to think about.

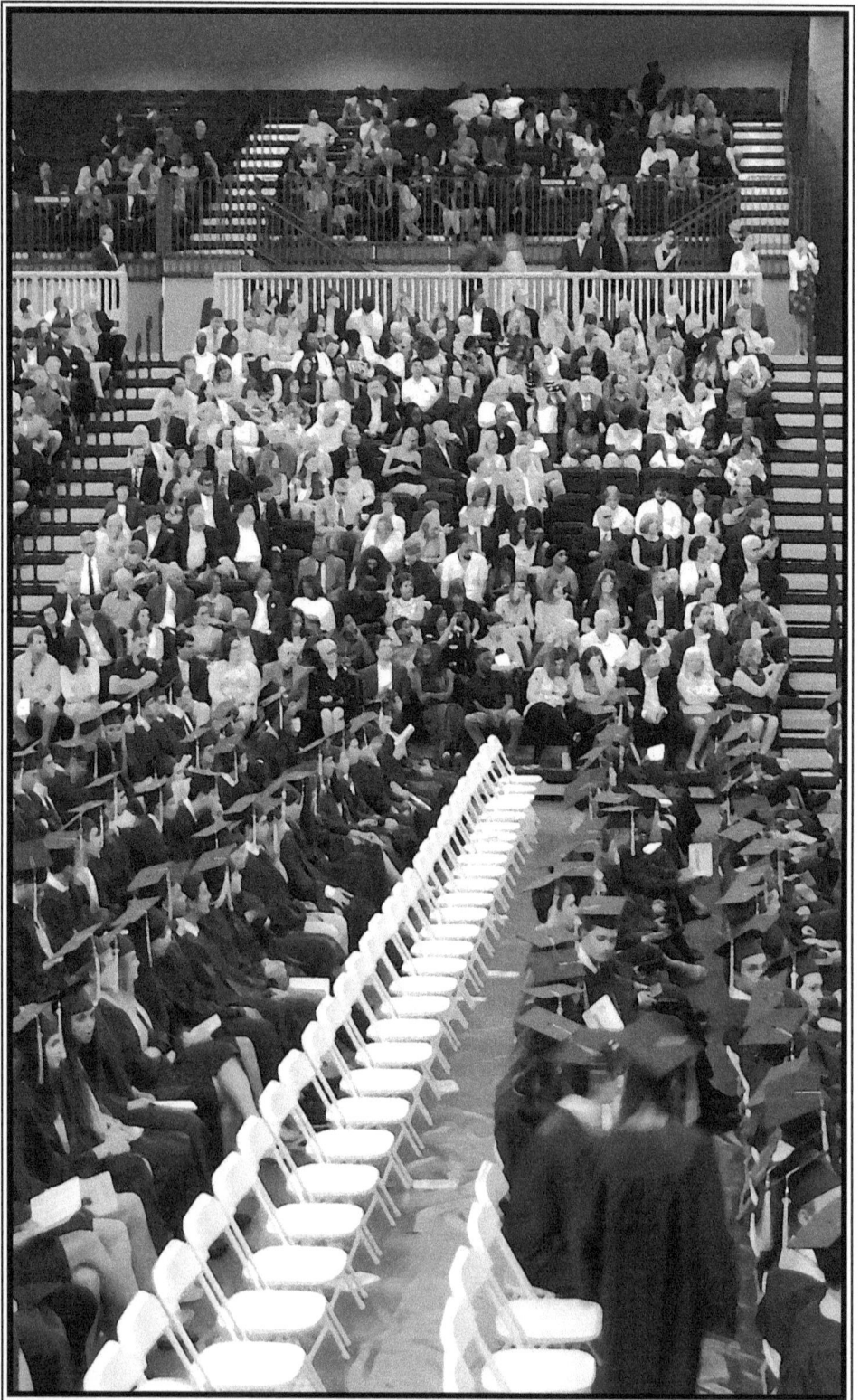

III. CRIMINAL JUSTICE

HEATHER TOSTESON

ACCOUNTING

Cardinal rustling in the tulip tree,
coyote sleeping near the creek.
Helicopters circling overhead
as if this were Watts, not
a quiet cul de sac in Georgia
where I am taking the whole day off.
A manic depressive on a short leash
feeling the bite of that tether.
I have to pull myself together.

Too many days spent imagining
my way into lives I wouldn't want to lead.
MLK, tears in his eyes, offers food
to a small child murmuring,
"It will get better by and by."
Decades later, freed from prison,
she wields a kitchen knife when she feels
short-changed of her grown son's attention.
How dare he favor his own children
when she's prepared a meal for him,
the decades she's dreamed of this moment,
of what might have been and still could be
if people just played by the rules
of her own psyche. He pushes his children
behind him, raises his hand.
"Try that and I will *do* you," she warns him.

She warns me too, eyes gleaming, voice
bright as a knife. "When I look at you
I see a business woman with an investment
in understanding but no heart, no
humanity." I feel like a spendthrift
even listening. What on earth was I thinking
to come here. She's hurt that I didn't offer
my roof when she was homeless.
I pick and choose my words like precious jewels
from a plundered safe. Not cold. Not fool.
Certainly not foolhardy. Not as hopeful
as MLK. Bankrupt. Maybe that's the word I'm seeking.
No one could every pay me enough to do this.
I envy her longer leash and reach. I want to say,
Do you have any idea what it costs me
to get this close. *Do* you?"

Instead I say, "I'm so sorry you see me that way.
But you're right. I do want to understand. This has been
a difficult time." "I know I got to you," she murmurs
with a broad smile. "Your face is red." Thin skinned, *my*
tell. I take a deep breath. I know she is honoring me
with her ruthless truth. Am I free to refuse it?

SHARON HILBERER

THE SHOOTER

was a sweet boy	*always a troubled kid*
showed up regular for work	*hard to catch his eye*
prompt and reliable	*wasn't much for small talk*
would stop by on Friday with a fish sandwich	*oh, sometimes a call on Christmas*
never caused any trouble	*generally kept to himself*
neighbors say he was quiet and polite	*relatives decline to discuss . . .*

JUDY CATTERTON

THE TEENAGE KILLER

*/Y/outh is more than a chronological fact. . . .
It is a time of immaturity, irresponsibility,
impetuousness[,] and recklessness.*
—The United States Supreme Court

It was late. Maybe I was concentrating on reading some legal document or engrossed in preparing a case for trial. So, I hadn't been particularly interested in the darkening sky out the window behind my desk. Perhaps I noticed that the only sound was the usual hum from the refrigerator down the hall in the small kitchen in the suite of offices my law firm rented in a high-rise building in Rockville, Maryland, a suburb of D.C. I was aware but not concerned that the other lawyers and staff had left for the day and that I was alone. Except, I wasn't alone.

"You don't remember me, do you?" he said. He was squatting in the corner behind my desk amid a bunch of wires doing something related to my phone. I must have noticed this repairman earlier in the evening when he arrived and then promptly forgot about him. I had to twist my body into an extremely awkward position and swivel my chair around to see him. Looking down, I saw a large man, mid to late twenties, short brown hair, clean-shaven, dark gray workman's clothes, muddy boots. Nothing about him seemed either remarkable or familiar. I stared at him for only a brief moment before he said, "Gene Miller." Then I knew. My heart raced and my breath quickened. Suddenly it mattered that we were alone.

How many years earlier had it been that I had prosecuted him for murder? Fifteen, ten, fewer? He was a teenager at the time, sixteen or seventeen, legally a juvenile, but able to be tried as an adult because of the seriousness of the offense. He had a juvenile record, for a housebreaking, maybe more than one. His father was a dentist. I don't recall anything about his mother. I knew the family was well off and lived in an up-scale neighborhood, in Montgomery County, Maryland, one of the wealthiest counties in the country.

It was a high-profile case that garnered a great deal of local publicity because the events had taken place during a holiday celebration at a County Recreation Center where a large number of teens were drinking alcohol and smoking marijuana. The gathering was outdoors. Was it Memorial Day or Fourth of July? Or maybe, it was Labor Day. I remember only that school was out and the weather that night was hot and humid. Much of the publicity centered on the fact that a county-sanctioned gathering had gotten out of hand. Who was supposed to be supervising these kids? Who bought the alcohol for this underage crowd? Where were the police and county employees when the trouble started?

The facts of my case in brief were these: Gene Miller and Stephen Groff were friends. Both were drinking. They started arguing. Somehow I recall that Miller wanted Groff to come with him to break into someone's house. Groff said no. The two were outside on a small wooden bridge that spanned a trickle of a creek, down a hill from the Rec Center building. They were not alone. The grounds were crowded with teenagers milling about, smoking weed and drinking. There was some pushing and shoving, wasn't there? Miller picked up an empty Coke bottle lying in the grass. Raising his arm he brought it down violently on a rock or maybe it was on the bridge railing. With the jagged end of the bottle leading the way he thrust upward, catching his friend under the armpit.

Maybe if the ambulance had arrived sooner, Groff would have lived. Certainly, if Miller's jab hadn't hit an artery, the boy wouldn't have lost so much blood so quickly. Actually, he didn't bleed to death right away. The emergency room doctors staunched the bleeding and resuscitated him. But he never regained consciousness.

One of the legal issues in the case was whether or not the death was actually caused by the stabbing. Groff stayed on a ventilator until he was declared brain dead and all life support was discontinued. At the time Maryland followed the common-law "year and a day" rule. If the victim died within a year and a day of an assault, his assailant could be charged with murder.

At a pre-trial motions hearing, the defense argued that by asking for the removal of life support the Groff family converted an assault into a murder. But a Maryland statute makes it clear that a person is dead when his brain dies, which actually occurred shortly after the stabbing. The defense also argued that it was negligence on the part of the rescue squad and/or the hospital staff that was the real cause of Groff's death. But the judge ruled that, since Miller put the chain of events in motion he was, therefore, responsible for the result even if someone else was arguably negligent.

But these were the legal questions in the case. The more important question to me now is why was I so determined to extract such a high price for this homicide? Why had I decided to prosecute Miller for murder instead of manslaughter? As an adult instead of a juvenile? And seek the longest prison term the law allowed? Certainly, it wasn't because the dead boy's family wanted me to take a hard line. In fact Groff's father came to see me in my office to try to talk me out of prosecuting the case.

Though it's been over forty years, I feel as though I should remember my meeting with the dead boy's father. I can't see him or hear his voice. I don't know if he cried or looked weary; if he dressed in a suit or casual clothes; if he had an appointment or just showed up. I remember only that he was furious and emphatic. But he wasn't angry with Miller. He was angry at the slow response of the rescue squad. The father hadn't been there but he must have pictured the scene in his mind's eye thousands of times: His boy lying on the ground bleeding profusely while someone searched for a payphone to call 911; people milling around as though in slow motion, waiting for the arrival of the EMTs, no one knowing what to do to stop the bleeding.

It would be many years before I would be near that kind of loss, the kind of loss that hits a parent, raw and with animal-like fury. When my twenty year-old nephew committed suicide, though my brother wasn't there, I know he could see his son standing atop a building about to jump. In the same way Groff's father must have agonized about the slow response of the rescue squad, my brother thought obsessively and angrily about the building's management carelessly leaving the door to the roof unlocked.

I understand better now how Groff's father grieved. I understand better now why he felt he should have a say in, if not control over, my decision. It was *his* loss, so why didn't *he* get to decide? No doubt, part of his argument was that Miller was his son's best friend and his son wouldn't have wanted him to go to prison. But at the time I whipped away these concerns. Maybe that's why I've obliterated all memory of Groff's father. All I really remember of the meeting is my impatience and my desire for it to be over.

Why was I so single minded, so unwilling to even consider the possibility of not going forward or at least to take a less severe position? Was it cold legal analysis or the excitement of trying my first murder case driving me?

When portions of my closing argument were reported in the *Washington Post*, my father called to say I sounded "blood-thirsty." At the time I was deeply offended. I explained that the reporter had taken my remarks out of context, quoting only the most virulent parts of my argument. But now that I reflect back on how strongly I wanted to convict this teenager, perhaps my father was right.

If you had told me before my last year of law school that I would become a prosecutor, I would have said, "no way." Like many children of my generation, I'd grown up on a steady diet of Perry Mason shows where the DA was portrayed as bungling at best, and perverse at worst. But the prosecutor's office I worked in was not that TV stereotype I'd come to accept as real. The head of this office was fair, ethical and conscious of the proper role a prosecutor should play. Even during my brief tenure in his office before this my first murder case, I had learned that here is where the real power in the criminal justice system lies. I knew also, even then, that this power should be exercised with discretion, with mercy. But looking back on the Miller case, I think now that I exercised my discretion with little regard for mercy. Actually, I refused to exercise my discretion at all.

☀☀☀

Imagine if you had the power to completely alter someone's life by writing two words on a piece of paper: *nolle prosequi,* "not prosecute." Would you really want that daunting responsibility? I had that as a prosecutor. The public sees only the trial played out on a courtroom stage. But decisions made behind the scenes about what charges, if any, to pursue determine the nature of the drama that will take place.

I could say that in the Miller case I wasn't the one who decided on the charges to present to the grand jury for indictment. I didn't. I could say that I was one of the more junior assistants in the office. I was. And that I inherited the case from the deputy state's attorney two weeks before trial because he didn't want to be burdened with it. I did. But, one of the things I loved about my tenure in the prosecutor's office was that we assistants were given autonomy over our cases. We might ask for advice and consult with others. But mostly, each of us decided what to do with our own cases. If we thought a plea should be offered, that was our decision to make. If we thought a charge should be dropped, that too was our decision.

Yes, this was technically a murder case, but it was not the kind of murder case that I was absolutely obliged to prosecute. The public wasn't crying out for it and my boss wasn't demanding it. So when the victim's father asked me to drop the charges, I could have. When the defense attorney asked me to take a reduced plea to manslaughter, I could have accepted his offer. Instead, I ignored their entreaties and paid attention only to my own inner drive, a force I didn't at the time really examine.

How wrong it seems to me now for society to have trusted me to decide the fate of this boy. Yes, I knew the law and I knew how to try a case. But what did I know of life? More specifically, what did I know of Miller's life?

In her book, *The Empathy Exams,* Leslie Jamison compares empathy to a kind of travel. She says: "It suggests you enter another person's pain as you'd enter another country, through immigration and customs, border crossing by way of query: *What grows where you are? What are the laws? What animals graze here?*"

I was at the time an alien in the "country" of troubled teenagers.

My decision to prosecute this case was "thoughtless." Not in the sense that I didn't do research on the law; interview and prepare witnesses; visit the scene of the crime; organize exhibits. No, it was thoughtless in the sense that I gave no thought at all to the real world consequences of my decision. Miller was a troubled teen. What did I know about that?

At the time, I didn't have children of my own. I knew from his juvenile records that Miller was an alcoholic, something else I knew absolutely nothing about. My parents might drink an occasional highball and yes, I'd occasionally gotten drunk in college. But alcoholism was not something I had any personal experience with. Nor had I ever suffered a loss as grievous as either the victim's family's or the perpetrator's family's.

The problem of entrusting these important decisions to such an inexperienced person was not unique to me. Sure, there are career prosecutors, men and women with years of experience in both life in general and prosecution in particular. But prosecutors' offices are also frequently places where young lawyers earn their spurs and then move on. And maybe to understand someone else's life, you have to live more of your own.

In my particular case, there were, no doubt, factors at play other than my relative youth and inexperience. My parents grew up poor and, though I personally hadn't suffered economically, I think their backgrounds caused me to be sympathetic to the plight of the poor while feeling a certain distain for the rich. So, I wonder if the fact that Miller came from a privileged family influenced my decision. Would I have been more empathetic if he had come from more difficult circumstances? Was there something about this kid being a "rich" boy that made me assume he felt a sense of entitlement and he needed to be treated even more harshly than someone from a more humble background?

Or perhaps my hard line approach had something to do with trying to prove that, though I was a woman, I could be tough. It was 1974 and I was only the second woman ever to be employed in this county's prosecutor's office. The first woman was hired a mere six months before me. At the time there were only one or two more women prosecutors in the entire state. In fact, there were precious few women trial lawyers of any kind; none in the public defender's office; none in the county attorney's office. Most of the women practicing law at the time were divorce lawyers who rarely went to court. So maybe I was what *The New York Times* columnist, Maureen Dowd calls one of those "hard-boiled alpha women trying to break gender barriers?" Was I, as she writes, "over compensating on Machismo?" My desire to show how tough I was at the time is evident in what occurred the weekend before the Miller trial began.

Maybe it was the pressure of trying my first murder case. Or maybe the pressure of knowing the press would be watching. Or maybe it was because I had so little time to prepare and had been pressing hard to get ready for this legally and factually complex trial. Perhaps I should have paid more attention to the fact that in the days leading up to the trial, I started to wheeze, a little at first. But then . . . .

It was Friday evening before the Monday trial was to begin. I had scheduled a meeting with the EMTs and the ER doctor who had attended the Groff boy after the stabbing. As I interviewed them in my office, my breathing became more and more labored. After they left, I knew I was in trouble. I could barely breathe. The only other person in my office called 911. The firehouse was only a couple of doors away from the courthouse where my office was. So it only took a few minutes for the rescue squad to arrive by which time my colleague had managed to maneuver me to the sidewalk to await its arrival.

The same EMTs I had within the hour interviewed were on duty. Ironically, it was they who lifted me into the back of the ambulance. They must not have realized how frightened I was as they placed an oxygen mask over my face and one of them said, "this is what we did to Groff." Yes, I thought, and he died. Then they took me to the same hospital where the same ER doctor who had treated Groff treated me. Now, I was certain I was about to die.

It turned out to be my first ever asthma attack for which I was admitted to the hospital where I remained over the weekend. On Saturday the judge assigned the case called my room to ask if I wanted a postponement, a request he would have readily granted. "No," I said. I was adamant. On Sunday, my boss and a colleague visited me and tried to persuade me to agree to delay the trial. "No way," I said. Or more likely, using my "I'm just one of the boys" vocabulary I said, "no fucking way."

Somehow, I thought postponing the trial would make me appear weak, something a woman professional in 1974 was loath to be. So instead, I appeared Monday morning pumped full of cortisone and Valium, powerful drugs that made my legs shaky and my mind fuzzy. I willed my way through an opening statement, the content of which I couldn't recall only moments after I gave it. What was that other than "bull-headed machismo?"

)()()(

Looking into the face of the man crouched behind my desk that night, I tried to see the face of the boy I watched in that courtroom so many years earlier. Since there were many eyewitnesses, it was incontrovertible that Miller had stabbed the victim. Therefore, when he took the stand in his own defense, he testified about how drunk he was; how alcohol had fueled his anger; how he never meant to harm his best friend. It was an accident, he insisted, for which he would be forever deeply sorry.

I remember quite clearly my strategy on cross-examination was to slow the action down. I broke down each of Miller's actions into as many pieces as possible. "You walked over to the grassy hill?" "You found a Coke bottle?" "You raised your arm?" "You brought your arm down forcibly?" And on and on. What I was eliciting was factually accurate. But, in a very real sense, it wasn't true. Making it seem like what Miller did took a lot of time was a trick. It was the way I suggested "pre-meditation." And premeditated acts are the polar opposite of accidental ones. But the truth was that all these actions, no matter how many tiny movements I broke them down into, might only have taken seconds. I must have known this truth even while I watched Miller squirm.

In his book *Law v. Life*, Walt Buchman despairs that: "Law is the only profession in which one is ethically obligated to hurt people." He's talking about the duty of a lawyer to advocate for a client with all the zeal the Code of Professional Responsibility allows even if someone, not the client, gets hurt.

Nowhere is this duty and it's potential for hurting someone more evident then in a skillful cross-examination. I can still see young Miller's eyes desperately searching the courtroom for someone or something to save him. At 5'4" and about 120 pounds I looked small compared to Miller who was over six feet tall and probably weighed over 250 pounds. I was well aware of the geography of the courtroom with it's elevated witness stand and purposely positioned my body in front of Miller so as to make him appear to the jury as menacing as possible. I remember rapidly firing questions at him that I knew he wasn't verbally agile enough to handle. I even tried to make him angry as if by doing so I could suggest to the jury that a quick temper in the courtroom was the same as rage that night at the Rec Center. It was all theater, really. A show designed to make him look bad. Though he looked for help from the judge and his lawyer,

✕✕✕

I can't precisely determine how many years in jail Miller actually served. A conviction for second-degree murder carries a possible maximum sentence of twenty years, which I think Miller received. He must have made parole at the earliest possible time, seven or eight years in prison. What, I wonder, was that like for him? Yes, he was big for his age, but still immature. Was he frightened, I wonder? Did he cry at night? But for this interruption, disruption, in his life, would he have gone to college? Would he have married, had children?

When now I think of a teenager spending time in prison, I think of my son. I like to think he never would have committed a crime like the one Gene Miller committed. But it could have happened. My own son would on occasion—no let's be honest here, on many occasions—drink too much and get into fights. So, he could have been Miller. I know that now. I see now how cavalier I was; how dismissive; how removed. By the time my own son was seventeen, I understood better. I saw in him the immaturity, the confusion, the uncertainty about who he was and how to be in the world, all things I never saw in Miller. Being a teenager is not just one characteristic like hair or eye color. Being a teenager is the lens through which a young person views the world.

Years after the Miller case, years after I had left the prosecutor's office for private practice, I represented a teenager who, drunk one night in Ocean City, Maryland during June Week, historically a week of rowdy partying after high school graduation, got into an argument and pushed another teenager who was flirting with my client's girlfriend. It was just a push but the boy fell backward and hit his head on a metal grate. One push, one nanosecond on a June night, and a classmate became a paraplegic. This time I found myself arguing a position opposite from the one I argued in the Miller case. This time, unlike Groff's father, I succeeded in talking a prosecutor out of going forward with a case. Was this situation really so very different than the homicide at the Rec Center? No, there wasn't a weapon, if a broken Coke bottle is a weapon. And no, no one died. Still, a drunken teenager in a singular, impulsive moment of rage caused grievous harm without intending to do so.

In the last few years in a number of cases the Supreme Court has recognized that the teenage brain is different from the adult brain and that, therefore, the criminal justice system should treat teenagers differently than adults, more leniently, more compassionately. This view is backed up by neuro-science.

"Children," the Supreme Court said in 2005, "cannot be viewed simply as miniature adults. . . ./D/evelopments in psychology and brain science continue to show fundamental differences between juvenile and adult minds"— for example, in 'parts of the brain involved in behavior control.'"

Miller didn't need to go to prison to turn his life around. I see that now. When I read the all too frequent news of a teenager driving drunk who rams his car into a tree and kills his friends, I'm sympathetic to both the driver and the parents of his deceased companions. Nothing about those events are really very different than what happened that night at the Recreation Center so many years ago.

)X()X()X(

Looking to fill in gaps in my memory about the case, I Google Gene Miller. I am surprised when I see his obituary on a funeral home website. I recognize him immediately from the photo on the page. His face is a little rounder; his hair is sprinkled with grey; and he has a short beard. But he doesn't look all that different from the man who repaired my phone some thirty years ago.

He was fifty years old when he died seven years ago. The cause of death isn't mentioned. I can't help wondering if his years in prison hastened his death in some way. I wouldn't ordinarily put much stock in comments left in a guest book at a funeral parlor posted on line. But these comments are heart wrenching and, as I read through them, an eerily consistent picture of the man emerges. He was a big man whose nickname was "Big Gene." Over and over again I read of his "big smile" his "big hugs." One woman says how his hugs lifted her off the ground. Several women friends talk about how they always felt "safe" in his presence. I remember that Miller's size seemed to have subjected him to teasing in high school. Unable to convert his mass into athletic prowess, it just became an impediment. Though it doesn't appear that he ever married or had children he was clearly adored by his nieces and nephews. "You were the best uncle, godfather and mentor a kid could have," one says.

I can find no mention of his time in prison or the case that sent him there. I do see references to him being active in AA and a family request that, in lieu of flowers, mourners contribute to a non-profit organization that works with adult drug court.

It appears that he was the "go to" guy for help. One note reads: "he taught me so much by his honesty, grace, compassion, empathy, humility, and his kindness." And then there is this: "He never judged another." But did he not judge me for judging him?

✕✕✕

I was scared when he re-introduced himself to me that evening he was repairing my phone. What was he thinking, planning? Was this his chance for revenge? Did the fact that we were alone provide him with a perfect opportunity? Was it really an accident that my phone wasn't working, making it impossible for me to call for help? My thoughts raced and my hands trembled as he spoke to me.

"In the beginning," he said, "I hated you." I held my breath and waited for him to continue. Would he say, in time he actually came to agree that he deserved to be punished for what he did? Or would he say he learned something of value in prison? He didn't say either of those things or anything like them. But somehow as his words hung in the air between us, I understood that he no longer hated me.

There were no hugs for me from Big Gene. As he gathered his tools to leave, he just gave me a nod that somehow seemed to say, "I forgive you."

I was relieved, though at the time I didn't think I had done anything that needed to be forgiven. Now, I do.

HEATHER TOSTESON

I AIN'T GOING TO LIE TO YOU

I would not be able to pick out his face in a crowd or in a line-up, but I have a strong kinesthetic sense of the two of us, shoulder to shoulder, me in my usual interviewing posture, feet folded beneath me on the chair, and Omar, to my left, tilting back in his armchair, the two of us staring together at the enormous oval conference table with its scarred veneer, the twenty or more empty chairs gathered helter skelter around it, and the little droid electronic recorder on its tripod, aimed directly at him, eager to catch his every, often mumbled, word. I remember how he kept toying with the broken arm of his chair, and the way I turned in my chair so I could both catch his eye and continue to write on my yellow legal pad. People were passing in the hallways on either side of the windowed conference room in the South Fulton Day Reporting Center, usually probation and parole staff in dark brown or khaki duty wear. There was some laughter and repartee, but, muted by the window glass, it felt we were watching fish in an aquarium, almost silent, weightless, other worldly. Whenever Omar toyed with the broken arm on his chair I thought of suggesting he take another, but the chair was the least of what needed fixing in Omar's life.

Omar was there talking with me because Officer Loretta Jackson had asked him to, and he either wanted to please her, didn't know he had a perfect right to refuse—or he had a story he wanted heard. But, somehow, from the beginning, we were in it together, woebegone Omar and me, not taking the artificial conditions personally, making the best of it, human being to human being. I assumed he didn't know I was talking to him because I wanted to understand more about those who are having difficulty on parole. "Just because" seemed reason enough since Omar didn't ask for more and, unlike my usual custom, I didn't launch into an extended description of our project—or any description at all. Later, I found this omission both lucky and odd.

Omar had been incarcerated for eleven years, from the time he was eighteen. He was released on parole in 2010.

"Eleven years is a long time. Especially from eighteen to twenty-nine," I said.

"Thirty-one. I was released when I was thirty-one," he corrected me.

Time warped frequently in his account—or in my understanding of it. But certain dates stood out. November 2017, for example. If he didn't successfully complete this Day Reporting Center program, his parole would be revoked and he would be sent back to prison to serve out the remaining three years of his eighteen-year sentence. This was both a threat and a reassurance. One way or another, in November 2017, he would be out from under his prison sentence. He had five years on probation following, but that wasn't the same thing.

Certain ages stood out too. His son was three. The same age he was when he was taken from his parents by child protective services. He was seventeen when he worked at KFC and rented his first apartment together with his friend Dante. "Freedom is being able to rent your own apartment, even with help," he said. His almost wife was the same age as he was (whether that was thirty-four or thirty-six).

What is hard to capture in any linear account is the intimate weaving back and forth of time, causation, consequence, and interpretation that allowed us both to feel known somehow by the end of our hour together. How easy it would have been, at any point, to miss Omar's growing edge, the poignant, half-buried, crucial possibilities of his life.

This was something Officer Jackson intuitively picked up on as I talked with her later: "I thought he'd have more to say than the others." When I shared some of my observations, she said, "He wants someone to play the sympathy card with him." I started to object, but she went on, "When I say sympathy, I don't mean feeling sorry for him, but that he needs his officer to understand, almost a put-yourself-in-my-shoes kind of deal."

But, as Omar had observed, "They all tired of me over at parole."

And even Officer Jackson shook her head when I suggested, with her intuitive understanding of him, that perhaps she could get him moved to her caseload: "He's a headache." When asked why, she expanded: "He has trust issues. He feels like everyone is going to do what the previous person did. It's hard to deal with somebody that has that mindset because you feel like everyone is against you." I wondered where in Omar's life trust would have been the appropriate response to his circumstances. I suggested it might help build trust if Omar's previous parole officer could at least say he was sorry for a very legitimate grievance Omar felt. If the officer could just say that he may have had to do what he did, but that he understood the cost to Omar.

"He won't talk to his officer to a manner where it will benefit him. He just needs to sit down and talk with his officer," Officer Jackson said firmly—but she seemed dubious about whether that would happen. At that point, Omar had had so many officers, it was difficult to pinpoint which one might be at issue. In addition, "Sometimes for us as officers, its harder because we're not in positions where we've ever lost anything, we don't have kids we've lost contact with, we haven't had to start over. We're not trying to be in a situation where we don't care. You have some officers that might not be able to sympathize because they just don't know the feeling."

But Officer Jackson was open to some suggested programmatic supports for Omar: "If that is something that is going to help him, I'll do it. We can try. I'm one of those who if it is going to put you in the right direction, I'll push you even if it will take you out of your comfort zone a little bit. You can't be afraid to change for the better."

Officer Jackson also believed in the power of conversation. "When it comes to my caseload, I treat everyone the same because it could be one of my family members. I treat everyone with respect. I *talk* with them. Its not so much a question and answer session as a conversation, because I feel you get more out of them if it is a conversation." She elaborated later, "We have people who never open up and people who open up from day one. It's really about trust and I've noticed a lot of them have trust issues so a lot of that information is harder to get out of them. That's why I take the conversational route. That's why I like to talk with the family because you'll get a lot of information out of the family versus the offender, and the family kind of gives you insight on how they were before, some of their triggers." She draws the family in because family support is the one variable she finds common to all those she has seen be successful on parole.

As I think about Omar's life, the challenges he faces and how he understands them, I try to imagine an officer like Loretta Jackson listening in on the conversation, how that might—or might not—make a crucial difference. For it is true that Omar is a headache for parole, a challenge to himself, and an improbable godsend to his son and almost wife. But for their sakes, and ours as well, his future needs to be a truly open question. I have my doubts, as does he, that it can be. But I have, as he does, as Officer Jackson does, my hopes as well.

When I asked Omar what he was giving back to his family now that he was out, he said: "Being there. Ain't nothing like just *being* there. See my little boy just three years old. Me and his mother the same age and whenever I go and get locked up it's *hard* on her, *hard* on her. But when I'm there, its instant comfort. And I like watching my little boy grow. I've been enjoying watching him grow."

Instant comfort. For Omar to know himself in this way is no small thing.

)X()X()X(

"You got to be the stupidest parolee in the world," his parole officer exclaimed when Omar reported to him after a long absence—and tested dirty, again, for marijuana.

"You know how they talk. 'You got to be the stupidest such and such and such and such. . .' I couldn't say nothing because you can't say nuttin. They'll put you in the situation where they *want* you to say something so they can lock you up, but I ain't never had nothing to say. But it came to me, I just had to tell him, 'You sent me to jail for nothing. You had me sign a waiver because you went and looked at the paperwork and you felt you knew I did it. Now it's a year and a half later and I just showed you I was found not guilty by a jury.'"

Omar looked at me directly: "*He was wrong.*"

Dirty urine or not, Omar wanted some acknowledgement of the personal cost of that misjudgment—not only on the part of his parole officer but also of the police, DA, and judge.

This is how Omar explained his grievance, which he returned to several times in our conversation, the recitations having the vivid but rote quality of a trauma narrative:

"I went with someone and they mistake us for someone who had committed a theft somewhere. I went to trial two months ago. They went and seen on tape that I wasn't the person Clayton County was looking for. But I went and did eight months on that thing.

"Parole said they didn't care. It was the fact I was incarcerated and I had that charge. I think that should change about parole because I ain't even able to sue and I lost a lot of money on this. Everything I built on with my son, my house around the corner, I lost in those eight months and I'm still down from it now.

"I'm thinking, if you're supposed to help somebody, why you giving them a waiver to go back to prison because in your mind they did it? That's what my parole officer told me, 'You did it.'"

"No, I didn't do it."

"'You did it.'"

"No, I didn't."

"'Well, sign this six months waiver anyway because you shouldn't have got arrested.'

"I did two months in Clayton jail waiting on a bed and then six months in all on the parole violation. After I got back from doing my eight months, I had to come home and go back to trial every month to Clayton County jail courtroom. I had to keep hearing the lies they were telling about me and their telling me, 'Go ahead and take the year they're trying to give you.'

"*And I just did a year!* Why would I do that when I know I didn't do this crime?

"And I had to spend $60 a day going there and coming back because there was no MARTA bus. $30 going there and $30 coming back.

"And my own public defender and the judge were lying to me and telling me to take time for something I didn't do. They had to go and see at the jury trial that it wasn't me.

"It was a lot on my shoulder. I'm not able to sue nobody because I don't have the money to get a lawyer. I feel I should be able to get back what I lost from doing time in jail. So, like that's a problem. I lost my apartment and my car. So when I got out I didn't have nothing anymore. I just got out to nothing. And it started stressing me. So I started back doing marijuana. I can't get my old job back and I started smoking weed when I was bored. Not to sit here telling you no lie.

"Right after that my parole officer came to me and said, 'You dirty. You going to jail.' But see, I went and did a couple days in jail. And now I came back because I was dirty again. So now I'm here at the Day Reporting Center."

Omar had been earning good money roofing and barbering before these setbacks. Omar felt that he lost more than employment or confidence in the justice system—he'd lost much of his personal support system as well: "The people who haven't given up on me are me, my son, and my wife."

His father, who was not there when Omar was growing up was a support for the years when he was in prison, providing money for his prison account. But his father did not support him in this situation and Omar felt that absence keenly: "I felt like he betrayed me when I was just in jail on that recent charge because everybody kept saying *He keep going back to jail* or *He did i*t and such and such. So nobody want to pay my bond which was $240, so a friend of mine ended up doing it. So I just haven't spoke to my father since then because I felt like none of them believe in me. Like none of them done went to trial with me when I went to choose my jury trial. I felt like he let his guard down on me. You know how you give up on somebody."

Even though his mother did come to his trial, Omar didn't necessarily feel she was a support. "Now, I ain't going to say my momma give up on me but I look at it like that cause I don't bring no drama her way." This is not purely protective of his mother, but also of himself, which he acknowledges: "That's another reason I don't have a good relationship with her, you know, because—well, I want to patch it up because I'm in this program—but when I was smoking weed and drinking a *lot*, you know I tried to stay away from her and protect her from looking at me in a certain way. Unhuh, judging, like yeah—like when I couldn't get no job, and she look at me like, 'You don't *want* no job–' and I can't *get* no job. So I'm going to stay away from you, mama, so we won't have no problems like that." He laughed at his reasoning.

This threw some doubt on his claims that his marijuana use was simply because of the very real stress he felt at a wrongful charge. It also revealed how much Omar felt the loss of the positive regard, and more importantly, the *hope* of his parents, however reliable—or unreliable—they had been in his life.

)0(0(

Officer Jackson, as she drove me over to the remarkably grim buildings on Sylvan Road that housed the South Fulton Probation Center and the Day Reporting Center, had told me that the purpose of the program was to help change thought processes: "Once we get them out of their negativity, then we can work to get them where they need to be. That is one of the major problems we have."

As I talked with him, it was not clear to me which of Omar's thinking processes he could realistically change. His keen sense of injustice about the latest charge against him differed markedly from his thinking about the relative fairness of the charges that originally sent him to prison. He went to prison for armed robbery. His five-year probation to follow was for aggravated assault. Omar felt both his parole and probation sentences were fair because the alternative in each case would be more prison time and anything was better than that. However, he mused on the relative fairness of the armed robbery charge:

"If everyone else getting the same time for robbery, I guess it's fair. I never had a gun in none of those situations. I guess it was a brick. Or a BB gun. I never meant to go kill nobody or hurt nobody. But how the law set up, I'm no different from no one else. But looking at the *nature* of the crime, it wasn't fair. I think you should be sentenced by the nature of the crime. Someone should look into the case and see what really happened. I mean did he try to kill someone? Was it over $2? I think one of my case was about like $2. I hit a guy with a brick. He stay in my neighborhood. DA made it armed robbery. I thought it was more like reckless conduct. We were out gambling, throwing dice, whatever. That dude, I hit him with a brick and for that it was armed robbery. Ten years.

"The probation was actually for me hitting the dude with the brick, so that's the five years. It's fair because I could be doing five years in prison. As far as the armed robbery part. . . They say I took money from the dude, but I never went nowhere that night. There was a big fight, but me and him, we waited on the police to come. He said he was going to call the police and I said I don't care. I ain't think it was going to be armed robbery because when you going to rob someone, if it was going to be armed robbery, you go with the intention you going to take their money and I ain't went with intentions like that. I thought it should have been reckless conduct because we was all out drinking and such."

When asked if he felt he would have any trouble with the man he attacked, since they both lived in the same part of South Fulton, he said immediately, "No, I'll walk the other way." When asked if he would like to make amends to the person he attacked, he said without self-consciousness, "I did. Same day of my trial. I was in a small holding tank and he in another little holding tank. I told him, 'G, I'm sorry. Don't do it.' I was trying to get him not to go in and give his testimony. But he was only mad because of his head because I hit him on his head with a brick."

Omar was also clear that he would not engage again in the behaviors that led to his criminal conviction and imprisonment. "I think my choices came from trying to be slick. I always analyzed it and always thought it was me trying to be slick. Trying to pull things off. But that right there was the big no no. I be looking at ten years—"

He said firmly, "I been done changed those behaviors. I never ever in my life thought about trying to rob another person. Or *looked* at another person like I wanted what he had. So I have *changed. For real.*"

)()()(

He was less clear about his willingness or ability to stop the drug use, which was not part of his criminal conviction, but was now threatening his parole status. Omar acknowledged that he had a problem with substance abuse—"Because I couldn't stop when they told me to stop." But he claimed that before the recent challenges, he had it under control. "I was maintaining. I was staying under the radar. There was nobody know about me. I wasn't giving him no problems—"

Staying under the radar was a very important principle for Omar. From the beginning of his time on parole, Omar tried to keep his distance from them. "I will say this, I never went parole way. I won't say they never gave any help, I never *seek* any help from parole. For one, I was using marijuana. If you using, parole the last people you want to be around. You just want to like live your life and get away from them. Because you don't feel you need no help. And you want to keep on getting high, whatever you using. I use marijuana. Let's say I'm scared to call in each month because I'm scared he will say, come on in and take a drug test. But not calling in, that's trouble by itself—"

This wasn't actually the first time Omar had been at the Day Reporting Center, he revealed as we were talking about ways that he might "rehab himself" since he felt that no program could do so. Sent there some years earlier in his parole, again for marijuana use, he was assigned to the Fatherhood Project. However, both the Fatherhood Project and the Day Reporting Center required that he be clean, which he wouldn't—or couldn't—do: "I didn't want to stop smoking marijuana or abide by the parole laws, so I just left. I let the police come git me whenever they come git me." Omar felt it was more efficient to do six months in a detention center than a year of counseling. "I did six months and I came home and I didn't have to worry about anybody worrying about me anymore. I flew under the radar, smoked weed, do what I wanted to do."

)()()(

Being left alone was important to Omar. Not returning to prison was too. The cost of staying out now was being clean and Omar wanted to—but he couldn't guarantee it because sometimes his mind did things: "It's just things can go wrong in your own head sometimes that will make you disregard not using. And that's what happen to me and that's the reason why I'm in trouble now. I couldn't shake what was in my head, you know. I came up through a lot, you know. I came up through a lot coming up as a kid, you know. I still be having—you know there be summat that be coming up, summat that's buried up under the surface, you know. I went through a lot as a four year old, probably as a three year old, you see what I'm saying."

When asked what kinds of things he experienced, he went on: "Like watching my mother get beat. By my father. Him beating me. Beating me in the face with an extension cord. Like stuff was in the newspaper. Like I had to leave him and maybe go to a foster home for like two years. I had to leave them because my mother wouldn't leave *him* and they said either I would have to be there and he would have to go, so they chose to put me there. So I went through that and my grandmother had to come and get me and I had to stay with her. Like I broke up with them for a *long* time because DFACS say I couldn't go there. A dude try to hit me with an axe at a young age. My step—That somebody my mama *chose* to have, you see what I'm saying. In and out of juvenile—"

As Omar was aware, he was his own most powerful trigger—because of the sense of anger and frustration he felt about his recent arrest and trial based on mistaken identification, and also because of all the childhood trauma he tried to suppress.

In addition, the program brought up some of the traumatic dimensions of incarceration itself. When I suggested that he might think about attending a support group of ex-offenders, he said: "I already told you I don't deal with many people out here. When you been locked up as long as me, your circle is limited. I don't even know how to deal with the big group I'm with here. I don't even know how to connect, you know, for real with nobody. Like my momma. I love these people but I done did so much time away from them, it's like I don't even go see her like I supposed to, like a mother—you know, a son supposed to. I just don't connect good. Because I'm so used to being like in a one-man cell. I been in a one-man cell as long as I been out of prison, you see I'm saying."

When I asked if he felt safer in a one-man cell, he thought I was referring to prison. "It will never feel safe. I don't know why they tell you that. People come in you room whenever. Officers will let em in and do something to you the same way they can out here on the street. I never felt safe."

When asked if he felt safe now, he said, "I always feel safe on my own. I'm a loner, we can just say that. Say I won't be doing nothing to anyone out here and—never think about doing anything. The only thing I be doing is the marijuana."

)(()(

Omar knew that he must get through this program if he was to help his wife and child, but he also realized it separated him further from his extended family: "I stay away from them for the most part. Not my mother, but my other family. They do a lot of weed. I stay away from them. Plus I work a lot. That's the kind of family—I can go there and fall into a trap because they're going to have marijuana."

Besides posing the temptation of marijuana use, Omar's family also was unable to give him any clear models of people successfully completing parole. His two brothers had both been to prison but were out now. "Everyone I know, they go back to jail. They never stay out. They come out on parole and some kind of way they be back in. They like me I guess."

We agreed that he would have to be his family's first parole success. This was not as far-fetched as it might seem because self-reliance was an obvious value and a source of pride for Omar. Omar, for all his self-doubt and reticent presentation, has a strong sense of confidence about his ability to support himself, which he began to do at seventeen. "I do multiple," he said proudly. "I can do anything. Cleaning. Roofing." Learning how to barber in prison, he eventually provided haircuts for prison staff. He was trained in roofing at Coffee Correction Center, where he said he had a number of vocational programs to choose from. While at the Day Reporting Center he was working demolition in the evening because he could combine it with his programs, which at present included Moral Reconation Training and Early Recovery Skills.

He also wanted to be there for his son and wife. He knew they wanted him to succeed. He and his wife had just learned that she had diabetes and an enlarged heart. "So it's like, whew, I wish I could get rich some day so she don't have to worry about it."

It may be that very combination of self-reliance and self-doubt that surprisingly opened up a small window of real possibility as we closed our interview, one that came from my mentioning that I had been a single mother as a young woman.

"You was? And you handled it? Business."

"But there were times when I thought, oh, I can't do this. And then I would look at my son, and he *believed* in me. And I didn't know how I would be able to do it. I had *no* idea."

"But you got up and did it. I'm glad to hear that. I'm sorry to hear that, but I'm glad to hear that. *For real,* though."

"And it doesn't mean that you feel that you can. You say, 'I don't have a choice here because it is this or—'"

"But you really can. And I'm going to try. I ain't going to lie to you, it ain't going to hurt me to try."

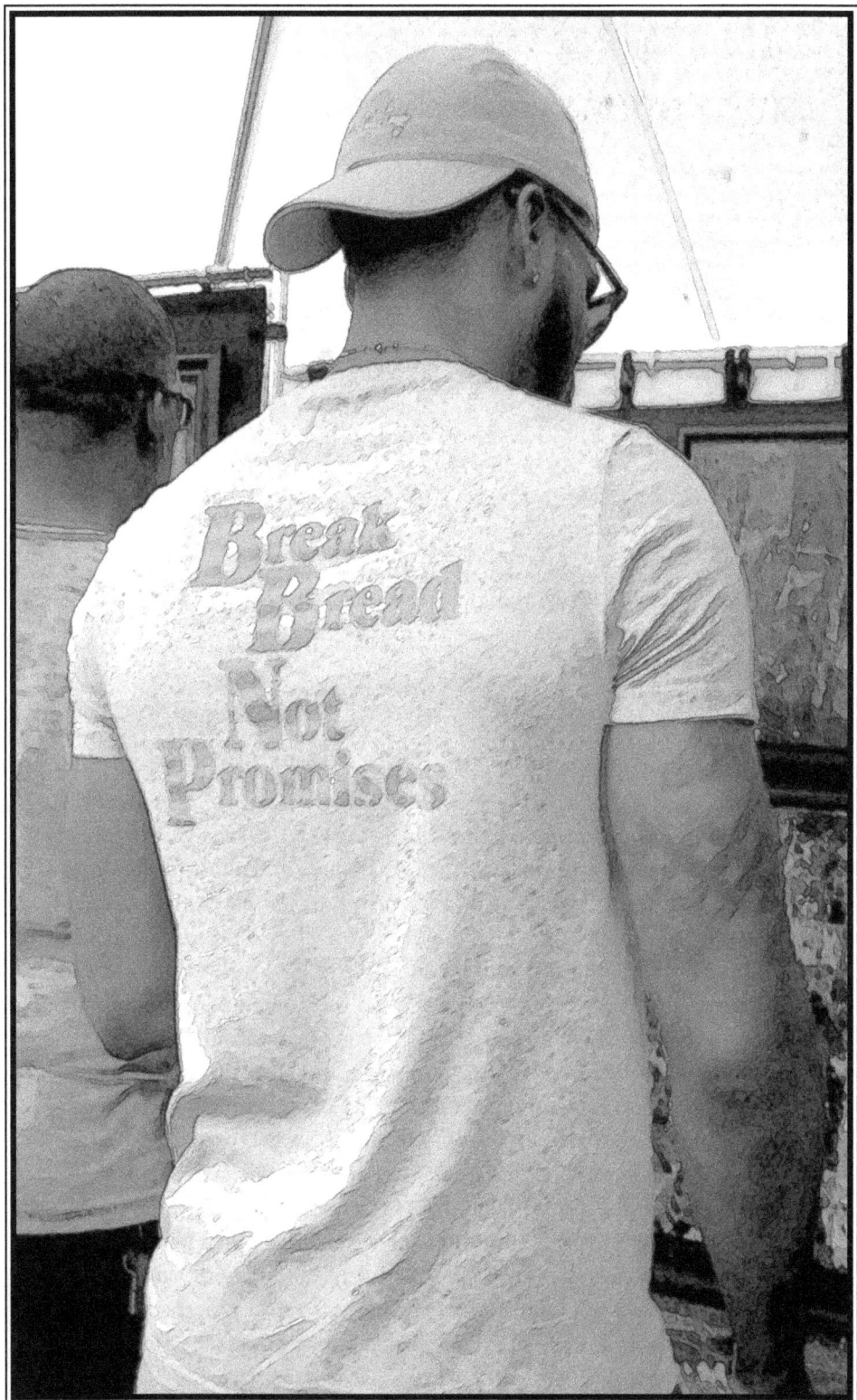

GAYE D. HOLMAN

POWER, RESPECT, AND THE CONVICT CODE: SURVIVING BEHIND BARS
[Book Excerpt]

Basically, you don't see nothing, hear nothing, or say nothing. You mind your own business. You don't run to the guards and tell them anything. If you have a problem with someone, you deal with it yourself or you lose respect. —Wayne

I believe there are two things at the heart of the prison experience: the need for power and the demand for respect.

Power

The bureaucratic structure of Corrections is similar to that of the military. Positions of sergeant, lieutenant, and captain are rungs on the career ladder. Current emphasis is on professionalizing the ranks. New officers graduate with formal ceremonies from their initial schooling and all employees regularly attend "training," which includes a variety of classes, martial arts, and practice on the shooting range. The officers wear dark uniforms laden with accoutrements of handcuffs, radios, utility belts, micro-shields (for doing CPR), flashlights, and pepper spray. Many in the ranks are former military, and they fit comfortably into the strict structure of command.

Once established in their positions, most officers are caring, sensible individuals who know how to manage a troubled population with consistency and common sense. Those are the officers on their way up the career ladder. Those with a mean streak or wrong mind-set often remain in the lower ranks, dealing daily with the inmates, and that is where the problems germinate.

Unfortunately, certain authoritarian personalities gravitate to Corrections and they cause problems and are often hard to work with. For the most part, I found the top administrators above the level of officers to be well educated, caring, and concerned. They had an interest in rehabilitation while

emphasizing safety and security. They were respectful to me and often surprised me, making themselves freely available whenever I jumped ranks to ask
for their help. That access did not sit well with other people in the rigid chain
of command, but it worked for my program as long as I kept the wardens well
informed about everything.

At all levels, I found if I acknowledged the staff's power and showed
deference to it, things were more likely to get done. I enjoyed the employees I
worked with in the prisons, but there was much more game playing required
than I liked.

The officers are still referred to as "guards" when the older inmates talk
about them, especially when they are angry. The officers on the yard have
complete authority over the inmates, collectively and personally, and some
make overt and subtle use of that power. The inmate who recognizes the
authority and accepts his place as physically powerless will serve easier time.
The inmate who constantly rails against his status and things he sees as unfair
will spend his years figuratively knocking his head against the wall and doing
harder time.

In writing this, I realize how my own emotions have been influenced
by my time behind bars. Of course, I had good experiences with officers who
were kind, helpful, and sensible. They followed DOC's "firm, fair, consistent"
philosophy, and showed respect for the men under their care. They deserve to
be highlighted, but they tend to be invisible as things around them are quiet
and uneventful.

In prison, I learned a lot about myself, and I find that I would not make
a good inmate. When I witnessed or experienced actions by an officer that
were unprofessional and personal, I could not let it roll off my back. I felt red
hot anger whenever one flexed his/her muscles with me, deliberately letting
me know where I stood in relationship to their unquestionable power.

Like the inmates, I was often treated disrespectfully, forced to wait much
longer than needed, refused help that would have made things much easier,
ignored when I was waiting to speak to an officer. I let the incidents sink
into my psyche where, to my surprise, they still burn with the same anger
that simmers within the men. As I write my memories of the years spent on
the various prison yards, and I think, particularly when I write about the
power-hungry officers, it is the piercing anger that comes to the forefront. I
never reported any of them. I never talked back to any of the rude ones. I just
simmered with things I saw and experienced. Had I done otherwise, it would

have brought trouble to my own house as Jack wrote earlier. I understood the feelings generated by the struggle for power and respect. And I started to understand the convict code.

In spite of the move to professionalize the ranks, there are problems throughout the country. As prison populations burgeon, money becomes an issue and prison salaries have not kept pace as demands for more officers eat into the budget. Long-term officers say that there is no longer an incentive to make Corrections a career for those who start at the bottom as officers. Pensions have been taken away; salaries are low. Turnover is extraordinarily high. Both long-term officers and inmates say the quality of the officers is falling.

"If they are breathing, they will get hired," one career officer noted.

Because of the high turnover, staffing is at dangerously low levels in many places and regular mandatory overtime is required. Money is at the heart of the problem.

This is not a book about officers, but as I interviewed officers, staff, and administrators, I found I had opened a can of worms. In today's prisons, there is as much distrust, rule-breaking, and anger among the officers, administration, and staff as there is in the inmate population. I learned very troubling things. An incredible amount of ugliness goes on behind the scenes. Cliques form and influence what information is passed upward to administration. Administrators support their friends, ignoring their shortcomings. A former administrator explained, "If the warden or officers feel they are invincible because they are friends with those above them, then ultimately the men suffer because there is no accountability." All the resulting tensions, anger, and mistrust is carried downward, often lying upon the shoulders of the powerless inmates.

Men and women, unhappy in their work setting, uncommitted to the importance of their jobs, quickly learn to build up their own egos by flexing their muscles in a system designed to let them do so.

When it comes to power, the inmate is going to lose. A prisoner with an attitude will be subjected to close scrutiny (some call it harassment)—frequent shakedowns, strip searches, and even body cavity examinations. The physical abuse has lessened greatly over the years, but it still occurs. The men have little protection against personal vendettas if they make enemies of the officers. The officers have to follow rules, but there are many ways to get at someone. Bill was not a man to handle officers with tact, and he paid the price:

During the counts when everyone is locked in their cells, the officer uses a flashlight in order to see inside the darkened cells. Most use a small flashlight that has a very dim light. This not only allows the officer to see, but also doesn't cause the disruption of sleep of the inmate. We have a few officers who wish to use nothing but the biggest possible flashlight and they purposely adjust the light so that it is at its widest and brightest setting in order to do just that; wake an individual up from a sound sleep. The "rules" state that they "must see flesh and movement." While most understand how to interpret this, a few use it to harass. They will shine the light directly into your eyes and shake the flashlight back and forth until you finally wake up. When I was experiencing this, they were counting every hour. He would repeat this scenario at every count, thus you would not be afforded a good night's sleep. The following day, things that would not normally upset you were suddenly irritating. They created a hostile environment through deliberate harassment.

He continued:

With the cell doors isolated at night from midnight to 5:45 a.m., one must press a button to get the tower guard's attention in order to have their cell doors opened to use the restroom. I have had the officer up there ignore my buzzer for as long as twenty minutes. There has been more than one occasion over the years in which I ended up going to the bathroom in a food container and just going back to bed.

Leslie, who was in the same institution as Bill, handled his incarceration differently, and thus managed to stay out of trouble with the officers. They basically left him alone.

I don't get into trouble with the guards. I don't cause them any problems, and usually they don't give me any problems. It's a matter of common sense. I know what's right from wrong, so if I do something wrong, I have no one to blame but myself—right? A lot of guys come in here and give the guards a hard way to go; then they get mad when the guards write them up. That's stupid. I believe you "get" what you "give" . . .

Yes, I've experienced the so-called harassment of having a light shined in my eyes, not getting let out immediately to use the bathroom. Personally, I don't let little stuff like that bother me. I've got enough to worry about. Those things are minor to me.

One of the most difficult things for me over the years was to have to stand by and watch, and thus subtly be part of, the cruel mistreatment. We had an officer at one school who took delight in making the men miserable. He would make all the encounters as difficult as possible. On the days of advising, for example, he locked the door of the school, making the students wait outside in long lines in a freezing sleet storm or pouring rain. Another more humane officer firmly set guidelines for behavior in the crowded set-ting, but made arrangements for the men to come into the warm building to sit and wait.

When vocational students leave their classrooms, they have to be checked and patted down for possibly stolen tools. One day, my least favorite officer, with another officer in tow, picked out one young, less savvy man to taunt. As the students were leaving for lunch, the officer stopped the line and went after this guy. He had him take off his belt, put it back on, empty his pockets, fill them back up while he was barking out more things for him to do: "Turn around; stick out your tongue; take off your belt again." The young man was fumbling, trembling like a leaf before they let him go. As soon as the inmate exited the door, the two beefy officers doubled over in laughter. One of them said, "I love doing that."

There is no question that the inmate is at the mercy of the officers and staff, and he must learn to swallow his pride at times to get along. In the early days of our program, for example, the college students frequently were taunted by some officers who felt they should not receive a "free" education, and the student had to act submissive during their ridicule. Generally, how-ever, the two groups get along well, and informal friendships evolve between the officers and inmates.

> *I feel there are things in here that do get on your nerves a lot and that is the uneducated guard hiding behind a badge, and also the inmates themselves making unnecessary problems not only for them but everyone in general. —Al*

> *There are good and bad correctional officers. The bad ones are like drill sergeants, not police officers. Most, however, are friendly and have some understanding of how the inmate might feel. Some of the young ones are over-zealous and hide behind their badge.*
> *—Don*

However, if a conflict does arise between an inmate and officer, the inmate can file a grievance. It is similar when an officer writes up an inmate for a rule infraction. In both cases, the defendants appear before a court-like committee.

It is more difficult for the accused prisoner. As one inmate who used to be a correctional officer himself told me, "If you testify against a corrupt officer, there is no one to side with you. You don't testify against a brother, and they think they are like brothers."

One of the grievance counselors says inmates seldom ever win officially in staff conflicts, but sometimes they will win without knowing it. The "innocent" officer might be assigned to hated tower duty for several months, for example. Officers insist that inmates sometimes win against the write-ups if there is not enough proof to support the officer's charge.

)X()X()X(

Respect

The concept of respect comes up over and over again, but it is initially difficult to understand within the context of the prison environment.

There is, of course, the constant struggle for the individual to find something within himself to respect. Other chapters examine that in more depth, as the internal conflict is ongoing and ever pervasive. The man who has failed so miserably in life does, most of the time, know, or at least hope, there is something salvageable within himself.

Some of the men have found the inner confidence and peace that allow them to not judge their worth by their powerlessness within the correctional system. They are the ones who don't sweat the small stuff, as the expression goes. If they are talked to rudely, they see it as the other person being a jerk, rather than feeling belittled. They accept their lower role without it affecting their psyche. Those men, to me, have found a sense of self-respect. But that is my interpretation from watching and listening over the years. They do not talk in those words or concepts. And those reactions, so helpful in free society, do not translate into respect from the other men.

To men in prison, especially the ones who have served many years, respect is something else. It is the difference between an inmate and a convict.

Some of the basic rules of respect as defined by us on the outside are understood within the prison setting, but are heightened in intensity. More than once, I've had to jump in and defuse a situation before one of the men got in trouble, thinking an officer had disrespected me. The men might accept a curt or sarcastic answer or an order without explanation, but they were protective of me and got their hackles up when I was spoken to that way. They didn't seem to understand when I explained that I could take care of myself or that words didn't matter as long as I got what I needed. It was the act of disrespect that bothered them so much.

Tensions from the visiting room often reached my ears. Depending on the captain, the warden, or who was on duty, families were frequently subjected to a variety of searches. When the fathers saw male officers laying their hands on their pre-teen and teenaged daughters to frisk them for contraband, sparks flew, tempers rose, and grievances were filed. (Today in these institutions, mostly female officers pat down other females.) The same happened if family members were treated curtly or rudely. One man refused to allow his family to visit because he couldn't stand to let them see him being treated disrespectfully. He was afraid it would make him less of a man in their sights.

It is an ongoing tension, and issues of respect fly around all aspects of visitation. There is another side to that, of course, when the inmates take advantage of the situation.

The men seemed particularly sensitive to how visitors were treated; all of our college teachers mentioned with surprise the protectiveness and respectfulness they experienced. It was always a puzzling contradiction to me, considering the many acts of the men that resulted in imprisonment. But the contrast between students on our main campus and the students within the prison was startling. Each semester, I struggled with boxes of books, lugging heavy loads into the institution on campus. But at the prison, once I left the sally port and entered the yard, men always approached, without exception, to take the boxes from me and help me along to the back of the institution—even men who were not part of the program. It was like stepping back into the 1950s; doors were opened, men moved back to let women go first, and all needs were immediately cared for. I often noticed men quietly shifting chairs around so I had the one padded, comfortable chair while they sat on the plastic or metal chairs. They did not usually have a sexual motivation. Their actions emerged from a politeness and appreciative respect for those who came to help them and who treated them respectfully in return.

But there was another facet to prison respect that took a long time to understand. It was respect among the men and it didn't depend on administration, visitors, or officers. It went back to the days when the convict code ruled.

XOXOX

The Convict Code

I met David many years ago. He had already been in prison more than half his life and he hasn't been a free man since. Short and scrappy, a prison tattoo on his forearm, David hated to be called an inmate.

"We're convicts," he would say with some pride.

He was assigned to work with me and he took his job seriously. Always convinced that women weren't safe in the prison, he watched me like a hawk, sitting outside the door when I needed a private conversation with a man. His fears were exaggerated, but were grounded in years of experience in some of the country's toughest prisons.

David started his prison career at the infamous Angola facility in Louisiana. He later served time in the notorious maximum-security prison in Michigan City, Indiana, before he came to Kentucky. He told startling tales of murders, gang rapes, violence, and sadness. At Michigan City, he was stabbed above his eye as he stepped out of his cell—a misidentification in a hire-to-kill situation. The attacker was trying to run an icepick through his eye but missed.

"For a carton of four-dollar cigarettes, you could get a man killed," he said.

In the 1990s, when I first knew David, things were peaceful in the Kentucky institutions. The prison system was under a strong consent decree—a federal court-ordered cleanup of the state's prison system. Programs were in place, old guards were replaced with more professional officers, and the facilities were clean.

Yet David kept insisting he'd rather do time in Louisiana or Indiana. In Kentucky, he felt physically safer, but he claimed, "They play games with your mind."

I came to realize he was distressed about the gradual change from the days of convicts to the new atmosphere for inmates. He was not alone. To my surprise, even the officers I interviewed wanted to make sure I understood the difference between the old convicts and the younger inmates who inhabit the prison today. And, they agreed, the difference had to do with respect—however twisted that respect was.

Convicts had a code of conduct that centered on respect for one another—the old "honor among thieves" that we hear about. If a man broke his word, it was a sign of disrespect and he was "taken care of." If he owed money and didn't pay it back, if he stole from another, if he ignored the unwritten rules of prison life, the other inmates dealt with him. They didn't go to the officers for help; they handled it themselves. To rat on someone was a weakness. If a convict refused to rat, he might end up in the hole, he might catch another charge, but when he re-emerged on the yard, he was more respected and not to be messed with. The unwritten rules were strengthened.

Weaker men broke under that system and there was certainly more violence. However, those who survived and followed the convict rules were proud and strong—and respected. And there was a predictable order to things both for the men and the officers.

In preferring that old system, David was railing against the new population where officers use men against one another, finding "rats" to tell on their fellow inmates in return for special privileges.

Today, with the convict code dwindling, you can trust no one—even those closest to you. And there was an unspoken order to prison life that is now missing. In David's words, "There are really no convicts these days. Convict is an old-school name for a man or woman who has morals and ethics in a prison setting."

I had to smile as David struggled to explain the issue of respect that is such a different thing within prisons than it is outside. But what he says is worth repeating as long as you read it carefully. I asked, how is respect in prison different than the concept outside?

> Outside, right is right and wrong is wrong. If a man steals your car, you can call the police. You have to. In prison, if a man steals my radio, I don't call the cops/guards because, unlike on the streets, it's wrong to call the cops. Respect kind of works the same way. You get respect in prison by handling your own problems. If you use that concept/scenario on the streets, you go to jail—no one out there respects you for breaking the law (to handle your own problems). In here, they do respect you for it.
>
> I'm not explaining this well. Try again. On the streets, if you do the right thing, people respect you.
>
> In prison, "the right thing" is often the wrong thing. You get no respect for doing the wrong thing in any setting.
>
> So it comes down to the fact that between the streets and prisons, what's right and what's wrong is completely different. Therefore, so is the concept of respect.
>
> Let me know if that makes any sense to you, because I don't really understand what the hell I just wrote, but I'm pretty sure it's close to right!

In another letter about the convict code, David told me the story of Dick, who committed the only murder at that particular institution in the twenty years I worked there—at least the only one that I knew of. David's conclusions are extreme—almost bizarre—to those of us on the outside, but they are helpful in understanding the convict code.

> Dick was my cellmate at the time he killed a guy in the print shop. That story might help to explain the difference in inmates and convicts. A more respectful and respected man I've never known anywhere in any prison system. At Christmas that year, Dick stole three Christmas cards

from the print shop. An inmate saw him and told on him. Another inmate heard him tell and informed Dick. Keep this in mind. In the old days (like my years in Michigan City and Angola), a snitch was killed for snitching. Also killed were child molesters.

So, we were searched and our cell tossed until they found those cards. Afterwards Dick told me he knew what the deal was and he'd have to handle it. I had no clue what was going on. Picture the yard in your mind—the grievance office was in education and the print shop two doors down. Dick and I walked to work together as usual. To make a long story short, Dick walked into the print shop, checked out a ballpeen hammer, and beat the snitch to death. After doing so, he reached down, snatched the wristwatch from the guy's wrist and held it up to the cop, who wisely watched it happen and did nothing, and said, "Now get it right this time. 'Robbery-murder.'"

I know what he meant. Robbery-murder brings the death penalty in Kentucky. He told me before he wished they had sentenced him to death the first time. He said something I have said many times, that he didn't have the guts to commit suicide.

At that time, if you'll remember, I was a grievance aide and my job was to go to segregation and handle grievances for the seg inmates. Dick was in the observation cell, which had a big Plexiglas window. He didn't have any of his property, just a jumpsuit. He asked me to get him something to read. I asked the unit manager of seg if I could bring him a couple of books. He said no. I tried to talk him into it and he finally said, "He killed a man. I'm not giving him anything."

To make a long story short, I told him that Dick was a convict and what he did, he honestly believed (right or wrong) was what he had to do, what he was supposed to do. Regardless of what you think, in Dick's world, he did what was needed and expected of him. In your world, he's a monster.

I told him that unless Dick is disrespected again or snitched on, assaulted, etc. you'll probably never have another problem out of him. He'll accept whatever punishment you and the system dishes out and won't hold a grudge about it because he, unlike you, understands that what's right in his world is wrong in your world. Not allowing him a book or a magazine isn't accomplishing anything.

I went back to seg the next day and Dick was reading a book.

I'm not saying that Dick was right to kill that boy. I'm just saying that he thought it was right. I remember the day clearly. He wasn't angry or vindictive. It was like, for example, a sniper shoots a kidnapper. It may be murder, but it's his job as a sniper. Dick felt it was his job as a convict. I personally wouldn't have done it, but to be honest I guess, though I have portrayed myself as such, I have never been a real convict. I draw the line short of killing and/or bucking the system to the point of rioting.

In short, an inmate just merely exists in a convict's world and, if he's smart, stays out of everybody's way. He's loyal to no one, staff or inmate, but tries to straddle the fence and make both factions happy, and that never works.

A convict lives by a code and won't be disrespected by any inmate. He also won't accept disrespect from staff when they go over and above their job description. He understands and accepts that staff members have the responsibility to make sure you serve your sentence as ordered by the court. He understands enforcement of most rules and regs.

That being said, that's the way it used to be. It's no longer that way. These days the word "convict" simply means you don't tell on each other. You do your thing and keep your mouth closed about other people's business and, truthfully, these days most so-called convicts will tell whatever they have to, to get or keep what they want. Pretty much these days, inmates are inmates. Back in the old days, if you had a problem you knew it and knew where it was coming from. These days you have no idea.

The bottom line is that for the convict, rules for successful living on the outside are turned upside down within the prison. That makes the transition back to the community difficult. Years ago, David's supervisor was complimenting his work ethic to me. He's smart; he is conscientious; he is capable. He knows prison life and operates very well within the prison environment, she said. Way better than he probably will when he's finally released, she added.

When I first met Al, he had already been in prison almost twenty years. He's now at the forty-four-year mark. The parole board served him out on his life sentence, meaning he can never be considered for parole again; he is in prison until he dies.

He was one of the men I had hoped most would answer my letters. In 1994, he was straight-talking, tough, and proudly declared himself a convict. I was anxious to see if he had changed and wanted to get his unique take on prison life. I wanted to see what had happened about some of the things he had talked about twenty years before. Someone told me he'd never participate—he considered himself too tough to do something like that. "He's an old convict and thinks he's better than anyone else," I was told.

It took several letters, but I finally got an answer. It was a short note written in a shaky, disconnected print. It was obviously difficult for him to write. Al's letter read:

Ms. Holman, I have received all of your letters. I am sorry for being so negative and unresponsive toward you and your project. Yes, I will help

you, but only if we have a one-on-one conversation. My writing over the
years has kind of hurt my hands. Too much fighting in here over the years.
    This will be short. So do let me know and I will answer every ques-
tion you ask me. But, I will only answer them honestly and to the best of
my ability. Again, I hope you forgive me for being so selfish. Hope to hear
from you soon and see you.

He got his way. I got permission to meet with him privately and we
talked for three hours. I know now that the old con "conned" me. Most of the
later letters have been written in a smooth cursive hand, no sign of debilitat-
ing arthritis, although I noticed his knuckles were indeed swollen when I saw
him. But I didn't care if he had conned me. Like conversations with him years
before, it was time well spent and a fascinating look into the mind and life of
a man who has spent most of his sixty-five years behind bars. He doesn't have
visitors except for a rare visit from a brother. He enjoyed the conversation as
well. Like years before, he was straightforward with his thoughts on a number
of subjects.

I asked about the difference between a convict and an inmate. He said:
    I'd a hundred percent rather be a convict. There aren't many old-
timers left. These new guys have no morals, no respect for selves. They don't
care who they hurt. Sixty to seventy percent of people here are sex offenders.
They don't have any morals. I hate sex offenders.

That negative feeling about sex offenders is indicative of the convict
and was pervasive years ago in prison—that was the one crime (especially
if it was child sex abuse) that inmates kept very quiet. They did it for their
own safety. It still isn't openly admitted. Al went on to emphasize that he
treats women right. Indeed, he showed a lot of respect for me, watching his
language, carefully choosing words as he explained how things work that had
a sexual context (like the smuggling in of drugs by females).

Like some of the other older guys, he had a disdain for programs. "The
guys ain't learnin' nothin'. Either you are or aren't going to change. You can't
teach that." He and David use almost the exact same words.

He continues about the life of a convict today.
    I have no close friends. A close friend is going to cut your throat.
With enemies, you know where you stand. Friends cut your throat—it's a
matter of time. They will get jealous. They will turn you in or steal from
you. It's a different breed today. In the old days, I could leave ten dollars on
this table and come back in a week and it would still be there. Not today.

I asked him what advice he would give to someone coming into prison
and facing a long sentence like his. It took him a long time to answer. He was

unusually silent.

I'd tell them to be prepared to handle things differently here than on the street. It's a mad house. It's crazy here—off the handle. You have to be tough. I'd tell them to buckle up and do things best they can.

Interestingly to me, the old-time officers also liked the days when the convict code ruled. It dictated the informal rules of the prison and there was violence among inmates as a result of it. But the old convict was (and maybe still is) the best ally of the staff, one long-term officer told me. They used the convict code to help run the prison and keep things in line.

"At any one time, we might have sixty-eight staff supervising fifteen hundred men. They can take the prison whenever they want," he admitted. The situation is dangerous with the understaffing that occurs with budget cuts. One of the old cons told him in a friendly conversation, "We let you run the place." And he knows it's true.

This man and others—officers and inmates alike—want to see things run smoothly. They respect the situation when rules and officers are fair. This particular officer, who later became an administrator, enjoyed working in the living units, whereas others hated it and talked about the danger.

"If you treat them right, follow procedures correctly, there will be peace and order," he said. "The old convicts will help you out if you're doing a job correctly. They will back you up. It's like 'treat a dog mean and he'll bite you.'" If you treat the men mean, you'll have trouble. They'll help you if they know you are fair, firm, and consistent."

He went on to tell about a time there was trouble brewing and there was about to be an uprising in the dorm. He was ready to call for backup when one of the old cons stepped in front of the men and, facing them, started cussing and yelling at them about their behavior, telling them to settle down. The convict emphasized that anyone who caused trouble would answer to him. All went silent and peace reigned.

I heard similar tales from a former female officer who told of incidents where men stepped in when their fellow inmates were getting out of line.

I was surprised by the number of staff who said that especially in the old convict days, they were sure that the convicts would have protected them in case of a riot. That aligns with what I was told during my years inside the prison. Both the men and older staff said that if trouble came up, the men would not let harm come to me. But they emphasized that wouldn't hold true for some of the staff.

All older staff that I talked with verbalized the same respect for the old, traditional convicts. They broke rules, ran stores, dealt drugs, caused headaches for the administration, but when caught, they never complained. They respected the fact that the rules were in place and calmly accepted their prescribed punishment.

The old convict code is fading away. I'm told by inmate and staff alike that the new group of young people bring more discontent into the prison. They say the young inmates won't take responsibility for anything. They blame everyone else for their crimes and their present condition. They keep things stirred up. They ignore the informally prescribed codes of conduct and cannot be trusted. It is all a matter of respect and they have none.

The new emerging order of things troubles the older long-term inmates. But still, there are portions of the old code left in place, and danger still lurks for those who don't understand or ignore them.

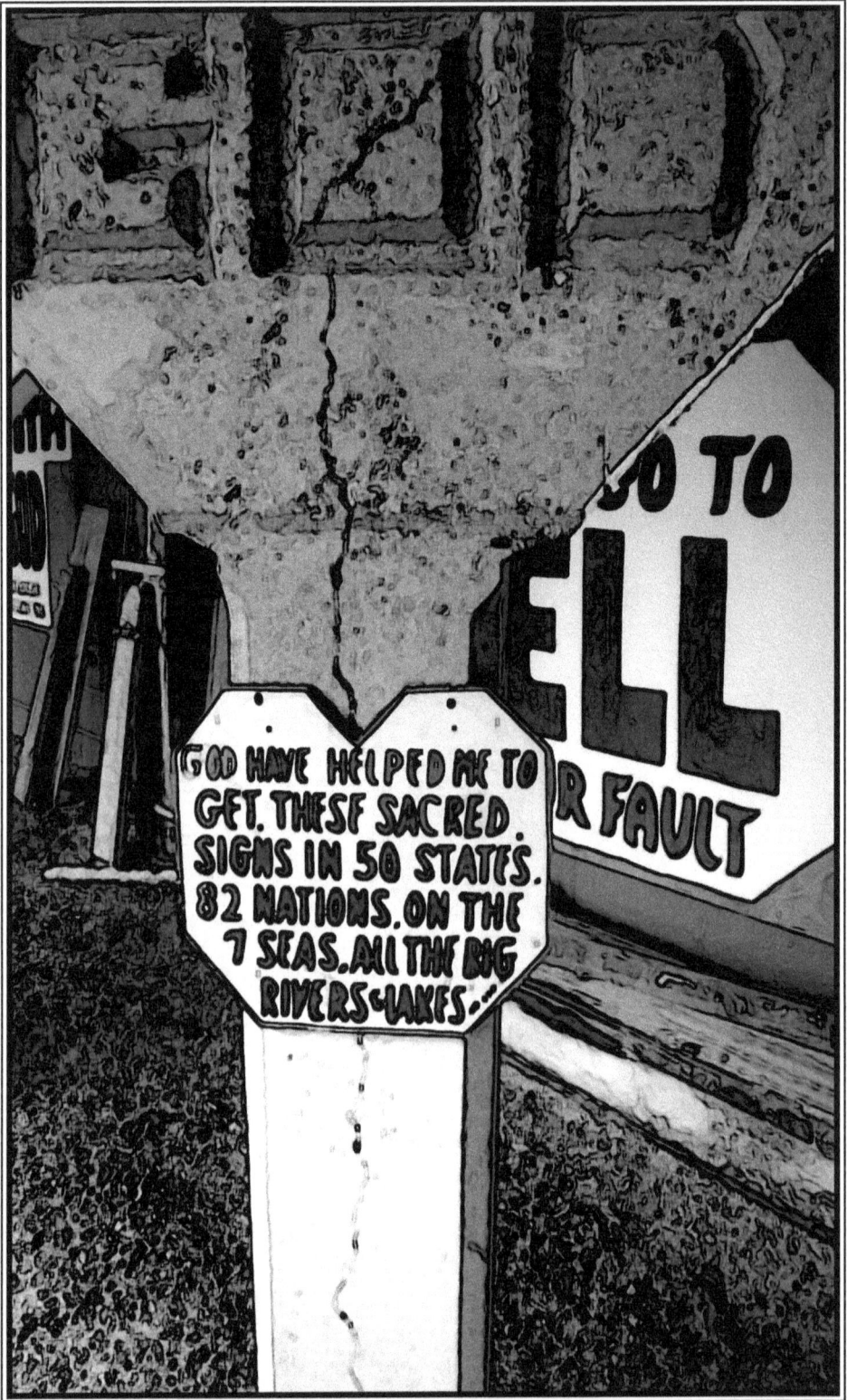

IV. RELIGION

MARIANNE PEEL

I AM PEACE

At first the Peace Rally on Grand River tonight
was a riot of horns, berserk wild honking,
exuberant waving out of car windows,
even a man leaning out of a storefront window,
giving a two thumbs up to our "No Fear"
and "Welcome to Muslim Refugees and Immigrants" signs.

Then a car screeched by
with its driver shouting *Muslims go home.*

Another shook his head at us.
Another yelled, *Yeah, until one kills someone you love.*

And then you stopped your car to talk to me,
recording our ragtag collection of activists on your cell phone.
You took pictures of our signs advocating
love over fear,
compassion over hatred,
welcoming over rejection,
trust over suspicion.
You tell me you don't know what to say.
You tell me *I am so grateful for all of you.*
I feel that I will cry, seeing all of you here, like this.

So I step off the median,
down the curb, to your car.
I reach out to touch your hands.
I am a Muslim man. I cannot shake hands with you, you tell me.

I am suddenly aware
of my femaleness, embarrassed
by this cultural faux pas I have made
reaching for the hands of this Muslim man.
But she can touch you, she can
hold your hands, he tells me,
pointing to his female companion.

And so I reach across the divide
to the woman in the passenger seat.
We embrace hands,
hold one another.

We stopped traffic with that touch,
our eyes fixed steady and pure on one another.
Love over fear.
I did not want to let go.

LAURIE KLEIN

EUCHARIST

Son, this man who built your bomb, has anyone lit
candles for him, some modest wife, who might be
pregnant, angry, afraid to raise a *jihad* child?
Still, to want him dead—

I will say this aloud, with the host, translucent within
my palm—has remained unconfessed. I nudge the wafer
aside, while far away, his praying wife likely threads
heaven, a needle's eye,

bowing over his extra robe, if he owns one. Does he
ever dream of a motorcycle? The man might possess
comedic timing, a green thumb. Or maybe, in secret,
the guy paints. I am trying to see

myself with forgiving eyes—instead of his, exulting
over your death. So I mouth words, wrung from the
throat of Christ, cradle the cup with its clot of wine
and cannot believe this man with his timed device is
one who *knows not what he does* . . .

But oh, he must long for paradise, this believer with
courage enough to worship a God, who, like the One
I've served, declares death sometimes—in the name
of faith. How the body sticks to my tongue: sulfur,
saltpeter, charcoal. Bread.

S. J. ENGSTROM

BREATH, BELIEF AND BELONGING

It was on my bucket list. I had wanted to attend a Parliament of World Religions conference since 2011, when I attended a study trip to Turkey. Along with eight other college faculty members, I had been granted a fellowship by the Niagara Foundation of Chicago for the purpose of cross-cultural education and inter-faith understanding. It proved to be a great gift in many ways and only increased my desire to connect further with people of many faiths.

Theology had been of interest to me since my teenaged years. I was raised in a restrictive born-again Protestant faith that brooked nothing that wasn't a literal interpretation of *The Scriptures* or on the list of forbidden behaviors. After Confirmation class when I was thirteen, I was not a very good believer in the One Way I was taught, so elected not to join our church in suburban Minneapolis. As I grew into adulthood, personally and professionally, my interests in religions didn't subside. In my fields of Sociology and Humanities, religion is a prominent aspect of culture that I continued to enjoy through study, teaching and experience. I traveled and lived in many countries including Zaire (now the Democratic Republic of Congo) and always put visiting worship services and sacred spaces at the top of my list. The first thing I went to see as a first-time student visitor to Paris, for example, was Notre Dame Cathedral. While in Turkey, I enjoyed several mosques and the monolithic beauty of ancient Hagai Sofia. And so I continued to trust that the day would come that I could dialogue and learn with others from all over the globe, at a Parliament conference that I could attend.

Besides intriguing testimonials, I knew a little history; The Parliament of World Religions is an international organization devoted to sustainability, faith, peace and justice. Its premiere event had taken place at the Columbian World Exposition in 1893 with the objective of starting an international dialogue open to all faith traditions. The centenary conference in 1993, also in

Chicago, had featured the Dalai Lama as keynote speaker. An estimated 7000 people showed up to listen to dozens of renowned faith-based speakers and religious leaders from most world religions.

So when I learned that the 2015 Parliament conference would take place in Salt Lake City, I intended to go. I was very reluctant, though, because my heretofore ninety-four-year-old healthy active father had just been told his congenital heart failure would likely end his life within six months. I felt compelled to help him come to terms with this harsh reality and wanted to uphold my promise to him that I would be by his side as much as I was able, offering whatever moral support and lovingkindness I could, as he slogged through his last months on earth. My decision was right; I was with him in his last weeks, helping him prepare to pass away as he had wished, at home in his own bed where my mother had died eighteen months earlier. So, a year or two later, when I learned that the next Parliament conference would be in November 2018 in Toronto, my only response was, *I'm going. Period.* On my long-range planner went the trip.

After making preparations for the November trip, I applied to serve as a volunteer. I liked to stay active, engage with people, and the bonus was a greatly-reduced registration fee. My part-time volunteer role at the speaker registration desk proved to be one of the most meaningful experiences of the event. I met dozens of people from countless nations, professions, and 200+ faiths, including those who identified with agnosticism, secular humanism and paganism. The rich palette of human skin tones, hair textures, cultural dress and movement of 8300 people in a massive urban complex created a kaleidoscope of human energy that remains sculpted in my mind's eye. Both the diversity and atmosphere of the conference were spectacular, encapsulating the theme of inclusion. The ambience was humble and tranquil, yet engaging and lively. Never did I hear an angry tone, discord, a quarrel, or even theological discussion. Rather, I witnessed people from all stations of life, living together, a microcosm of global life, sharing two ideals—inclusive love of all humanity, irrespective of social variables, and extreme love of Planet Earth, which was given to all of us for sustenance, pleasure, beauty and stewardship.

There I was, on day one, putting my friendly foot forward in front of the desk, as two Indian women walked up speaking Hindi. "Do you know where we can get a cup of tea?" asked the middle-aged woman in English. I extended my hand and introduced myself, pointing the way for her on the map. Just as I was preparing for my customary handshake with the elder woman, divinely dressed in white linen from head to foot, she reached out to me with two hands on my shoulders, looked squarely into my face with her soulful dark eyes, and said, "You are my *sister*!" Then the full embrace and holy kiss, or so it seemed, and, "You *know* that, don't you?" My planned conventional handshake and greeting lost their power as I smiled an "I do" and nodded, watching them walk away.

"Breathe and push, breathe and push." Those are the three words I heard emphasized at the next evening's plenary session. Spoken by Valerie Kaur, a global leader in human rights, ecology and the Sikh faith, the phrase engraved itself in my mind. When things seem too dark or stagnant to keep us hopeful, it behooves us to think about the literal birthing process. Women are told when the going gets really rough and tough in delivery, to breathe and push. Painless, no. But essential, yes. The process of invoking life from womb-darkness to new light reassures that we never stop aspiring and that we keep pushing towards our own chosen values, whatever they might be. "Breathe and push, breathe and push," I repeated to my friend as we walked out of the session at the end. "Nancy, would you please remind me of those short, precious words when I complain to you about the challenges in my life, or impatience about our culture or whatever annoyance I can't abide?" Just breathe and push, breathe and push. So simple, so difficult.

A Catholic priest, a Jewish rabbi and an Islamic imam. The Three Amigos, as they called themselves, were religious leaders from South America. They were on a panel, along with three peers from the USA and Canada, so six religious leaders would be speaking about their faith and theology, or so I presumed. But no; my expectations would prove false.

"I know. We sound like kind of a joke!" said the Rabbi. They all chuckled. Listening to their panel discussion was a highlight of my Parliament adventures. The six panelists obviously delighted and inspired the audience, as we smiled along with them. Excellent storytellers, the six smiling men discussed their interfaith friendship of twenty plus years. Their obvious focal point was their faith in God and their common heritage in branches of the Abrahamic faith tradition so prominent in the Middle East. The speakers shared anecdotes and photos, chiefly focused on friendship, families and fun more so than on faith. They joked, poked fun, and teased each other. They lauded each other's cultural and religious traditions, never explaining or defending their own point of view. It was clear that they cherished their interfaith friendship, respect and genuine love above all else. They mused about the regular meetings and visits they have on both continents, enjoying the nostalgia of past and ongoing celebrations and visits. They knew the names of each other's children and grandchildren, as if they were all in the same family. At the end of the session, to hearty applause, I felt like I had just born witness to pure interfaith friendship and love. And these questions pummeled by mind: *Why is this so rare? Why don't we see more demonstrations of this in religious and academic institutions? Why doesn't every city in the U.S. have an interfaith council or coalition just for the sheer purpose of forming alliances and friendships? Why? Why not?*

The last day of the conference, I had time to finally enjoy what was on my list as a "must-see" art exhibit, one of dozens throughout the venue. Having dabbled in quilting and mosaic art, I began imagining what I had so far only heard about. The *Quilt of Belonging* took up an entire wall on the lower level of a massive exhibition hall. Created in the 1990's by Canadian artist Esther Bryan, it is truly something to see and has been viewed around the world by millions who follow the traveling phenomenon. Over 120 feet long, it is a collage of 263 pieces, originally designed and hand-stitched, each section representing a country or a tribal nation in Canada. It appropriates every hue of the hundreds of variations on the color spectrum, repeats the shape of the hexagon, and has an intense fringed, crimson border. I spoke with the cordial artist, who explained all the symbolism in the piece, in a one-on-one show-and-tell tour. More accurately called a "textile mosaic" by Bryan, every piece was amazing in its detail and symbolic portrayal of a culture. One of the most noteworthy aspects of the ten-year process was that Bryan and her team had secured textile artists living in Canada from almost every nation on the globe; when she couldn't, she somehow located someone who knew someone willing to do the job in his or her native land, until the vision was complete. As I wandered along the artwork, I thought of the cultures I had enjoyed, the nations I had visited and especially pondered one of the best times of my life, when I had taught and lived in Kinshasa, in the Democratic Republic of Congo. I found the piece that symbolized this vast, rich, spectacular country I had grown to love; it pictured the natural beauty of the land, its exotic animals and warm people. Imagining the countless number of onlookers who had enjoyed the art exhibited in many lands, only magnified my experience. The *Quilt of Belonging* is indeed a stunning spectacle that has enough warmth and breadth to cover the whole human family.

As I concluded my time at The Parliament, I recalled that I had read that there are more than seventy names for The Divine— Alpha and Omega, God, Great Spirit, Allah, Lord of Lords, Jehovah, Higher Power, Creator, Dios, Abba and the list goes on. It seemed "providential," as my mother often told me, that I was able to enjoy the unity of thousands of people who had different names and concepts of the Divine Source of all Life. No matter how we address our Almighty, we share three fundamental values—faith in a creative Supreme Being, devotion to care for The Earth, and the full embrace of all Abba's beloved children.

LORI LEVY

TAMING THE BEAST

Compassionate listening, their website said.
A Dialogue group for Jews and Muslims.
Just what I wanted: a chance to meet *the other.*
I went to meetings, almost hungry for conflict,
so I could hone my skills, practice tolerance.
I waited for action—but we smiled, supported, agreed,
all of us moderate, peace-loving folks, opposed to war.
We listened to each other's stories
and ate Middle Eastern food, gushing over
each other's lentils, salads, spices.

Who would have known I'd need my daughter
to teach me tolerance? Where she believes *A,*
I believe *B,* everything from politics to religion to
raising children. How, I wonder, can the daughter of a liberal,
secular Jew who barely knows who Abraham is
become a faithful believer in the Bible? And Jesus.
A conservative, there-is-only-one-truth, Messianic
kind of Jew. How can the granddaughter of a physician
become an ardent anti-vaccine mother
who home schools her kids partly to avoid vaccination?
We argue, insist, eyes bulging from our faces,
trying to convince. She speaks the language of *discipline, obey,*
stricter than I ever was. I chafe against these words,
against her rules for what is and isn't allowed.
The beast in me roars, aching to pounce and
tear to shreds. So easy to forget

it's her life, her kids, her choice. So easy to judge and blame.
I grab the beast and attempt to restrain it.
Sometimes I succeed. Mostly I fail—
wishing it were as easy as listening to a story being told
in my Jewish/Muslim Dialogue group
where *the other* was always respected.

PATTY SOMLO

A NIGHTLY INTERRUPTION

Lou might have said, if anyone asked how it began, that Mohammed offered him a cup of tea. Not even raising his head to look Lou in the eye, Mohammed, almost in a whisper, said, "May I offer you some tea?" He held the dark thermos in his right hand, next to where Lou sat behind the gleaming mahogany counter in the lower lobby, poorly lit at that late hour because no one other than Lou and Mohammed were usually around.

Lou's first thought was to say no, that he disliked tea, its bitterness so unappealing. But seeing how Mohammed bowed his head, a sign of respect, Lou said, "Yes. Thank you. Let me go get a clean cup."

They did not speak more than that after the tea was poured. When the sun came up, the streets outside the hotel that had become slick with rain during the night started to shimmer. Lou and Mohammed both left their respective posts in the bowels of the building, nodded and said good night. Then each, separately, headed home.

It might have ended there and the nights would have passed without incident, one after the next, for years to come. Lou coming into work, taking his post at the desk, as he had done now these past five years. Mohammed, in this last year, following only moments after, picking up the mop with its long thin lines of rope and starting in on the tile floor. When Mohammed first came to the job, there was a simple nod of his head to Lou as he arrived and a second nod when he left. Later, English flowed more easily through Mohammed's mind and he enjoyed trying it out. Along with the nod, Mohammed added a "Good evening," and then, a month or two after that, he stretched it out more with a "How are you," to which Lou would raise his head momentarily and respond, "Fine."

The next night Mohammed offered tea again. This time, Lou understood. Unlike what Lou had experienced before in his life, a bitterness that lingered on his tongue, the tea that Mohammed served him was sweet. If pressed to say more, Lou might even have added that the tea tasted a bit like flowers.

After offering the tea, Mohammed raised his head an inch or so. Lou thought he glimpsed a smile, trying to sneak out the corners of Mohammed's lips. As quickly as Mohammed raised his head, though, he lowered it again. Lou considered making a comment about the tea. Instead, he simply said, "Thank you."

The tea turned into a nightly interruption from the dull monotony of watching the time pass on the fine Rolex watch Lou had bought himself when he'd been doing a lot better than he was now. In a matter of weeks, though he might not have been ready to admit it then, Lou began looking forward to the tea. It wasn't just the taste, its sweetness a sudden surprise on his tongue, but Lou also enjoyed the ceremony.

"The tea is very good," Lou finally told Mohammed one night, weeks after the tea interruption began.

Mohammed, without lifting his head, raised his eyes to stare intently at Lou. Lou's strong face, with the deep-set dark eyes and prominent nose, stared back. A Jew, Mohammed thought, likes my tea. All Mohammed could do that night was smile.

After sipping his tea quietly, Lou began to wonder. Where had Mohammed come from? Before Mohammed, there had been a guy named José. But then, in these jobs, there had always been a guy named José. José smiled and sometimes hummed when he worked. Lou almost never spoke to José. He knew that José didn't understand much English.

Two months into the tea ceremony, it seemed to Lou that Mohammed had always been there. And now that Lou thought about him, he had to admit that Mohammed seemed as ill fit for the job as Lou believed he was for his. Lou would have guessed Mohammed to be in his early to mid-forties. With square shoulders and a trim mustache, a handsome proud face, Mohammed appeared the sort to be an engineer or a doctor. An Arab, Lou said to himself, and that made Lou wonder if Mohammed knew. A Jew was drinking his tea.

Around the start of the third month, Lou decided it was time. Looking back, he might have said the change came because he was bored. Bored with the long nights of sitting in the lower lobby of the hotel and waiting next to a phone that never rang. The hotel prided itself on service. If a guest needed anything in the middle of the night—aspirin or a cup of coffee, a bottle of booze—Lou was there to provide it. But no one ever needed anything and so he sat, reading the thick novels that he bought used and sold back to the bookstore to buy other novels he could lose himself in during the long nights.

Biscuits, Lou decided, would go very nicely with the tea. He had stopped at the grocery store a block from his house to pick up something for breakfast. Lou had never eaten anything he would classify as a biscuit but he'd seen them there. A long way back, still a student at the university in New York, Lou recalled the characters in Victorian novels he'd been forced to read sipped tea in the afternoon and ate biscuits.

Not surprisingly, the biscuits turned the tea ceremony into a more formal event. As soon as he offered Mohammed a biscuit, Lou understood. Biscuits meant eating. And eating required a table and, dare he think it, two people sitting down together to eat.

Mohammed's first reaction to the biscuit offer was fear. He noticed his heartbeat suddenly speed up and his neck and face grew warm and flushed. If he said no, Lou might take it the wrong way. He might think, *That Arab. He refuses my food because I'm a Jew.* But if Mohammed accepted, what then?

Unaware of the time, Mohammed had stood silently for several minutes after Lou spoke. It was only then that Lou realized what he'd done. Tea was simple and polite. But a biscuit was asking for it. A biscuit demanded something. Yes, a biscuit even said, *Let's be friends.*

"I thought the biscuits would go nicely with the tea," Lou said to break the awkward silence. "In case you wanted something else on your break with the tea."

Mohammed could feel the relief dripping down the sides of his face.

"Yes, yes," he said, probably too quickly, but the relief had taken over, like a transfusion of fresh new blood racing through his veins. "Yes, thank you. A biscuit would be nice," he added and held out his hand.

An hour later, in the small janitor's room behind the lobby where Mohammed sat to rest, he bit into the biscuit and slowly chewed. The biscuit was dry and not that sweet, unlike the pastries he was accustomed to eating back home, filled with warm dates, honey and walnuts. His teeth crushed the biscuit into fine dust. He was accustomed to a fruity chewiness that clung to his molars and left a sweet flavor on his tongue. So, this is what Jews eat, he thought, understanding at that moment that the food he was accustomed to had a bold liveliness this biscuit sorely lacked.

Interestingly, the realization made him feel sorry for Lou. As much as he'd disliked Jews his whole life, Mohammed always believed the Jews had it better than the Arabs. This biscuit made him see that he may have been mistaken after all.

DANIEL M. JAFFE

A BLESSING ON YOUR HEAD

Sitting across his desk from me, Rabbi Katz patted his stiff hand on a yellowing translation of the Torah. "My boy, according to the Torah, we must obey the Almighty's laws in order to receive his blessings. So, what you're requesting is obviously impossible." This conversation took place decades ago, in my youth, before the Conservative movement came around to authorizing gay weddings, so I pretty much expected Rabbi Katz to turn me down. But I didn't want to make it easy for him. I told myself back then that my motivation was purely political, an attempt to force a rabbi to confront the issue head-on, so that one day, maybe, his mind might change and then he might change another rabbi's mind, and so on. But now, as I recall that conversation, I wonder whether part of my motivation for confronting him was a need to vent anger at some symbol of religious intolerance. And who better than the Rabbi of my upbringing?

"I have to turn you down, of course," Rabbi Katz continued. "Nothing personal."

"Nothing personal?" I exclaimed with a mocking laugh. "Rabbi, how can you say that refusing to perform my commitment ceremony is nothing personal?"

"I mean that rabbis must act on principle, regardless of who poses a request, even generally good boys like you."

"A Reform rabbi would help me."

"Ethical relativism." Rabbi Katz closed his eyes momentarily, then, "Not to speak ill of other rabbis, but the Reform are too quick to ride the tides of social fads, giving people what they want instead of what they need."

"No disrespect, but don't the Orthodox say that about you Conservative rabbis?"

"Nonsense. We Conservative rabbis balance strict standards against fanaticism."

"If you're not a fanatic, then be flexible enough to bless my union with the man I love."

"Look, my boy," said Rabbi Katz, rubbing fingertips across the volume of Torah as if massaging or polishing. "A wedding ceremony between you and your friend wouldn't even make sense. In the Jewish wedding vow, one spouse takes the other 'according to the laws of Moses.' But the laws of Moses expressly prohibit your sort of . . . coupling."

"So we'll come up with a different vow. We can be creative."

"It's not up to me," said Rabbi Katz. "The Rabbinical Assembly doesn't permit me even to attend a marriage between a Jewish man and a non-Jewish woman, so it certainly doesn't permit me to officiate at the sort of union you want, which is—you'll pardon the expression—a perversion."

If I had known, before that conversation, about Rabbi Katz's infidelity decades earlier, would I have thrown that misstep in his face? Would I have said something like, "You're willing to violate your marriage vows, but unwilling to grant me the chance to create and honor my own?" In anger, I might have spouted such a thing, and maybe that argument would have shamed him into considering my request more seriously. But how ashamed I would have felt forever after.

"I'm a member of the Rabbinical Assembly," he continued, "and must abide by its rules."

"How convenient to hide behind a group," I said. "Can't you think for yourself?"

"You used to be a respectful boy."

"You used to be a respectful man."

"You want I should disregard the Rabbinical Assembly? Collective wisdom is greater than any one man's. Our tradition gains its strength from learned men's discussion and debate of Torah. That's the Talmud, the spine of our heritage, our unity despite Diaspora. I won't betray it." Rabbi Katz's eyes gleamed, the raised beauty mark on his chin bulged.

I looked down at my lap, embarrassed at where my anger had led me. I stood, slid and scraped my chair around to the side of his desk, set it beside him, sat. "I drove all the way from Boston to you in New Jersey because you're the rabbi of my childhood. You bar mitzvahed me, Rabbi."

Rabbi Katz reached out and patted me on the cheek. The instant he touched me, my anger dissolved and I nearly started to cry.

"You're right," said Rabbi Katz, "I'm the rabbi of your childhood. So I feel partly responsible for your moral failings. All the more reason I must do right by you now."

I felt totally calm. "Rabbi, when I was fifteen and graduating from Hebrew High School, you gave our class an inspiring lesson."

"I did?"

"You talked about your first landlord, the one after you married Mrs. Katz. From a Polish *shtetl*. He followed every ritual, you said, attending daily *minyans*, laying *tefiln*, eating strictly kosher, spending every Shabbes with a volume of Talmud on his lap. But if a tenant was one day late with the rent—eviction! 'That man,' you told us, 'was observant, but not religious. There's a difference.' I never forgot that lesson, Rabbi. Compassion is fundamental to religious observance."

Rabbi Katz tilted his head, smiled. "You're right. For us compassion is central. My decision to observe the Torah's prohibitions is my way of showing compassion to all our people. You included. Matt, you shouldn't do this thing."

"You're trying to save me from myself?"

"I can't stop you, of course," said Rabbi Katz. "The Almighty grants each of us free will. But I can refuse to condone—for your sake and for the good of our flock, so that our people as a whole may receive the Almighty's blessing."

I sat back in my chair. "I don't mean disrespect, Rabbi, but aren't you Conservative rabbis behaving like a flock of obedient sheep?"

"The Lord is my shepherd—reread your Psalms. There is no shame in following His guidance. Obedience, too, is exercise of free will."

"So that's it, then?" I said. "Each of us exercises opposing free will? No compromise?"

Rabbi Katz shrugged.

I stood slowly, saddened by the totality of the impasse.

Rabbi Katz raised his hand, palm facing out, "A blessing on your head." In low tones, he began murmuring, "*Yevarechecha . . .*"

I let him finish the *brachah*. Then, "Thanks a lot, Rabbi." I shook my head, turned, and left.

Despite my anticipated disappointment, I did take something of value from that conversation—Rabbi Katz's statement that obedience is also an exercise of free will. That was a new idea and it stayed with me, actually changed my thinking over the years, helped me become more tolerant of those who are intolerant of me. Of course, out of hurt and resentment, I never told this to Rabbi Katz, although I know full well he'd have been heartened by my acceptance of another of his ethical lessons. Am I wicked for withholding comfort from a man who withheld comfort from me?

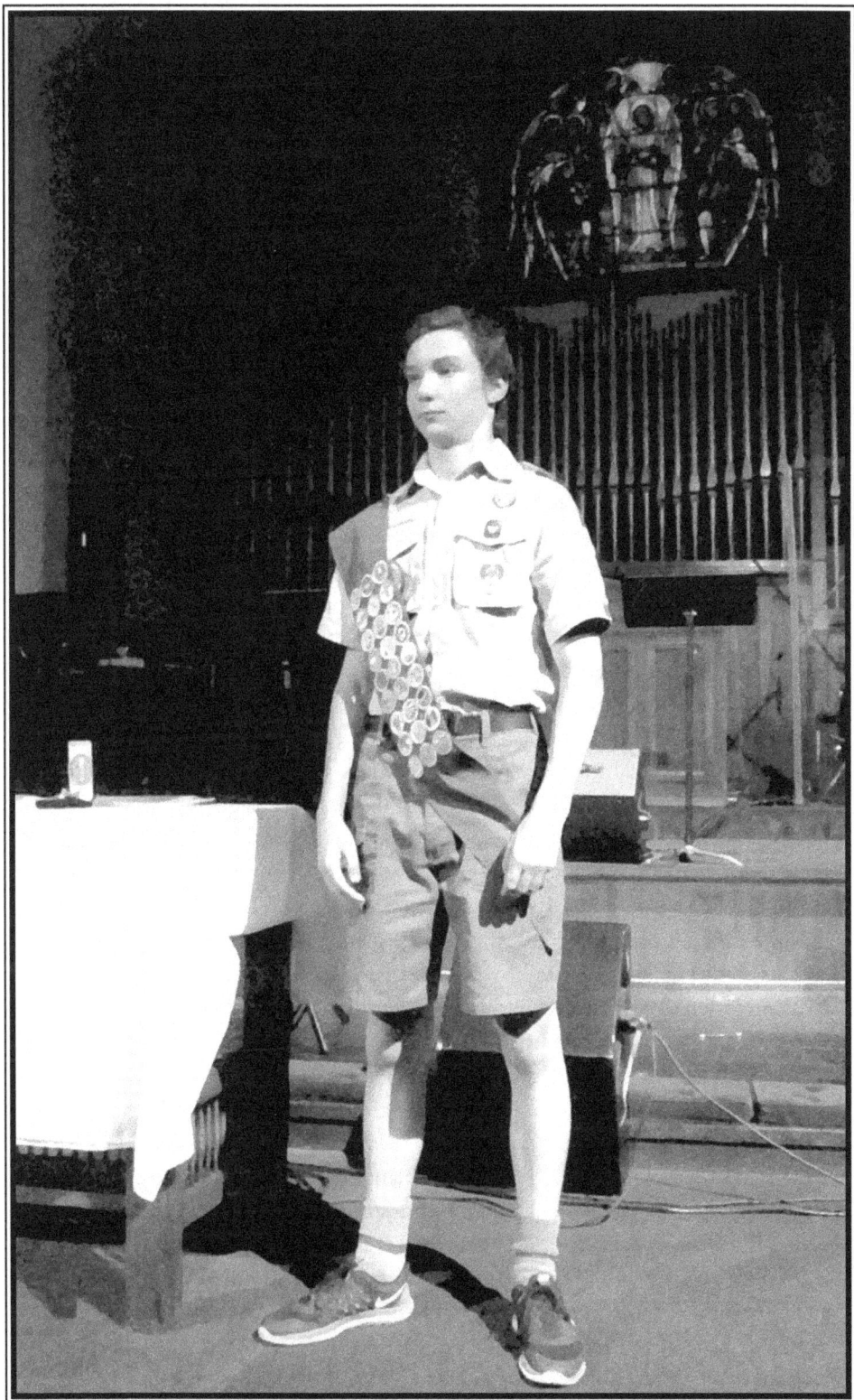

DAVID ARANGO-DIMITRIJEVIC

SAM DALCA

Sam Dalca was the smartest student of my career. He aced every assign-ment and exam. Reading his papers was a constant revelation. His insight into literature and the humanities was that of a college professor, not an eighteen-year-old high school senior. His comments in class would traverse psychology, history, ancient cultures, sociology, and classical philosophy. In a roomful of hands raised, I would often call on Sam last, because his remarks couldn't be topped by anyone, myself included.

Sam was an unusually tall high school senior. He paid no attention to his appearance: his understated clothes, his blond haircut too short to ever be messy, his bouts with teenage acne. One day he walked in to the classroom, and with his typical intensity told me that he hadn't had a chance to finish his homework. This meant he'd only read the assigned pages *once*, instead of two or three times as usual. When our AP Literature class would flip through a chapter trying to find a specific passage, Sam would not only know the page number, but he would have the lines nearly memorized. If we were stumbling over a difficult pronunciation, we could just turn to Sam and ask, "How do you say 'Ozymandias'?" and he'd tell us. In an e-mail to me, he critiqued the valedictorian's speech at his graduation by writing: "It was truly a masterpiece of vacuous pomposity; verily, 'twas exacerbated in large part by the magni-tude of the orator's pathological superciliousness."

Teaching, at its most draining, moves in one direction: I guide the stu-dents, I impart knowledge, I make them think, I ask them questions, I create the dialectic and debate, I try to have them absorb whatever I have to give, I struggle to give them energy and enthusiasm to replace their teenage mal-aise. But Sam reversed it. His comments energized me, and in the midst of a discussion I could feel my neurons crackling with a hundred new thoughts about a piece of literature I thought I'd known completely.

)X(X(

Though Sam should have been renowned for his intelligence, he had a different label at our high school. He was the resident Christian. Sam was an uncamouflaged, exhibitional, proud, vociferous believer in God and Jesus. He owned shelves of Bibles and gave me two within the first few weeks of class. He had a wooden cross glued to his locker; above the cross he taped a "prayer sheet" where anyone could write down his or her wish, and Sam would pray for it that night. Some requests were sincere: "end the war in Iraq," and some were pure high school: "I want the football team to win. Go 'Stangs!" I don't know what Sam did with the athletic requests.

His junior year, when the class was reading Hawthorne's "The Minister's Black Veil," Sam wore a black veil to class. It reminded me of the Sex Pistols shirt I used to wear in high school. A black veil or a punk rock T-shirt helps mark you as someone who has given up on fitting in.

)X(X(

One day Sam dropped by to tell me about a speech he was giving in Oral Communication class. I asked, "What kind of speech is it Sam?"

"It's going to be great. It's a demonstration speech."

"And what are you going to show the class?"

"How to exorcise a demon."

"Really?" I thought for a moment. Then I asked, "Sam, how *do* you exorcise a demon? How do you bring the demon in the classroom in the first place? Do you have to find someone who is possessed? Put an ad in the paper? And then, even worse, what happens when you *do* excise the demon right there in speech class? Then you have a demon loose in the room."

"Oh Mr. Arango, ye of little faith," he said. "I haven't seen any demons yet in the building. My speech is just about its possibility. I'll show the signs of the demonic possession of the human body, read essential Biblical quotes, and talk about the types of priests required for the exorcism. As long as I'm at here, you'll never have to worry about demons."

)X(X(

As a workaholic teacher I didn't date, I left for work a 6 a.m. and got home at 8 p.m., and I rarely saw friends. I let myself be consumed by a profession that wanted to take every last part of me. So my relationships with students took on increased importance. I always remained their teacher, but I would turn to them for a moment of humor, or reflection, or friendship. I saw Sam all the time, and we spoke with the ease of two people who know each other well, who enjoy each other's company. We let our endlessly shared minutes feel like home. Weekend visits with my adult friends had to be scheduled and often required a period of reacquainting; talking to Sam was effortless and fun.

⟩⟨⟩⟨

Once Sam said, "Mr. Arango, if I wasn't so religious, I'd be psychotic."
I chuckled, "C'mon Sam. 'Psychotic' is a strong word."
"No Mr. Arango, I'm serious."
It did seem like Sam was always on edge. If he sat in the back of the room, he would lightly bang his head against the brick wall. Other times he would silently conduct an imaginary symphony with his arms, or take out a pretend sword that was sheathed on his back and swing it around. And for the entertainment of teachers and students alike, Sam would take requests to do a split, dropping to the ground immediately, both long legs impossibly stretched.

All these physical antics made him a strange kid. Didn't he want to fit in? Is that a universal need, or can someone prefer to live without it? Sam's classmates never made his life miserable. The saw him as a strange one, but they would still invite him out to lunch. He seemed close to his intensely religious father, a minister who translated Christian texts from Romanian into English. He had a good relationship with his mother and brother. But I still wondered if Sam was lonely, and if he was, if he even knew it. His hyper-intellectualism and religiosity could form one hell of a painkiller, one that Sam may have been clinging to with all his might.

⟩⟨⟩⟨

Just as there are blue and red states, there are blue and red high schools, and I'm a liberal who works at a red high school. My high school is far away enough from urban and suburban sprawl to have some of the Bible belt conservatism found in rural communities. Many parents vote only for Republican candidates, and countless students have told me that Jesus Christ is the only way to heaven. Sometimes people ask why I don't work at a high school that better suits my politics. My response is that I enjoy the friction, the argument, the debate, the volley of words. And Sam was the most enlivening of all. For all his religiosity, he had an incredible understanding of most of my positions, and then would try to knock them down with his pre-set doctrines.

I asked him once if, when we talked, either of us was truly willing to hear the other. We would share our beliefs and enjoy the intellectual exchange, but would we be open enough to move, even to the slightest degree, towards each other's position? I was as dogmatic in my political views as he was in his religious views. He would argue against homosexual unions, I would argue for them. He would claim Jesus was the only path to heaven and God, and I would dispute such exclusivity. I was sure I was right, he was sure he was right. Would we hear each other? We had to do more than just tolerate each other's thoughts, more than just encourage open debate. Even as an atheist, I had to get inside his head and see things his way. I had to actually consider the existence of God not for Sam, but for me. I couldn't just be a teacher welcoming all viewpoints, a detached yet encouraging referee of any perspective. I needed to open my mind . . . but I could never quite do it. I don't think Sam could either. We were both ideologues to some degree, an atheist and a deist who had shut down our minds years ago. But Sam helped me identify this foreclosure of my thinking, which seemed like an important first step.

And yet our ideas converged occasionally. I found capitalism incompatible with ecological balance and true human happiness, and Sam found it incompatible with core lessons of Christianity. I would argue for the deep ecology of Thoreau and against the menace of materialism, and Sam would find the Biblical quotes to support it.

Sam wasn't only as smart as a professor, he *was* my professor. He quoted relevant Bible passages, he referenced Hegel and Kant, he wrote up annotated supplements to class conversations and gave them to me the next day before class. He helped me intertwine disciplines, expand my thinking, and move beyond my intellectual and personal comfort zones.

)X(X(X(

When Sam was a senior, a former student of mine named Joey Flynn died a mysterious death, his body found floating in the Chicago River. Joey and I had been close and had stayed in touch after he graduated. The day after I got the news of his passing, I was emotionally wrecked.

Standing in the freezing snow at his burial, I wondered, where is Joey now? Does he still exist somewhere? I didn't know, but I was sure if hell existed, he wasn't there. Joey was beloved by everyone, including me; he couldn't be burning forever in eternal damnation.

Back in my classroom after the funeral, I talked to Sam and a Jewish student named Leah. I asked Sam if he thought Joey was in hell. He looked down at his hands, hesitated, then said yes—though it was hard to say aloud—since Joey hadn't accepted Jesus Christ as his savior, he was in hell. He then looked at us with a face more concerned than righteous, and told Leah and I that we were going to hell too unless we brought Christ into our lives.

I smile at that conversation now ("A Christian, a Jew, and an atheist are standing in a classroom . . ."). But at the time I needed Sam. I felt raw from the funeral, and I was in no mood for any of the artifice of most conversations. I had been stripped down to my bones, and I only wanted to talk to someone who could speak from his marrow as well. Sam knew it was a tough time to be saying that Joey was going to hell. He knew this was a time of grief for Leah and me, and it would be no relief to tell us we would suffer eternal damnation. But he also knew that to say anything but his true beliefs would be a betrayal of our relationship. I was comforted by Sam being himself, and whatever he was saying about heaven and hell just didn't matter.

After years of teaching I've noticed students make use of me in various ways. At some point I realized that I might be a surrogate father, or a mother, or a disciplinarian, or a friend, or an intellect, or an activist, or whomever else they need. An adolescent continually flirts with what the world might be and who they might be in it. When some new part of them wants to surface, they need to make use of a teacher to affirm whatever is emerging. So I had to be scores of different important people, often at the same time, every day of the week. While my students make regular use of me, I sometimes do the same with a student; and I did this most of all with Sam. When I needed a college professor to set my brain afire, I would find Sam. And when I needed a friend after Joey's death, it was Sam.

⚜⚜⚜

I knew I didn't have much to give Sam as an English teacher. He had been reading books at a fevered pitch his entire life. I put the likes of Ibsen, Ellison, Dostoevsky, and Morrison in his blazing path, which he consumed (often in a couple nights) before moving on to his next undertaking. But his intense devotion to scholarship and religiosity always seemed like a fleeing of sorts, not just a running to but a running from. I thought his dogmatism and nervous energy must be some type of defense. I didn't want him to be so adult so soon. I wanted to make sure he was also a teenager.

I always reminded him that he was funny. Very, very funny. A teacher is well practiced at knowing his audience, including its sense of humor. And the subtle thirtysomething humor I use with my most intelligent adult friends was more than suitable for Sam. A sly, understated, comedic insinuation wouldn't be missed by him, and it was a pleasure to know one student in the room would be in on my joke. Sam poked fun at the administration and absurd school rules, he criticized standardized exams for ignoring creativity and nuanced thinking, and he would even mock his reputation as the resident Biblical scholar.

)()(

I saw a part of my past self in Sam. Not in his intelligence, but in his tendency to live in his head, in his suffocation of a teenage body. For various psychological reasons, I was dead inside my own body during my adolescence. I punished it in cross-country and swimming, but I never luxuriated in it. I didn't sleep well, I didn't take pleasure from eating, I didn't have sex, I didn't drink or do drugs. Most significantly, I wasn't interested in girls. I didn't date them, I didn't fantasize about them, I didn't stare at their body parts in math class. I sensed that Sam's hyper-intellectual and intensely religious life was doing the same to him. I wanted him to be interested in girls. I felt I had lost valuable years of my teenage life by ignoring my erotic self, and I wanted him to make up for it.

One day after school his senior year he walked into my empty, sunlit classroom, pulled a chair up to my desk, leaned in, and spoke confidentially: "Mr. Arango?" he said in a low voice.

"Yes, Sam?"

"There's a girl I like."

"Really?" I was thrilled. This was unprecedented, uncharted territory. I wanted to encourage him. "Tell me about it."

"Well, for one, she's a Catholic."

"That's a problem? That means she's Christian, right?"

"Well, yes, but I'm an evangelical fundamentalist."

"Oh. O.K." I needed clarification, but I didn't want this to veer into a religious discussion. Not this time. I wanted to stay focused on girls. "Well, so she's a Catholic. But what about attraction?"

"What about what?"

"Attraction. There's some part of you that's attracted to her."

"What do you mean?" Sam asked.

"I mean, is there some part of you that's acting beyond the 'you' that you're used to? Isn't there something compelling you that's beyond the reach of your intense intellect?"

"You see, that's the problem. That's what's happening."

"And it's something a little out of your control."

"Right. I don't let things exist beyond my control."

It was making a lot of sense. Much of Sam's intellectual work was about maintaining control, about having a monopoly on what was in front of him. When he read his homework assignments twice, he dominated them. With the Bible memorized and seventeen different copies on his shelf, he *owned* The Good Word more than anyone I had ever met. And now there was some primal part of him, this crush on a girl, that was beyond his control.

"Well Sam, some things *are* beyond our control," I said.

"I don't like it."

"But isn't that where the excitement comes from? To sort of surrender to the unexpected? To allow for surprise? To let something outside of your control have its way for awhile?"

Another student came into the room, and Sam quickly changed the subject. I don't think Sam ever approached the girl before he graduated, but this felt like a critical first step. Sam discovered he had desires, urges. Maybe, at least for a moment, Sam discovered he was a teenager.

⚬⚬⚬

After Sam completed his first year of college, he surprised me at the high school with a visit before my first period. He had been studying Christian history and theology at a nearby Christian college. He walked into the classroom, about ten pounds heavier, oblivious to the twenty-five high school freshmen ricocheting off the walls.

I said, "Oh my goodness. He leaves a mere boy, and he comes back a man. As I live and breathe the prodigal son has returned. Sam, how are you doing?"

He sat down, a breathless bundle of conversation. We had a year's worth of backlogged conversation and only fifteen minutes to talk. I threw out rushed questions to get a sense of his last year: he still lived at home, he had gotten straight A's, his most fascinating class was about intelligent design, and my AP Literature class from a year ago had prepared him well. Sam paused for a moment and asked how I was doing. It's a rare student that asks such a question of his teacher, and means it. I told him I was thinking about getting a second degree, about volunteering abroad again, but I was constrained by an empty bank account. I explained that I was truly worried I'd have no money one day, or no health insurance, or no retirement.

Sam sat back a little, smiled, gave me a soothing hand gesture, and said warmly, "Mr. Arango, God will take care of you. Don't worry."

I'm not sure why, but I felt like a burden was lifted. Sam would say that's the comfort God provides. I would say that's the comfort Sam provides. I don't know who was right, but I do know that for the first time in months, my muscles loosened and I took an easy, relaxed breath.

(Note: Names have been changed for this essay)

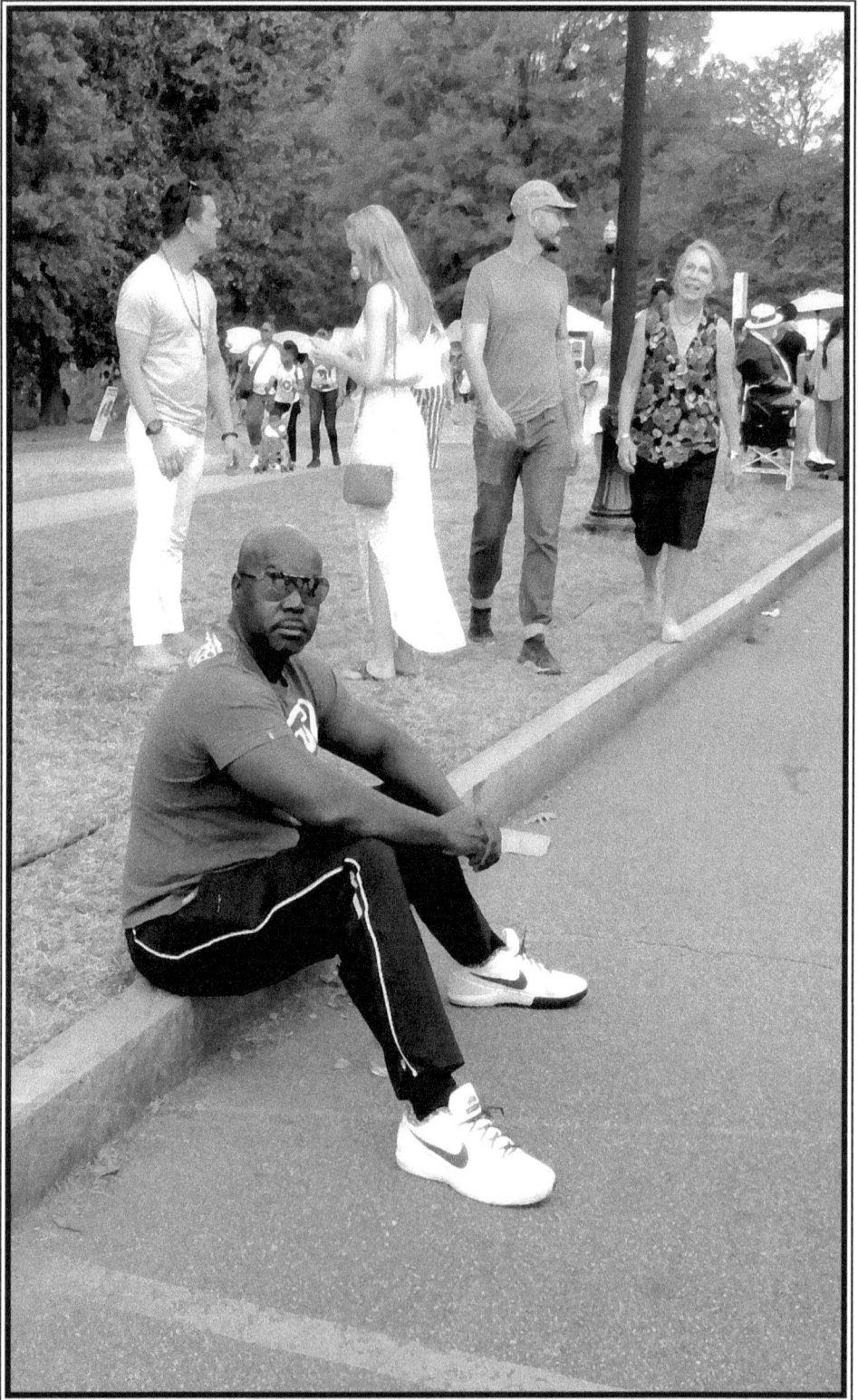

V. RACE

LORETTA DIANE WALKER

STILETTO

The sun is on sabbatical.
Aquarius is wearing its February self
when three white teenage boys
in a white pick-up truck shout
from the window, "—you—."

When I walked into the store, my head was high
as the moon floating in its freedom.
Now, it's hanging limp with anger—disbelief.

I feel the shame my mother did when she was a little girl,
and the mother before her, when hatred was hurled
with such openness and conviction just for being.

And *that* word they use is as pointed,
not sexy, as a black stiletto.
I refuse to say it.
Use whips, water, ropes or chains—
they've been used before.

I've trained my tongue to make it silent
although I hear it blasting from car CD players,
watch heads bop hypnotically
to its new financial meaning. I remember the old one.

Oh, Ancestors, our brothers spit on your graves
with gold teeth and chains, expensive cars and bling—
use that word to gain fame
and the ones in the pick-up—you knew their type of fury.

I want to move where that word does not exist
but there is nowhere to go.
Ignorance like greed pollutes every artery of air.
I inhaled their hate,
but have decided to exhale forgiveness.

SHARON HILBERER

FIRST ENCOUNTER

I remember the narrow cracked walkway
along the side of the building.
Heavy trucks filling the width of the gravel alley
and the sound of coal rumbling down the chute.
I remember the breath-held fear of the empty space
yawning behind the open steps
leading down to the cellar—
the damp smell, the dim shapes,
the flickering orange glow
around the mouth of the furnace.

The mix of fear and fascination
standing near the open throat of a storm drain,
water rushing down the gutter,
plunging out of sight.

I remember a mellow light on warm afternoons
the drone of radio dramas,
my mother humming or sighing
as she dampened and rolled clean laundry. I remember
the smell of steam and starch
and the hissing of the iron.

On a day like that, one particular day
hearing the clank of garbage cans,
the shouts of workers,
I remember climbing onto a chair to lean
out the unscreened second-floor window
and for no reason that I can remember
picking up a bottle cap that was lying on the sill
and throwing it down into the scene below.

And then I remember the big man,
black and gleaming, glance up.
He shook his head. He laughed.
He looked right into the eyes
of little white me.

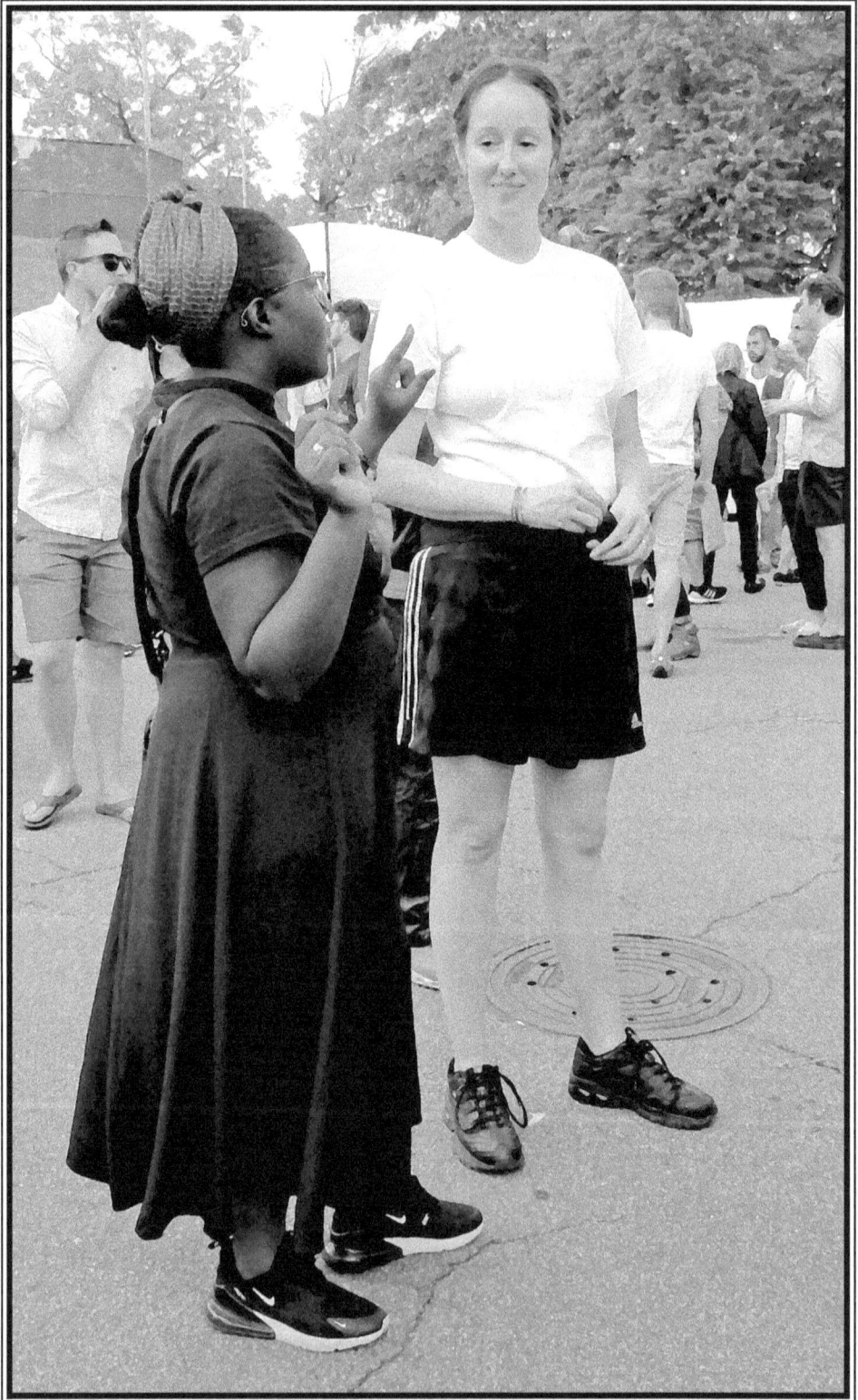

LUCIA TALENTI

CAUGHT BETWEEN GREEN GABLES
AND LILY WHITE

In the summer of 1990, behind the wheel of a speeding car on a major highway leaving New England for New York City suburbs, I was confronted with the brutal facts about white privilege for the first time. A particularly dear, particularly beautiful, brilliant black friend was riding shotgun, and something had tripped her trigger. Something had compelled her to carry on at length and in high volume in close quarters about how clueless white people were regarding the lives of black people.

Erica is incredibly photogenic with a gorgeous smile. Smart, well-educated, well informed with deeper perspectives on politics and history that always elevate our discussions. Oldest of three children of hardworking, loving parents, she is intricately connected to extended family. I am of a discontented brood. My disgruntled parents, who were largely at odds with their extended family, were most successful at combining discontented sperm with anxious ovum and spent what time they had under the same roof undermining their resultant offspring's mental and emotional stability.

The ferocity of Erica's outpouring on that drive took me by surprise. Good friends since high school, though life had sent us in different directions over the years, we'd stayed close, talked for hours on the phone or during visits, often fans or critics of much the same things. She called me a 'Sister From Another Mister,' yet, there she was ticked off and loaded for bear over something my white self truly had no clue.

The power and intensity of her emotions were so shocking, so out of the blue and relentless, to this day I still do not know exactly what triggered the sudden storm. Did it have anything to do with the recent unexpected death of her handsome, charismatic father who adored her, and whom she loved and admired for the way he'd overcome poverty, segregation, and disability to survive and thrive in mainstream America and, along with his hardworking wife, provided a solid middle class life for his family? Could it have been the prospect of returning to a basement apartment in Queens after a spending a couple of days at my little house in the woods?

All I remember, what I can never forget, is how she unloaded in no uncertain terms, in high decibels, how a white woman like me was inherently an adversary, even a kind of enemy, who could never understand what it meant to live a black life.

Anyhow, by the time we were in that speeding car, Erica and I were in our late twenties. She'd known me, warts and all, for a long, long time. Over the years, we'd bonded over so many things: clothes, books, work, politics, concerns over body shape and size—but, on that afternoon, it was if we'd never known each other at all. Before that torrent of reproof, it's true, I'd never stopped to think in specific day-to-day terms of what black people had to put up with or how they had to act as they put up with it. Within families, I knew about being unloved, bullied, abused, but not necessarily in the larger world. Accusing looks in stores? Suspicious salesclerks who follow closely, expecting you to steal? The neighborhoods you must never walk in. Or drive in. Or visit friends in. Or where to go out to eat. Why and how to teach your children from a young age to live in a state of vigilant awareness of what their skin signals to others. And more and more and more. Every facet of daily life has an edge to it that whites rarely have to take into consideration.

By the time I dropped her off in Queens and made my way to the relatively bucolic, tree-lined streets of the outer burbs, my head spun, my ears rang, and my heart ached. I struggled to parse out her anger. Her pure, unreconstituted anger. What had I done? What had happened to us? Were we still friends? Would our visits back and forth end? Did the diet and exercise plans we'd constantly made and broke matter anymore? What about the hilariously chatty phone calls and holiday get-togethers?

Over time, the disconcerting pain and shock from that initial nuclear meltdown eased, but not enough to quell a wariness on my part. Had I learned what she wanted me to know? Did I change enough to ease her frustration with my limitations? Even though she was affectionate and thoughtful, planned trips together, and reminded me I was a sister, I never completely relaxed, always on my mettle, I felt supremely conscious of my shortcomings, of being white, of being *culpable*.

Several years later, the stars aligned, Erica and I were pregnant around the same time and had healthy baby boys within a couple months of each other. There are pictures of our infant sons side by side on the couch bolstered up by pillows, of us mamas nursing. It seemed like a fresh start, the little boys became fast friends, considered each other as cousins, and we visited back and forth several times a year. Accustomed to strong-minded mothers and aunties, when one boy stayed over at the other's house, there was no middle-of-the-night panic or homesickness, their sense of family and closeness was built in. Both similarly soft around the edges until adolescence, Erica's athletic son grew tall and lean, while my boy hardened muscle by weight lifting. To this day, the two young men text or talk daily, share a wicked sense of humor as well as a bone-deep trust in each other.

These days, Erica's default mode seems to be soapboxing in strident tones. Since I've witnessed her lecturing her husband, siblings, and in-laws, I've realized it's not my particular shade of stupidity that brings out her frustration or rants of disenfranchisement. Oftentimes, her topics and thoughts and criticisms are hard to hear and hard to respond to. This brilliant, beautiful, talented woman is constantly set on edge by pain and worry and fatigue, by subtle and not so subtle racism, by being overworked and overlooked in a career that isn't as promising and exciting as it once was. She's distressed by the money some friends spend on luxuries they consider needs—the kind of needs that only the wealthy are accustomed to.

We still talk health, but it's no longer about attractiveness or size, it dabbles around a looming sense of mortality: both her parents died too young of diseases that plague her race particularly cruelly. How chronic pain keeps us from exercising enough and how to find the time to cook the healthiest possible foods at home rather than to order out.

One afternoon, when the kids were little, we were on a visit to New York and Erica met me at my mother's house in the town she described as "lily white," meaning it avoided selling properties to people of color. As per the plan, our boys went off to play baseball with her husband and we took Mom on an amble around the neighborhood. It seemed like every car going by us slowed down dramatically, the drivers scanning from Erica to me to Mom and back again. It had never been so clear; these white people had a kneejerk reaction to a black woman on the block, even one carefully accompanying an elderly white woman with walker.

After tea at Mom's, Erica and I headed to her house in a town not too far away. Since the boys weren't there yet, we decided to take a much brisker walk around *her* neighborhood. There it was my turn to be on the receiving end of side-eyes or full-on glares, questioning looks or shakes of the head by passing drivers. I had never felt so conspicuous, called to account over the lack of color on my skin. Or maybe it was the first time that I was aware of noticing it.

There's been no easy resolution. Eventually I realized there wasn't much I could do to make her feel better. My job in our friendship became to be whatever she needs. Mostly, I am stoic in the face of her vehemence and speak really quietly in order to make as much room for her to voice whatever thoughts, opinions, or emotions as she needs.

As with any of us, life has offered up crazy twists, turns, and betrayals in the last thirty plus years, and Erica has a need to lament loudly and with vitriol. Has she lost friends as a result? Yes. Only recently has she verbalized inklings and wonderings about why various friends take extended hiatus, occasionally to return. This happens when the anger drops and the fun-loving, sparkly, charismatic Erica appears.

In the meantime, I've learned about how unrelenting racism-related stress weathers black women's bodies, how the inexcusable oversights in OB/GYN care and treatment of black women through all stages of pregnancy, childbirth, and postpartum needlessly and tragically endanger both mother and child. How the lack of substantive research in health care and outcomes puts all women at increased risk, but even more especially for women of color.

Erica and I need our friendship and our shared history more than ever. We're thrilled that our boys are best friends. Her son is so much like my son. But one brutal fact separates them: when my boy gets pulled over for speeding and goes for his wallet, the odds of him being misread, mistreated or fatally shot are immeasurably less. White privilege is real.

In the fall of 2018, at the end of PBS' Great American Read favorite novel voting, we were on the phone discussing our top picks. Mine was, *To Kill a Mockingbird*. Erica asked me to guess hers. I wracked my brain and made a few suggestions, all of which fell flat.

"I can't believe you don't know!" she admonished. "It's been my favorite since I was little, *Anne of Green Gables!*" The story of a spirited little white orphan girl grudgingly taken in by elderly white siblings on Prince Edward Island. No way had I seen that one coming, though it fit with the Erica I used to know, back in the days we were both idealistic.

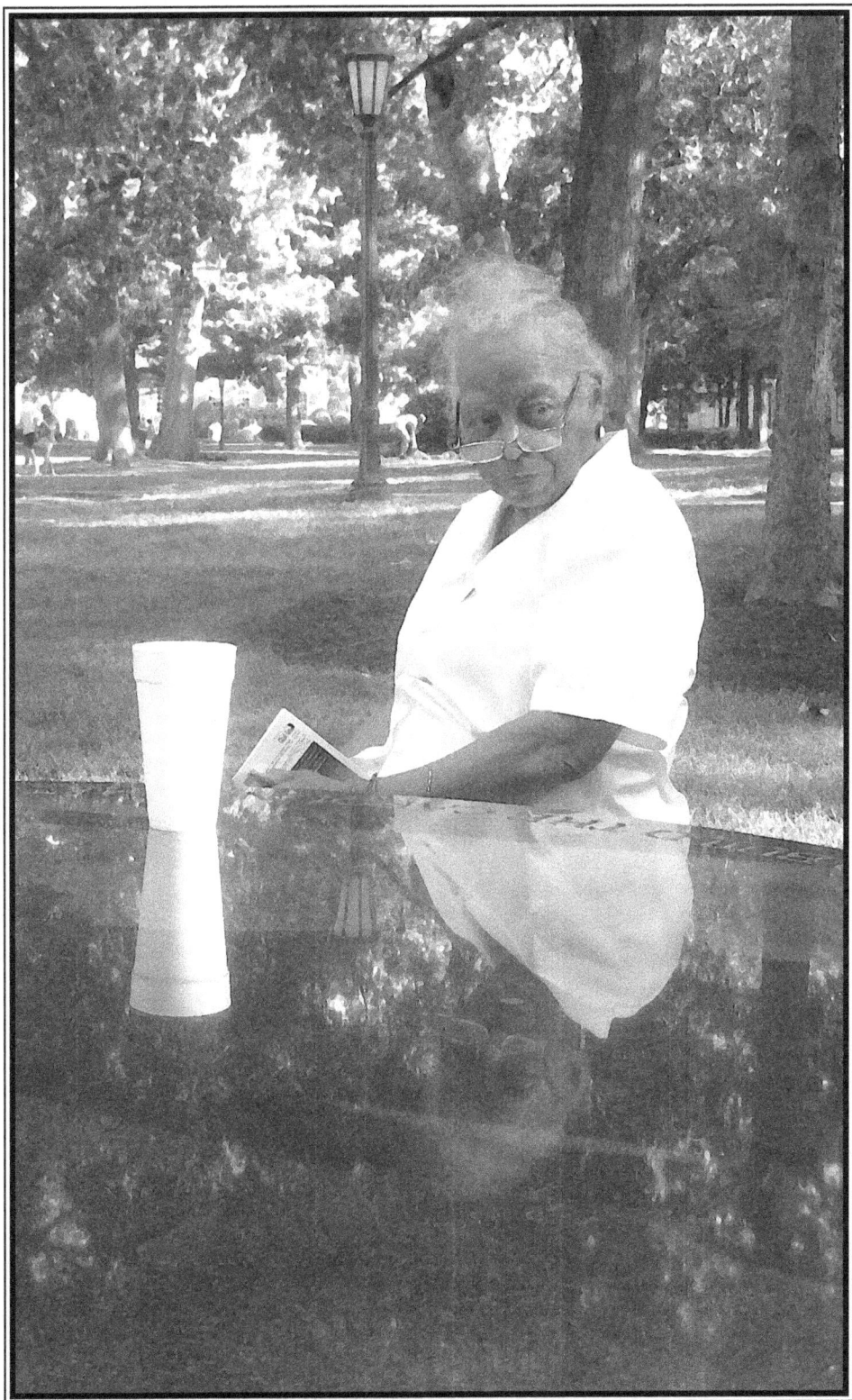

LORETTA DIANE WALKER

BLACK HISTORY MONTH ENDED YESTERDAY

When the sun comes back, and the first quail calls,
follow the drinking gourd. For the old man is waiting
for to carry you to freedom—Follow The Drinking Gourd

February laughs with heavy warmth.
I swim with slow strokes in a pool of cream
and caramel faces with sprinklings
of dark rich chocolate.

Listen. These words are a map.
The song swirls around the classroom,
lifting souls into the melody.

When the sun comes back, and the first quail calls,
follow the drinking gourd. For the old man is waiting
for to carry you to freedom

I parade the book in front of them,
my fingers a map to the title:
Follow the Drinking Gourd.

Children gather at my feet like seeds
dumped from a package.
I read—the characters an ambiguous shade of black,
an attempt to sanitize slavery.

We are a rainbow shade of people
my mind roars my mouth, mute.

I flip to a man standing on the auction block.
Arms folded across his loins, head bowed,
muscles rippling waves of strength,
    NEGRO FOR SALE.

Your caramel face colors with recognition.
Eyes fix on the page then dart
around the room searching for a safe way
to tell me, "Negro means black."

"Why is he for sale?"
The seeds are a forest now, tender limbs growing
with curiosity as they wait for my answer.
"Slaves were property like animals."

My words drain expression from your face,
silence settles on us like a gray fog. I read on.

I walk into a red hibiscus with March
blocked beneath it; your eyes following me—still,
your question traveling on my shoulder.

Child, this is what I cannot teach you.
Black History Month ended yesterday,
but not for me.
I am rooted in blackness still fighting the past,
those who blame me, my ancestors
for everything wrong and evil in the world.

Their names for me are not polite.
They want me to go back to a place
where I've never been.
I inherited America, too.

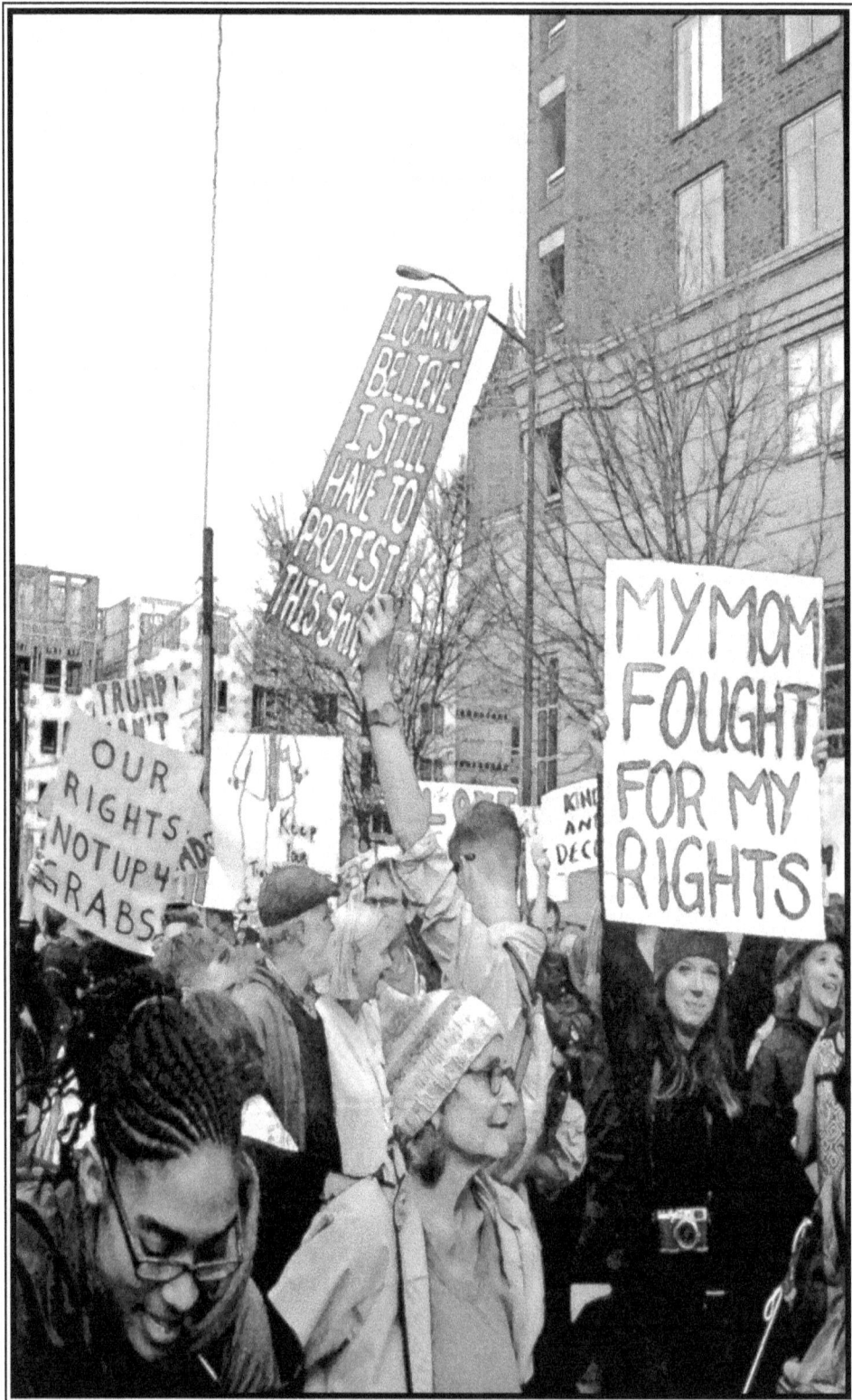

VI. POLITICS

J. J. STEINFELD

THE CHESS MASTER

I

The old men seated at nearby tables, playing chess, paused briefly to wave at the bearded man, but Lionel Siedelman did not notice them. He stared through the front window of Kruger's Grocery until he caught the owner's attention. Heinrich Kruger raised a fist and shouted for Lionel to go away. Lionel failed to move. Instead he blew kisses at the grocer through the window and yelled with mock affection, "*Sholom, sholom . . .*" Lionel wanted to break the window. In the last week he had dreamed about the destruction of the grocery—by explosives, by fire, by the wrath of God, but mostly by his bare hands, pulverizing each brick into dust, blowing the dust out of time.

Lionel could see his reflection amid the signs and advertisements in the store window. The shadows of sleeplessness on his face were sharp and incriminating even in the glass. In his mind every can and box and piece of produce was thrown to the floor and crushed under his wild, vengeful dance. Somehow this local grocery had become the source of all his frustration and anxiety and hatred. He swore at the grocer, uttering the most vivid Yiddish curses he knew; he made flamboyant, obscene gestures. Yet every word and gesture was inadequate, hardly more than breezes against a brick fortress. He considered urinating against the front window but had not yet lost all his control.

"Why do you still come here? He's dead," Heinrich Kruger said as he came through the grocery's front door, repeatedly wiping his hands on his apron.

"Sentimental reasons," Lionel said, trying to imagine the grocer forty years younger. He would have punched Kruger in the face had the grocer not been so old, had he not resembled so closely his brother, Ernst. The eighty-year-old man, trembling with anger, nonetheless appeared rejuvenated by his fury.

"I don't like you around my store."

"Your brother liked me around. I was good luck to him," Lionel taunted, stepping closer to Kruger. Lionel thought he saw the dark secrets that were embedded in the old man's wrinkled face, the lines of treachery and disgrace, the traces of an undissolved malignancy.

"He's dead. Go to the cemetery. Play chess by the grave."

"I told your brother I would kill you."

"So try to kill me, big mouth," Kruger said, pushing Lionel with all his furious strength but not budging him. If Lionel could have gotten closer to the old man, devoured him with his own body, he would have.

"And turn me into you, perish the thought."

"You pathetic and pitiful fool," the old man said with the conviction of a youth defying the world. "I have no trouble understanding how your brain thinks."

"*Mazel tov! Mazel tov! Mazel tov!*" Lionel screamed in a voice louder than he knew he had, feeling himself losing control. Ernst Kruger had taught him that control and concentration were essential if one wanted to win at chess.

"Try to kill me now . . . go ahead." The old man opened his mouth and noisily sucked in air, as if attempting to swallow his adversary.

Shoppers stopped to watch the afternoon confrontation, most from a safe distance. Storekeepers and their customers were summoned outdoors by the arguing voices.

"I loved him. For fourteen years I loved him," Lionel declared.

"Ernst was my twin brother, don't forget that. We were together during World War II. *Inseparable.*"

"You bastard," Lionel said, his fingers curling into fists, sealing themselves into an ill-boding permanence.

"Then he was a bastard. Twins are twins, even you must know that." The old man's face gradually displayed a swollen smile. His eyes indicated enjoyment; the prospect of both calamity and triumph overcame the hard downward slope of his mouth.

"Ernst was not an evil man. He regretted what happened during the war. You enjoyed what happened, you goddamn murderous old bastard." Lionel moved away from Kruger, closer to the window. The lettering on the signs and advertisements blurred. The old man began pounding on Lionel's back. Lionel thrust his right fist through the window, shattering the glass. The blood that flowed reminded both men of different times.

II

Riding on the yellow school bus home from Hebrew school made Lionel ill, so he usually walked the three miles from the school to his parents' house. Only the most heavy rains prevented him from walking. Lionel enjoyed walking and thinking, swinging a leather briefcase at his side, imagining himself anywhere but on the streets of Toronto. The briefcase had been a present from Lionel's older brother, Zvi.

It was during one of these walks home that Lionel, then twelve years old, first saw the old men playing chess. There were five tables in front of three adjacent stores. As long as the weather was agreeable, even in winter, the men played chess. The young boy associated the sight of the ongoing chess games with an old, orderly, tranquil world.

At first Lionel, always shy with strangers, observed from across the street. Then he would slowly walk past the men. Finally, when the school term was almost over, he stopped and watched, a feverish eagerness running through his body.

"You play chess, boy?" the old man sitting with his back to Kruger's Grocery asked Lionel. At the old man's elbow was a copy of *Deutsche Schachzeitung*; to the side of his chessboard was a bowl packed with large apples and moist grapes.

"Not very well," the nervous boy said, feeling the eyes of all the old men circling him.

"Sit, sit, play with me. This tree stump is no challenge," the old man said as another man got up from his chair and moved to the next table. "If he lasts twenty moves it is a miracle. . . . Move first, boy. Do not be bashful. Have fresh fruit," he said, lifting the bowl toward Lionel, "it is energy for the brain. For chess, brain energy is required. The great Goethe wrote that chess is the touchstone of the intellect."

That afternoon Lionel played the old man seven games, stopping only when he realized he would be late for supper.

"Come back soon," the old man said. "You have potential."

"You beat me seven out of seven," Lionel said sadly.

"You are learning. One day I will submit to your mastery. . . . What is your name?"

"Lionel Lazar Siedelman."

"Such an elegant name for such a small boy. I am Ernst Kruger. Play me

tomorrow again. I am here by my brother's store all the time. I will teach you
to play smarter," the old man said, pointing to his head.

"I can't tomorrow. I have to go to synagogue."

"Go, go to synagogue, boy . . . "

)()()(

"*Schoch and matt* . . . That is how you say checkmate *auf deutsch*," the
old man said as kindly as he could to the young loser.

"I can lose in two languages. Wonderful," Lionel said.

"But see how good practice and concentration are making you."

"I'll never beat you."

"Already you almost win. You are no pushover. I tell you this from the
heart. You are a real schachspieler now. Patience, you are such a little boy."

"I'm just about a man," Lionel said with an attempt to sound older,
locking himself into a rigid and serious pose.

The old man's face was tugged by delight and pleasure. He reached a
hand across the table but did not touch the boy. Suddenly his hand felt heavy
and inflamed.

"Come to my bar mitzvah next week, Mr. Kruger," Lionel said eagerly.

The old man shivered, as if something icily foul or pitiless had entered
his system. "I cannot possibly, Lionel."

"Please," the boy begged, leaning over the chessboard.

"You will understand why not when you are older."

"You're my friend, Mr. Kruger."

"Let us play one more game," the old man said abruptly, casting away
the fear that was beginning to dominate him.

They played and Lionel won after a struggle in which neither player
spoke or even took his eyes off the chess pieces. The men who were watching
the game could not believe the outcome, charging in German that the old
man had allowed the boy to win. He accused them of being lifeless old cynics.
Soon there was a heated argument, all in German.

Before Lionel left, the old man gave the boy his personal copy of *Modern
Chess Openings* as a bar mitzvah present. Lionel ran the entire way home,
jubilantly, clutching his new book, knowing full well that Mr. Kruger had
not tried his hardest. Ernst Kruger, the other old men had told the boy, was
a chess master.

III

My brother's not well," Lionel told the old man when he asked why Lionel was not concentrating, why so many silly moves today.

"What is wrong with him?"

"My parents won't tell me. Only that it has to do with his nerves. My brother has a bad nervous condition."

"No one is spared; life is full of problems," the old man said sympathetically.

"He's in hospital and they won't let me visit. I'm supposed to be too young. My father told me he fought in the Underground in Poland when he was fourteen. I'm fourteen and he treats me like a baby. I'm not too young, am I, Mr. Kruger?"

"Your parents know what is proper. Your brother will get well, you'll see."

"I told Zvi about you once," Lionel said, stopping and pinching his chin in thought. He started and stopped his next sentence several times before he could say, "Zvi says you're a Nazi."

"Let us play chess," the old man said with a sudden, stiff resolution. "I have an interesting opening strategy to demonstrate to you."

"Were you a Nazi, Mr. Kruger?"

"I tell you, let me show you what is called the Ruy Lopez Opening and a few of the more potent defenses against it."

"Were you a Nazi?"

"That nightmare still lives too odiously in my heart for words."

Lionel held his white queen in the air, squeezing it. Had the queen been a blade it would have severed his fingers.

"One day I will tell you about that nightmare. When you are more historically inclined."

"Tell me, Mr. Kruger . . . Tell me," Lionel said, an interrogator caught in the trance of his own questioning.

)()()(

"This is a beautiful story, Lionel," the old man said after he had finished reading the manuscript, kissing the last page in praise.

"My parents think it's foolish. *Narrishkeit* they call my writing. Science and math, my father says. You can always use science and math."

"This is a quite serious topic you write about. Your mother talks in such detail about being in the camps?"

"No. She won't talk about the war at all. I read all I can about the war and the concentration camps. The story still needs work. I'm going to rewrite it tonight."

"So you definitely want to be a writer?"

"Nothing else, Mr. Kruger."

"*Nothing else?* Can you be so sure at sixteen?"

"Yes."

"Sixteen is not a time for irrevocable decisions. I wanted to be a violinist when I was your age. I was so sure also."

"Why didn't you become a violinist?"

"Why? Simple: war changed me," the old man said casually. Then, as if harshly struck by the realization that he might have disclosed something too terrible for words, he quickly added, "The First World War."

"Nothing will change me, Mr. Kruger."

"Do not forget that life is a formidable opponent."

"I learned to beat you."

"Yes, on occasion . . . only on occasion."

"I'm still young," Lionel said, smiling, balancing a pawn in his palm, lightly blowing on the chess piece.

The old man shook with a pleasurable laugh, as if a dear friend had poked him teasingly in the sides. "That is true. So move, my brilliant precocious writer . . ."

)X(X(X(

"Why doesn't he like me?" Lionel asked as Ernst Kruger's brother went back into his store.

"Do not worry, Lionel. He sees you differently than I do."

"As an enemy?"

"Worse. As a reminder of what he was. What he did."

"What did he do? You're never specific about the past."

"Let us just play. Chess is more important."

"Chess *and* writing, Mr. Kruger."

"Yes, chess and writing. You have a new story, I know."

"How can you be so positive?"

"I know the expression of artistic delight. It ignites your whole body,

Lionel. You are very outward with your emotions and expressions."

"I haven't typed it out yet," Lionel said as he pulled out a cluster of papers from his old briefcase.

"And you are starting to grow a beard. Quite literary."

"It'll take me forever and then some," Lionel said, picking at a few of the immature strands on his cheeks.

"Nothing takes forever, my friend. I can see you one day with the most beautiful full beard," the old man said, pulling at his own trim white beard. He was going to say that he had not grown a beard until after World War II, but caught himself. "Read to me. My eyes bother me so much lately. Horrible headaches."

"The Chess Master' by L.L. Siedelman," Lionel began as the old man closed his eyes and concentrated, thinking of when he had played the violin and had an abundance of dreams.

)(O)(O)(

"My brother's dead, my brother's dead," Lionel screamed as he ran toward Ernst Kruger. Lionel was not carrying his briefcase; his eyes reflected terror.

"How is that possible? He was a young man."

"Zvi killed himself in the garage. I found him."

"I am sorry for you, my poor Lionel."

"The funeral's tomorrow. I won't go, I won't go. I want to know why Zvi's dead."

Lionel started to cry, and the old man embraced him. Aside from casual handshakes or a random pat on the back, they had never touched before, as if touching might unearth or destroy the past. Six years of chess playing and afternoon conversations and now they held each other wordlessly, like father and son. The old man let out a wail. The other chess players turned their heads toward Lionel and the old man, and imagined the worst.

)(O)(O)(

The early afternoon was warm, but Ernst Kruger was not at his table. The gap made Lionel think he was on the wrong street, in the wrong world. Lionel sat down and stared at the empty place. He made several moves for the old man, attempting to think the way Ernst Kruger thought. Some of the other men called for Lionel to play with them, but he refused their invitations. He played the game out with his absent friend, Ernst winning with his usual brilliance.

From inside his store Heinrich Kruger tapped at the window and told Lionel to leave. When Lionel did not stir, the grocer came outside, striding with a heavy-footed hostility.

"No more chess playing for you and my brother. He's blind now. Eyeless," the grocer said in a tone that was at once predatory and overflowing with satisfaction.

Lionel looked up at his friend's brother. The old man could see that Lionel had been crying. Ernst and Heinrich Kruger looked so much alike that Lionel could barely detect any physical dissimilarities.

"What hospital is he in?"

"None of your business."

One of the old chess players told Lionel where Ernst Kruger was recuperating, then said something to Heinrich Kruger in German.

The grocer's hissing, open-mouthed breathing turned into a fierce discharge of spitting sounds. "You are bad luck for my brother, a curse," he finally said, saliva spraying wildly from lips that had lost their durability years ago.

Lionel crossed the street to the northbound bus stop. He wanted to go to the hospital and read a story to his friend.

)X(X(

"You play better than ever, Mr. Kruger."

"You are my eyes, Lionel."

"It's incredible how quickly you've adjusted. That's really important."

"I like being blind."

"*Mr. Kruger!*"

"I've seen enough, Lionel. I have seen too much. Think of it, now all distractions from concentration are taken away. I can see the pieces perfectly in my head. The most exquisitely crafted chessmen are within my head. I wish I could have had this extraordinary vision when I was a young man . . ."

)X(X(

"I'm my brother's age now," Lionel said with a solemnity that frightened the blind man. "Twenty," Lionel added with a fearfulness that made the word sound grotesque, a denunciation of life and hope.

"You are not your brother. You have a destiny to fulfill," the blind man said with such determination that his dead eyes momentarily appeared sighted.

"No one wants my stories."

"In time they will, you wait."

"I'm more and more like my brother. You never met Zvi. He was always so sad. Sadder than my mother. You're not at all like your brother."

"Who can explain these things? Read me a story."

"I get extremely depressed like Zvi did. I know I have the same nightmares. My parents want me to see a special doctor. Doctors didn't help Zvi."

"Don't talk yourself into such a dark frame of mind, Lionel. Read me a story or shall I defeat you in ten moves today?"

Lionel smiled and tenderly touched the old man's hands. "I wrote another story about you," he said.

"You shouldn't, Lionel."

"About when you played the violin and soothed all the savage beasts in Germany . . . "

◊◊◊

"I can't believe a story's going to be published. At last an acceptance," Lionel said, his face radiating excitement like a man bursting forth from a long and profitable solitude.

"Congratulations! See, perseverance pays off. And you are not twenty-one yet. By thirty you will be world-famous. I feel this in my soul."

"Let the egomaniacs have the fame, I'll settle for a few kind readers."

"Which publication will be honoured by your story?"

"*Jewish Dialog.*"

"A good start. And which story?"

"The millionth rewrite of 'The Chess Master.'"

"The first of many acceptances. You are a natural storyteller. We should have some schnapps for a toast to your success and future."

"I feel good now, Mr. Kruger . . . I'm going to quit school and write all the time."

"Finish your degree, Lionel."

"No, it would be a defeat . . ."

ⵜⵜⵜ

"Nothing really interests me. Nothing makes much sense. Except for the writing. If I didn't write, I'd end up like my brother. It's as if I was there, in the concentration camps."

"You have inherited painful feelings from your parents. The past can be transmitted from generation to generation, even through any silence or deafness."

"Will I pass it on?"

"Through your eyes. Through your stories. Write about your pain and being a Jew. Write, and perhaps the suffering will make sense, Lionel."

"Zvi's been dead five years and I dreamed last night I walked into the garage and found him again. I was hanging next to him. I wasn't unhappy with my dream."

"You have witnessed so much already in your life."

"My brother couldn't take it."

"You can take it. Listen to a foolish old blind man who has stumbled around this world for as many years as Methuselah."

"Why won't you talk about the war with me? Let me take you to Germany for a trip."

"Absolutely no."

"I could do research for some stories and for you it would be a homecoming. Let's confront the past together."

"That nightmare . . . That nightmare is still there for me."

"But you never killed any Jews, right?"

"That nightmare was bad for everyone. It damaged the souls of so many people, even the unborn . . ."

ⵜⵜⵜ

"I'm sick and tired of the bullshit and excuses I hear. Goddamn it, I don't want to listen to any more crap from people."

"Calm down, Lionel. Let us play chess. What is your move? You have not used Bird's Opening in ages. Try Bird's Opening today." The old blind man reached across the table to touch Lionel's face, but the young man moved away, as if fearing a slap.

"I've figured out how to deal with my past and my future at the same time. I'll kill your Nazi brother."

"You should not think like that, Lionel."

"I'll be sent to jail and I'll write there. I'm not writing enough lately."

"You have written seventy stories."

"Not enough! I don't belong in this stupid forgetful world anyway. I'll write all the time in jail. If I ever stop writing I'll—

"Kill me instead, Lionel."

"I love you."

"I was a Nazi, too."

"No!" Lionel screamed as he pushed the chessboard off the table. All the old men got to their knees and began to pick up the fallen chess pieces.

"That nightmare suffocated everyone. I did not fight it. I did not hold back a single salute."

"You did! You did!"

After a silent, painful moment, Lionel, with his index finger, gently traced a number on the blind man's left forearm.

"Your mother's concentration camp number?"

"Yes."

"I am not worthy, Lionel Lazar Siedelman..."

❊❊❊

Lionel began his novel a week after the old man died. For a week he had brooded and drunk excessively. Then he put his fist through the window of Kruger's Grocery. He required twenty-nine stitches to close the wounds, but he began writing that night, fighting the pain. The novel, about a Jewish boy growing up in Toronto and playing chess almost daily with a displaced old German, started out with a grocery in flames.

STEPHANIE HART

ENCOUNTER WITH THE RED DEVIL

A mean rain drilled down on Richard Singer as he entered a bar in downtown Washington D.C. The bar was dark and smelled of grime and spilled liquor. Richard took a stool, ordered a beer, and let it sit for a while.

"Same as usual?" The bartender said to the man in a crumpled gray suit jacket at the end of the bar. The man nodded in assent, took the whisky he was offered, downed it, and ordered another.

Richard took in the man's bloated cheeks and blood shot eyes. He watched him shrug off his jacket and let it drop to the floor in an unruly heap.

"God damn commie bastards," the man said, "I'll show them what for. Gotta keep America safe."

Richard said nothing but slid onto the stool next to him.

The man slapped his fist on the bar. "At first they cheered me on. 'Go get those commies.' Now they're after me. When you're up, everybody loves you. When you're down, they wanna take everything away from you. After all I did for them. What do I get in return?"

The man made a grimace, lifted his head and raised his voice as if he was addressing an audience. "War is war. And war has casualties." He waved his arm, knocking over his drink. Glass chards splattered on the bar, and the bartender came with a rescuing cloth. As if waking from a dream, the man stared at Richard. "Who the hell are you anyhow? What are you doing here?"

Richard didn't answer, taking a pull on his beer. His older brother, Josh, had been pegged as a communist sympathizer; Richard was sure his brother had no such leanings, but he could lose his job, his standing in the community given the turn the society had taken. When Josh had his hearing, Richard, a criminal attorney, would be right there with him. Right now, not saying a word, he was looking after Josh as well.

The man looked off into the distance again. "I'm a good man," he muttered. "I never turned anyone away who asked for a handout. I did what I had to do to protect the country; no one but me has the guts or the grit to take on the job."

In the man's tone, Richard heard the rush of his own anger, his own righteous indignation. He had decimated opposing witnesses on the stand, bludgeoned opponents in street corner debates, rebuked his brother and father for not acknowledging his accomplishments. If anyone accused him of being too tough, he would say, "They got what was coming to them."

The man slurred his words. "Life was so simple when I was a boy. My mother was an angel. My father would give you the shirt off his back. We worked the land together." He sighed, "I was willing to do what it took. IT WASN'T EASY. IT WAS NEVER EASY."

Richard thought of his own pugnacious will when somebody got in his way. Once a man had heckled him when he was making a speech, and Richard had stomped down from the podium, stormed up to the man, and socked him in the jaw.

The drunk's sixth drink finished him; he put his head on the bar and began to cry quietly. Richard felt a surge of emotion he never expected to feel; he felt compassion.

Where had anger ever gotten him? He had resented his older brother for being his father's favorite, for leaving home to become an architect, for being tall, handsome and composed, in contrast to his short and stocky dominance. Now he felt a protective fervor toward Josh as he faced these hearings. Like a lamb to the slaughter. God, he was angry. What had Gandhi done with his anger? He must have been angry.

The sleeping drunk began to snore with a low humming sound, and the bartender came over and positioned him more comfortably on his arms so that his cheek was resting on a napkin. "He'll sleep it off," he said. "He always does."

Richard paid his tab, but instead of leaving the bar, he sat for a while, gazing into the darkness. Then he stood up, put his coat on, put his hand on the drunk's shoulder, leaned down and whispered, "See you again, Joe."

SUSAN K. CHERNILO

INTENSE ENCOUNTERS
OF THE EDUCATIONAL KIND

I teach English as a Second Language to adults. For the last twenty years I've taught students of all ages from many parts of the world. I've taught young and old, rich and poor. I had a student who grew up in a house with ten kids and dirt floors, and a wealthier woman from the same country whose biggest culture shock here was that she no longer got carted around by limousine. I've had students who were Catholic, Protestant, Muslim, Hindu and Jewish; students from Europe, Africa, Asia, Central and South America, and the Caribbean. It's been a wondrous, amazing encounter with so many different kinds of people.

Needless to say, I've dealt with all kinds of issues. One year I had a class that was mostly Protestant with a couple of Muslim old men who always sat together in the back, while everyone else pretty much ignored them. One day I asked the rest of the class what they knew about Islam: pretty much nothing! I did a lesson on the five pillars of Islam. As the Christian students watched in amazement, I wrote such benign words as "prayer" and "charity" on the board. "What do you think?" I asked. "It's like us," they said. "Exactly!" I said.

There was the year when a woman came to class and happily proclaimed that she had learned from her minister that gays are an abomination and a sign of the last days. Because I didn't necessarily know the sexuality of my students, I felt that I needed to protect them from discrimination. I stopped the class and asked if everyone agreed with her. They all did. I said that I did not, that I have a gay family member, and I did not agree. One by one, the stories poured out. This one had a cousin, another had a friend. Finally, a young man from Haiti told us in tears that he himself had had such feelings. His confession was followed by awesome silence, and then one by one everyone telling him he was okay. It was most likely the first time he ever came out. Our class had gone from being critical of gays to a supportive environment in a half hour.

So I'm used to dealing with diversity in the ESL classroom. I did a workshop for our staff this year about it in fact, and I said that the hardest thing for me to deal with is political differences. I'm a dyed in the wool progressive and almost everyone I know is as well. And that, of course, is what I'm dealing with now.

This year, my ten intermediate level students are all elderly women like myself, mostly in their seventies, grandmothers all, and we meet in the community room of a local senior housing building. Most of them are from the former Soviet Union. They're all retired now from pretty decent careers. They're smart, opinionated, and feisty, which I love. Since part of my job is to get them to express themselves in English, they make that part easy; no pulling teeth here to get them to open up!

They often talk to each other before they tell me what they think. They come to a consensus and often they're like a block. They remind me sometimes of these twins I know who if you ask them a question, they'll whisper to each other in front of you, and then tell you what they both think. So for example this fall, as soon as I got to class, one of my students, who was the group spokesperson de jour, asked me what I thought of the Me Too Movement. Before I could say two sentences about how I think it's terrific, they interrupted. "We think it's silly," several said at once with everyone else nodding. I asked them why and they had their reasons, so we had an interesting discussion. I didn't tell them that I'm a survivor, and being able to tweet "me too" felt awesome. I asked them about the rules for protecting women in the work place in the former Soviet Union, and pointed out that they had better protections than we did here, and maybe that's why they don't understand what it's like for women here.

When we talked about the election in November and I expressed joy and relief at all the new diverse people in Congress, as well as the reelection of our wonderful, *persisting* Massachusetts senator, I faced a blank wall of stares. "We grew up under socialism," one of them explained, "so we know what it's like." I was irritated and annoyed that they would equate the democratic progressiveness of our Elizabeth Warren with the totalitarian regime they grew up with. But that is what has formed them, and they look at the world through very different lenses than I do.

They're conservative about immigration too. When the caravan was making its way to the U.S. border, and the Trump administration was whipping it up for all it was worth, my students were also very upset about it. They agreed with the conservative idea that the U.S. is already full (never having seen, as I did, hitchhiking across the country in my youth, the vast open spaces in our heartland). One actually said that her nephew told her that even though the U.S. military could go to the border, that unfortunately it was against the law to shoot. "Unfortunately?" I echoed, and she nodded.

This was something everyone did not agree with, and some were clearly embarrassed. "Because in our country," one of them explained, "the military would shoot!"

"But you're in the United States now!" I said, feeling a gush of appreciation for what's good about this country.

I had a male teaching assistant. After that class he expressed irritation and disbelief. "But they're immigrants themselves!" he said.

"I know," I said. "It's frustrating. But our job is to help them express themselves in English, not tell them what to think."

He quit. I pressed on. I want to say that I really do love these people. They're honest and warm, forthright and smart, with terrific senses of humor. My grandparents emigrated from that part of the world a century ago, so maybe I feel a natural affinity. A couple of them also had grandparents who spoke Yiddish like mine did.

Around President's Day, I gave them brief synopses of six presidents that some people consider great, with basic bio information and key accomplishments of their tenure. I made a point of including some who aren't my favorites, to balance liberal and conservative. I told them to pick one president that inspires them, do more research and write an essay about why they think *he's* a great president (because of course they're all still *he*).

Being the bright and prolific people that they are, my students came up with amazing essays. I had them read them to the class before collecting them. Three people read about Lincoln, and we followed up with a good discussion. I was impressed that they understood the subtle distinction that the Civil War was fought to keep the Union together, not specifically to end slavery. Three others wrote about Ronald Reagan, and we went on to him. They read glowing accounts about *The Gipper.* They loved everything about him, but most especially how he turned to Gorbachev in East Berlin that day and said, "Mr. Chairman: Tear down this wall!" and we had a chance to go over a useful phrasal verb.

After each had read, I praised their essays, and was eager to go on to what I thought were the safer waters of FDR. "Wait, Susan!" One of them interrupted, "aren't we going to have a discussion about Reagan, like we did with Lincoln."

"Actually, I'm trying to avoid it," I said.

"You don't like President Reagan, do you!?" she pursued.

"Actually, I don't," I said.

"Why?" several asked.

I lived through those years, I told them. I explained to them about "trickle-down economics," how he cut back on social programs and benefits to the poor. "Like the program that runs our school," I pointed out. "Yes, President Reagan helped the economy," I concluded, "but he did it on the backs of poor people."

Ten pairs of eyes were staring at me. I waited for them to yell at me or at least disagree. Finally someone spoke. "We didn't know," she said.

"Yes, thanks for telling us," others said.

I breathed a sigh of relief, and happily went on to FDR. The student eagerly read her essay. She wrote how FDR helped the United States out of the depression with programs like The New Deal. But then she said, "But Roosevelt abandoned Europe," going on to point out that he didn't let the U.S. enter WWII until after Pearl Harbor was bombed, after Hitler invaded several countries and many thousands of people were killed.

I was stunned. Growing up in my liberal New York Jewish family with parents who lived through the depression, I'd only heard accolades about Franklin Roosevelt. And in school and documentaries, I only remember learning and seeing how we were liberators in Europe. We came in and fixed everything; lots of shots of our "boys" walking into the camps and freeing the people. I don't remember ever hearing about all the years before we entered the war, the suffering and loss of life. It was obvious, but somehow I never really thought about it.

I told this to my class, and they nodded gravely.

In this way, we learn from each other. And we struggle on.

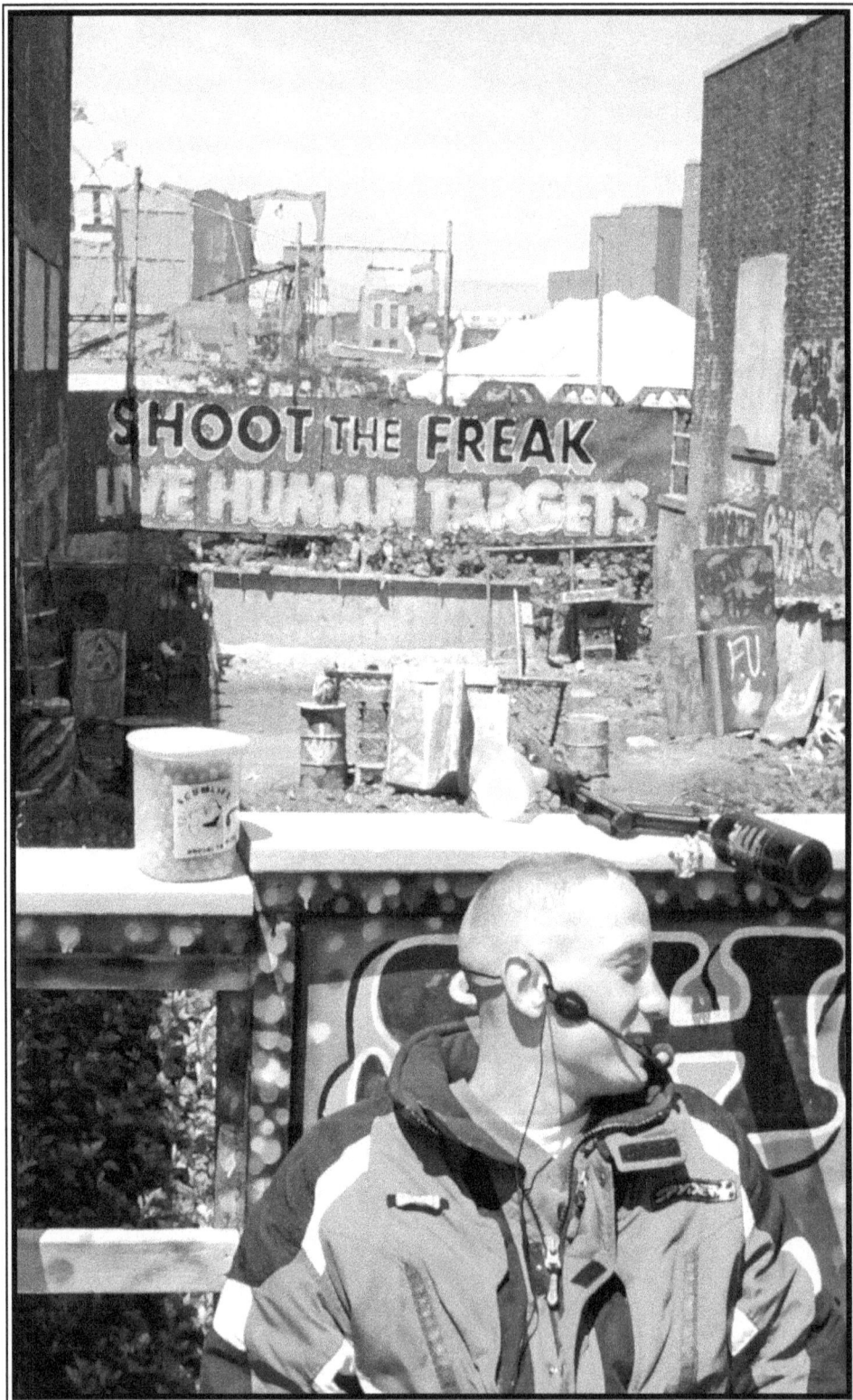

HEATHER TOSTESON

I WANT TO ASK THEM

I keep thinking about how the mothers
didn't want their babies, even stillborn, to decay,
how one left her newborn infant, lifeless,
in a cooler patterned with bright watermelon slices,
handle extended, in the middle of a barren field
along a busy highway, an open secret,
and another kept her stillborn home with her
for six months in her freezer.
Or the mother who, drunk, desperate,
took her whole universe—
wife and six adopted children—
with her over the cliff, so sure
no one could ever care like her.

And about those rowdy adolescent boys
with their red Make America Great Again caps,
gathered in front of the Lincoln Memorial,
high from hormones and the excitement of marching
for the right to life, for the right to extinguish
a woman's right to choose to bring them,
such primed, loose, sperm-laden canons,
into this world. How one of them,
still pumped, still plump with baby fat,
stripped off his shirt, bent his knees
to thrust out his pelvis, and jumped up and down
like any belligerent young primate inviting
someone, anyone, to tangle with him, skin to skin.

I want to ask them too, seriously,
What does love have to do with it?

MARIANNE PEEL

FEAR IN THE SHADOW OF PULSE NIGHTCLUB

I.   Two days after graduation
my daughter shaved her head.
                Mostly.
        Leaving a crop of short stalks
        like splintered toothpicks
        protruding from her scalp.
She asked me to touch her hair
feel it bristle
we both laughed
as I discovered the resilience of her new hair.
        How it rises   without any self-consciousness
        between my fingers
        and then settles
back
when I let go.

II.   I can see the shape of her skull now,
like when she emerged from the only epidural I ever had.

        Wanted to have all four daughters   natural.
        Wanted to dig a deep hole with my fingers out in the bush
        wanted to squat on my haunches
        and birth these babies pushing life out of heaving life
        alone circle breathing through my labor
                wanted to severe the umbilical cord
                with my own incisors
        wanted to plant the placenta under a Linden tree
                wanted to comingle her blood and my blood
                with the raw dirt of the earth.

And this planting would guarantee
she will always return home, feel connected to the earth,
grow to be a gardener herself maybe,
be eternally rooted to this firm ground.

III.   After Pulse nightclub
     with 49 lives gunned down,
     I worry
     she may be a target.
     Scripture wielded as a weapon.
        Don't ask that guy – he wants to hang them all
        45 says of Pence.
     Taking aim at her with *abomination* or *blasphemy*

IV.   She identifies as a woman.
     Prefers the pronouns she/they.
     Abandoned the strappings of a bra years ago.
     Refuses to line her eyes with kohl.
     Paints no blush on her lips.

     I remember how the freckles appeared every June.
     Across her nose and her cheeks.
     We would count them in the evening
     by the light of a jar of lightning bugs.
     Catch and release.

V.   Last night we saw *Love, Simon*
     An auditorium bursting with LGBTQ folks and their allies.

     My daughter turns to me.
        Are we all just sitting ducks
        for someone filled with hatred?
        Bumpstocks   Military assault weapons.
          Easier to wipe out so many   So fast.

I wonder if someone will enter,
desiring to rid the world of who and what he refuses to
understand.
An advocate of conversion therapy.
Or a victim of such torture.
Someone repulsed by his own gay leanings.
Someone filled with self-loathing, unable
to embrace his own sexuality.

In the bathroom, when someone mistakes her for a male.
On the train to Chicago, roaring out of the Midwest, gathering
for the Pride Festival.
Standing in line at Hucks Station,
where cars are draped in confederate flags.
Where affection between two women
is shouted down as *detestable*.

And so I ready myself
for an onslaught.
    Pivot my body toward hers,
    determined to cover her
    with my mother self
    if bullets ever take over the soundtrack.

SUSAN MARTELL HUEBNER

BATTLE AT THE LOT LINE: EITHER/OR VS. BOTH/AND

Summer 2016

My neighbor, who once brought me a prayer shawl for healing my cancer, now walks toward me across the bumpy lawn between our houses. Her new knee requires careful stepping over the lumps and dips. We haven't spoken in many weeks.

There was that one day, when we shared a glass of wine on her patio, and she said, "that's the way all men talk" and followed it with "some women ask for it." That one day, when we finished our wine, I walked home wondering how to navigate the hard ground that lay between our two properties, the divots and exposed roots glaringly obvious. Minor obstacles, until now.

Today she says she trimmed her houseplants and she offers me some jade cuttings. I say I already have a jade plant, but politely note that mine is not as brightly green as the stems she holds in her outstretched hand. I accept the jade and place it in a glass of water where it sits on my kitchen counter, waiting for me to place it in nourishing soil.

✕✕✕✕

Fall 2016

I struggle. The cuttings sit in water.

I seriously consider throwing them away. My ideas about who my neighbor is have changed. I don't want to plant these things and have them growing in my home. I don't want anything personal from a person so ignorant. I read somewhere online that jade is considered a symbol of friendship. I watch the news. This friendship feels impossible.

I reconsider. I contemplate finding a pretty pot and planting the cuttings. I could place the plant in my sunny living room window, next to the tall, healthy one I have growing there. I could do this if I think of that prayer shawl. If I think of the cookies we exchange each Christmas. If I think of how we wave to each other when we are outside working in our gardens.

We are neighbors. I plant the cuttings.

)(()(()((

Winter 2019

Two years later and we are still neighbors. We still watch over each other's properties when vacations call us away. During the summers, vegetables crisscross our lawns—asparagus from their garden, tomatoes from ours. Today I call my neighbor to say thank you. Her husband has plowed our driveway, unbidden, again. We talk about our families, exchange news about the neighbor across the street who is recovering from serious illness. She tells me about her Women's Club excursion over the holidays. We laugh, recalling my September backyard birthday party, how much fun it was despite the wind and temperature. She teasingly chides me for spoiling her dog with treats. I answer how nice it is for me to have a dog to play with but without the responsibility of owning one.

I still struggle. The news has certainly not changed for the better. My head doesn't understand and I ache and rage with the nightly news. How can people be so unfeeling, so loyal to faithless cruelty? But my heart insists, observes from a different viewpoint, sees the people next door—good people.

The struggle persists. It is clearly defined, with no easy resolution other than what is true: We remain good neighbors.

KELLY TALBOT

THE SHOOTERS

"How the hell can they see us? We should be invisible."

"I don't know. Maybe they don't see us. Maybe they're looking at something else."

"They're looking right at us. They're staring."

"Why don't you talk a little louder, Tanya? Then they'll be able to hear us, too. Don't worry about it. They'll move on in a minute."

"I don't like it." Tanya pointed her Winchester in their direction.

"Jesus, Tanya! Don't do that. It's dangerous."

"Calm down. I'm just trying to get a better look at them through the scope."

"I don't care. It isn't safe. Lower your rifle. Now."

"Alright, but they're being rude. Besides, they're going to scare the wood ducks away."

"Except we haven't seen a wood duck all day."

"And we won't with that couple staring at us. What's their problem? Hey, look. What are they doing now?"

"They've got cameras. They're taking our picture."

"What are they doing that for? Now they've gone too far." Tanya shifted her weight, getting ready to stand. Mark grabbed her upper arm and gently pulled downward.

"Don't do it."

"Why not? We should go tell them off. They can't just go around taking pictures of people. It's inappropriate."

"Even if they can see us, they can't get a good shot. There are too many reeds between us and them. If you stand up, they can zoom in on your face. Not to mention you'll give away our position."

"They *know* our position."

"I'm not talking about them. I'm talking about the ducks. Just keep cool, and they'll go. We have a sweet spot here. All we have to do is wait and keep quiet."

"Doesn't it bother you at all? They're taking our picture. They could put it on the Internet."

"Our picture's already on the Internet."

"You know what I mean. What if they're with the National Audubon Society? What if they're reporters? What if they're working on some sort of anti-gun story? We have every right to be here. We have our licenses, and we're in season. Who the hell do they think they are?"

"Like you said, we have our licenses, and we're in season. Who cares what they think? Look. They're leaving. I told you. If you ignore them, they'll get bored and move on. Now try to relax, keep your eyes open, and listen for the duck calls."

✕✕✕✕

"I was wondering if we'd see you again." Tanya strode up to the couple and put her hands on her hips.

"I'm sorry. Do we know you?"

"You were staring right at us about six hours ago. You took our picture."

"I'm afraid I don't recognize you. Margaret, did you take these people's picture?"

"I don't think so. I took some pictures of a group of hunters this morning, but they had bows and different clothes. Ma'am, where were you when you saw us?"

"We were in the reeds up there at the northwest side of the lake. You watched us for two whole minutes, snapping away."

"I think you're mistaken. I'd remember that. Bill, are you sure you didn't shoot these people?"

"No. The only thing we shot up on the northwest side of the lake was that beautiful duck with the striking colors and the bright red eyes."

"You saw a wood duck?" Tanya's tone softened.

"Is that what they're called?" Margaret took the cap off her camera's lens, turned on the power, and scrolled through the images. "There. Is that a wood duck?"

Tanya and Mark leaned in for a closer look. Margaret had managed to zoom in to get a vivid close-up, and the clarity of the image was striking. Mark started chuckling.

"What? What is it?"

"That's *our* wood duck."

Margaret's face fell. "You shot him?"

"Not hardly." Mark reached into his bag and pulled out the wood duck. He rapped on it with his knuckles, making a hard, knocking sound. "Not a wood duck. Just wood. He's a decoy."

"Wow. That's amazing. He looks so lifelike." Bill couldn't resist reaching over and touching it.

"Well, at least now we know he works. If he can fool you with that zoom you have, he should be able to fool another wood duck. You know, you've got some terrific shots. You should try sending them in to the hunting magazines. I'm sure they can always use pictures like those."

"So you didn't see us at all?" Tanya asked.

Bill shook his head. "No, but we weren't looking for you. We weren't looking for ducks either. We were hoping to get some shots of a blue heron."

Mark grimaced mildly. "It was a little late in the morning for herons. They tend to be more active at twilight. We saw a couple by our campsite this morning at first light."

"That's right. They were pretty big, too. Hey, would you two like to come back to our campsite? It isn't far from here. We've got sandwiches and pop and beer. You might be able to get a few shots of the herons by now."

"That sounds great. I'm famished. What do you say Bill?"

"Sure. I could really go for a beer. You know, you meet the nicest people out here in nature."

"Wonderful. And I'd love to see more of your pictures."

CHUCK MADANSKY

WHAT WE FEED THE EARTH

Why did I ask to meet him at the coffee shop?
I didn't want him to know where I lived.

His letters on immigration were filled with pain
and enough self-righteousness to match my own.

I made the invitation. He agreed to meet, and we met.
We lived in the same town, were about the same age,

found enough to laugh at together. When I asked why
he felt so strongly about ending immigration

he said something about not wanting to lose our way of life,
which I took to mean white, and in control.

Later, I learned something else beneath the pain:
his brother had died of an overdose, and he blamed

that death on the drugs and the drugs on immigration.
The last time I wrote, I said I was sorry to learn of his loss.

Why haven't we ever met again? I don't know how to meet
his grief. If the earth isn't fed with tears, we feed it with blood.

MURALI KAMMA

THE VISITOR AND THE NEIGHBOR

That morning, for the first time since he landed in the U.S., Prasad does not acknowledge his son's greeting. Although awake, he remains quiet when Vijay, stopping by the closed door as usual, knocks and says, "Good morning, Papa." Pause. Getting no response, Vijay drops the newspaper on the floor and walks away briskly, his footsteps resounding in the hallway. Every morning for about three weeks, Prasad has been opening the door to return his son's greeting and take the paper from him. But not today.

Reluctant to get out of bed, Prasad listens to the sounds of the household. Doors open; patter on the staircase; chatter in the kitchen; plates clatter; the microwave hums. The morning routine reaches a climax with the rumble of the garage door, whose rapid descent sounds like the closing of a prison gate. Prasad once heard a friend say, with a laugh, that when he was visiting his daughter in America, her suburban home had felt like "a five-star jail" after she went to work. He didn't know anybody else there, and couldn't go anywhere without her—but every comfort he could think of was readily available.

Prasad's daughter-in-law, Uma, who has a longer commute, is the first person to leave the house. Then it is Vijay's turn, and he leaves for his office with their daughter, Mala, whom he drops off at school on the way. Having quickly eaten their breakfast in the kitchen, they exit through the side door leading to the garage. And then comes the silence that seems to have sneaked in through the same door, even at the same time, like a taciturn cellmate.

Prasad switches on the radio next to his bed, and a reporter's excited prattle fills the room. What happened to the sprightly music he used to hear on this station? Now that everybody has left the house, he feels guilty that he ignored his son. But it couldn't be helped. Following the previous day's incident, Prasad wanted a break—and so, rather than face Vijay and relive the embarrassing moment, he pretended to be asleep. Rising now, he gets ready and makes a cup of coffee using the Keurig machine. How easy this is compared to what he's used to, he marvels, as the coffeemaker gurgles and the brew's rich aroma fills his nostrils. After finishing his yoga routine, Prasad picks up the paper—but today he is unable to concentrate.

Switching off the radio, whose nonstop chatter has begun to grate, he paces back and forth in the empty house, going from the front door to the back door that leads to the yard. A few rounds later, still feeling restless, he steps outside through the front door. But he's not going to walk in the neighborhood, as he used to. While his son hasn't placed any restrictions, he did gently suggest that Prasad would be better off sticking close to the house. So from now, until he heads back to India, he'll only walk on the property.

The throbbing sound of a lawn mower draws his attention. Walking towards it, he sees Vijay's neighbor, Ethan Cooper, pushing the mower in his front yard. Prasad is, once again, struck by the old man's energy. And what about his clothes—or rather, his shorts? Prasad has never worn shorts as an adult. As for yard maintenance, his son hardly does anything on his own, having outsourced the job to a landscaping company. But here's this neighbor, who seems to be about Prasad's age, doing work that only gardeners do in India. Amazing!

Giving Prasad a friendly wave, Ethan turns off the mower. Then, mopping his face with a handkerchief, he walks over. Ethan looks tired, but he is smiling and seems happy to see Prasad, as if this is an agreeable break from a taxing chore. A baseball hat with an unfamiliar logo partly conceals his snowy white hair, and he's wearing a pale blue T-shirt that bears the name of a charity walk. Seeing the wrinkles on his face, Prasad wonders if Ethan is older than him.

"Hello, Mr. Cooper. How are you? You're working hard."

Ethan laughs. "I'm fine. I was wondering about you, though. Yesterday was not a good day. Awfully sorry that you had to experience such abuse. Hope you're okay now."

"I . . . I'm fine," Prasad says, flustered. It didn't occur to him that Ethan had heard the motorist shout at Prasad as he was crossing the street. That explains why he'd pulled over, even before he recognized Prasad. But Ethan hadn't said anything about the motorist then, probably because Prasad was shaken and Ethan didn't want to upset him further. It's only now that Prasad sees how Ethan would have been close enough to hear the motorist yell, "Are you fucking crazy? Go back to your country!"

That's all. Then he was gone, the flashy car roaring as it accelerated. Struck by the man's vehemence, Prasad froze, though only for a moment. Pulling himself together, he slowly continued walking—only to stop when he saw Ethan pull over in his SUV.

"It was my mistake," Prasad says now, facing Ethan as they stand at the edge of Vijay's property. "You see, I was looking in the wrong direction. I don't know why. Although I'm used to left-side driving in my country, I know the traffic rules here."

"Mistakes happen, so there's no need for such rudeness, such abuse," Ethan says, shaking his head. "Motorists have to be careful when they see pedestrians. I don't know what this country is coming to!"

"It's no better back home, Mr. Cooper. In fact, motorists can be worse. I haven't properly thanked you for the lift—"

"Please . . . there's no need. It was my pleasure. I'm glad I happened to be there. Do call me Ethan. What's your name again? Sorry, I'm bad with names."

"Prasad. Looks like you stay pretty active, Mr. . . . I mean, Ethan."

"Well, I try, Prasad." He chuckles. "Did you come alone from India?"

"Yes, I did." Prasad, whose wife died a couple of years ago, doesn't elaborate; he has heard from Vijay that Ethan is a widower as well.

They chat for a few more minutes, mostly about their grandchildren, before Ethan asks if he'd like to join him in the house for a drink.

"I'm not used to alcohol," Prasad says, showing hesitation.

Ethan laughs. "I meant apple cider, Prasad. Or lemonade. Your choice."

After locking the front door with the key Vijay had given him, Prasad enters Ethan's house and follows him to his living room, comfortably furnished with a cushiony sofa set, an easy chair with a lamp beside it, a bright rug, and an oval coffee table covered with books and papers. The blinds of the bay window are open, giving Prasad a view of the sun-dappled backyard and a birdhouse dangling close to the glass. An upright piano is in one corner. A computer on a carved desk is in another corner, which probably means the room doubles as a study. What strikes Prasad the most are the wooden shelves on both sides of a black stereo system. They're filled with rows and rows of CDs and vinyl records.

"That's quite a collection, Ethan," he says. "You must be an aficionado. What sort of music do you like?"

"I'm open to different genres, but these days I tend to listen to classical music. Please have a seat, Prasad. I'll be right back with the lemonade."

They touch on various topics—weather, children, health, travel—before circling back to their interests. Prasad mentions that he used to sketch a lot and even contribute satirical cartoons to a magazine in India. But now he has no such hobby, he admits.

"Personally, I think it's important to continue doing what we enjoy," Ethan says. "I'm guilty of neglecting my own advice. But while I've given up carpentry, which I loved, my interest in music hasn't abated. I'm more of a listener these days."

After confessing that he knows little about Western classical music, Prasad asks if he could listen to something. Ethan, noting that a few CDs have already been loaded in the player, picks up the remote control and presses it. As the lush first movement of Beethoven's Sixth Symphony ("Pastoral") fills the room, he silently hands Prasad a boxed CD set and returns to his chair. The opening melody unfolds at a leisurely pace and the piece has a soothing, elemental beauty, even as it gradually builds in intensity with thrilling variation and repetition. Is it painting musical pictures of pastoral life? Flipping through the CD booklet as he listens, Prasad is startled to see that the symphony's five movements have titles. "Awakening of cheerful feelings on arrival in the countryside," reads the first one, aptly summarizing the mood it evokes.

Prasad gives himself up to the music. The next two movements are called "Scene by the brook" and "Merry gathering of country folk." Ethan seems to have chosen the right piece for a novice, given how effortlessly this bubbling, delightfully meandering symphony, with riffs that mimic bird calls, transports Prasad back to a youthful jaunt by a serenely flowing river in rural India. The flute, so recognizable, is imitating a nightingale, he learns. On that long-ago picnic, overcoming his shyness, he'd spoken to an attractive girl from another group—only to be teased by his friends. Floating in the music's inexorable current, Prasad knows that the descriptions are not meant to be taken literally. But he can't help himself.

)⚡)⚡(⚡(

The previous day, after signing the form his banker had asked him to send, Prasad set out on his regular walk in the neighborhood. But this time, instead of taking the same route back to the house, he planned to walk past the mailbox he'd seen from his son's car. After mailing his envelope,

Prasad would return to the intersection where his granddaughter's school bus stopped. Uma usually picked her up from school. However, since an office meeting would delay her this afternoon, Vijay had asked Prasad to meet Mala at the bus stop.

Prasad missed the mailbox, unexpectedly. As he recalled, it was in a little plaza near the intersection where Vijay often turned right onto a avenue. But the plaza wasn't in sight, and rather than being close to the avenue, he seemed to be deeper in a maze of residential streets with unrecognizable names. He must have made a wrong turn somewhere. Now he understood the wisdom of owning a smartphone, which he'd been resisting for a long time; even his son seemed a little embarrassed to see him using the outdated flip phone. Prasad, though, could be obstinate. Trying not to panic, he focused on retracing his steps.

It didn't work, and Prasad realized that he was lost. How did that happen when he hadn't walked very far from the house? This area wasn't easy to navigate, apparently, if you were a newcomer and a pedestrian. What his friend had said about the suburbs—"if you don't have a car, you're stuck and out of luck"—was true. Prasad had smiled then, but he didn't feel like smiling now. Determinedly, he turned in what he thought was the right direction and kept walking, quickening his pace and looking around to see if he could speak to anybody. But there was nobody—and the imposing houses he saw, with their tidy yards, were silent and ghostly, as if their owners had abandoned them. It was eerie.

Where were all the people, Prasad had wondered on his first morning in the U.S., as he stood in his son's front yard and looked down the leafy, orderly suburban street? At work, he'd surmised, or behind closed doors in their lovely homes. Cars had gone by every now and then, although he barely caught a glimpse of the passengers. Yes, he did see walkers and joggers later that day. A few had smiled or waved at him, while the others—looking purposeful, as if they had to get somewhere on time—were absorbed in the sounds emanating from their headphones.

What a contrast it was to the way he lived in India, where the hustle and bustle outside his building never seemed to cease, and one couldn't avoid people. Sometimes, it's true, the bazaar-like atmosphere was a little too much, too chaotic. But Prasad was grateful to be in a building where he knew everybody. With his wife gone and his only child living abroad, some of the long-time residents were like family to him. They looked out for him.

Loneliness, he'd heard, was common in highly individualistic societies like America. Yet, despite living in a country that wasn't very individualistic, he'd also experienced loneliness.

A car, turning at the corner, moved in his direction. Eager though he was to ask for help, Prasad hesitated to raise his hand. It felt awkward—what if the driver didn't stop? And then, when the car passed him, it was too late. However, as luck would have it, when he turned at the same corner, the avenue came into view. While this was a different intersection, it looked familiar and he knew that if he crossed to the other side, there was a petrol station. Or, as they liked to say here, a gas station. It had puzzled him at first, until Vijay, who often filled up at this station, told him that gas was short for gasoline.

Crossing the avenue in a hurry, Prasad neglected to look in the proper direction.

After the motorist who yelled at him took off in his car, Prasad—who was walking again—became wary when another vehicle pulled over and the driver, rolling his window down, asked if he needed a ride. But his apprehension turned to relief when he saw Ethan Cooper, Vijay's neighbor. On a couple of occasions, they'd exchanged quick hellos. Ethan recognized him as well, and when Prasad stated that he was trying to reach the bus stop to meet his granddaughter, he merely said, "Hop in."

The ride was short, giving them barely enough time for some casual remarks. Alas, the school bus had already left—again. Saying that Mala would be at her friend's house by now, Prasad asked Ethan to drop him near his son's front door.

Uma, when she came home after picking up her daughter, acted graciously. But Prasad could tell that she was a little annoyed, for she scarcely paid attention to his explanation. He forgot again, she seemed to think. No need for excuses.

Later that night, Prasad stumbled upon a conversation that his son and daughter-in-law were having in the living room, where the TV was on at a low volume and the lights were dimmed. They must have thought he was sleeping. But he hadn't been able to fall asleep, although his light was switched off and he lay comfortably in bed. Feeling thirsty, Prasad got out of bed and left his room—only to stop when he heard their voices. Afraid to announce his presence, he leaned against the wall.

"I'm not making a big deal, Vijay. But how do you expect a young girl to know whether her grandfather is home? That's why it's better for Mala to go to

Amy's place when I can't pick her up. And I don't understand why the suitcase was near the door. I almost stumbled—"

"Papa was looking for some bank documents. He just forgot, Uma. We'll be lucky if we're not forgetful when we reach his age. Think of your dad—"

"Come on, Vijay, this is not about my dad . . . and you know that!"

Soundlessly, Prasad withdrew into his room and got back into bed. As he pulled the blanket close to him, the silence and darkness around him felt like additional layers of protection. The glowing digits of the clock next to his bed said 11:23—which meant that it would be close to 10 in the morning back home. The building would be buzzing with activity, even though a bunch of residents would have left for work or school by now. Homemakers would be busy, while retirees like him would be puttering around in their flats or outside. Prasad imagined being on his little balcony, gazing down on a street that reminded him of a procession during festival time.

One evening, after dinner at Vijay's home, Uma had mentioned that Ethan's daughter came to see him on weekends. And sometimes Ethan visited his daughter and her kids. This bit of information, shared during Prasad's first week in the U.S., had surprised him. Since Ethan's daughter's lived in the same city, why hadn't he—after his wife's death—downsized and moved in with her? Why did he choose to live alone? Was it because people here, as Prasad had once heard a commentator say, were more I-centric than we-centric?

But now, as he was about to drift off to sleep in Vijay's house, Prasad could see Ethan's point. Despite the solitude, perhaps it was better to live on your own as long as you could.

✗✗✗

Shortly after listening to the symphony in Ethan's living room, Prasad walks back to his son's house. And that afternoon, before it's time for Uma to return home with her daughter, he heads to Ethan's house again, holding a manila envelope. In it are two Indian classical music CDs that he hopes Ethan will get a chance to sample, given that he'd expressed some curiosity. The lawn mower is in the same spot, as if the job was abandoned halfway.

When Prasad presses the doorbell, there is no response—and he hesitates to press it more than twice. Not having heard the chimes outside, he wonders if the doorbell is out of order. Maybe he should give the envelope to him later, when he is home, rather than leave it on the doorstep. But Ethan's

SUV is in the driveway, so he couldn't have gone anywhere.

On a whim, Prasad decides to go to the back of Ethan's property and return to Vijay's house that way. Catching sight of the bay windows, he is reminded of the symphony, especially the last two movements. They were listening to it just a few hours ago. "Storm" and "Shepherd's song"—that's what they're called, aren't they? In the penultimate movement, the rousing music builds to a climax with spectacular sound effects that mimic the foreboding rumble of thunder. Almost involuntarily, as he hears the vigorous beating of drums in his head, Prasad approaches the dangling birdhouse, his attention drawn by a pool of light in the living room.

Ethan might think he is spying on him, but Prasad doesn't care. Is he okay? He looked weary that morning, probably because he'd been mowing. Prasad peers inside. Ethan, at first glance, appears to be reading in his easy chair. But he is not. Slouching forward, with his eyes closed, he seems to be drifting in a tranquil river of dreams, while the lyrical but imagined music of the symphony's finale—the calm after the storm—gently washes over Prasad. An open book is lying on Ethan's lap. What if he is not sleeping?

His pulse racing, Prasad bangs on the glass window. To his relief, Ethan looks up with a start, turns his head towards Prasad—and smiles.

VII. FRIENDS & FAMILY

ADA JILL SCHNEIDER

NEAR THE NANCY A. MESSINGER TRAIL AT THE MARTIN WILDLIFE REFUGE

At a distance, we presumed it was mother and foal.
The perfection of caring, the protection of giving.

But it was a white mare and a white donkey.
Grazing the same patch of grass tells you they are friends,

says my friend who knows these things.
They have worked something out between them.

My friend grew up as a New England barn girl who lived for riding.
She has trained horses and dogs but opted out of having children.

I was a New York City girl who rode trains and never had a pet.
A family woman, I am devoted to my children and grandchildren.

My friend is Protestant; I am Jewish. She swims the bay and cycles
    marathons.
I garden and birdwatch. She can speak Chinese. Me? Urdu.

Our differences fascinate us. Our writing unites us. We can spend hours
contentedly grazing synonym finders for a perfect word that means
satisfaction

ELIZABETH BRULÉ FARRELL

A DIFFICULT LANGUAGE

She uses the Latin names of flowers
when we walk in the garden. I nod
silently as she remarks about the history
of each plant, never daring to utter
the common translation she finds too ordinary.
She cannot just say chamomile
when we come upon a clump ready for harvest,
only Anthemis nobilis. After she is gone
I steep the yellow tops in boiling water, slowly
sip the medicinal promise that it might calm anxiety,
and maybe help the difficult language between us.

SHARON LASK MUNSON

SPEAK UP

i

At a year and a half, Clara uttered
a word here, a word there.
"Water. Mama. No."

At almost four she speaks in complete sentences
displaying plenty of spirit
when asked to smile at the cell phone.
"When I say no, I mean no."

ii

Avoiding giving an apology
for spreading tall tales
about a beloved member
of our Knit & Sew group,
my friend cries,

"I'm sorry for everything
real or imagined."

iii

Before Mother's dementia progressed
to a point where dialogue
would no longer be possible, I state,
"You never laid a hand—
not a slap, a belt,
not even an occasional spanking."
She nods and responds,

"You speak gently to a child.
Children can't protect themselves."

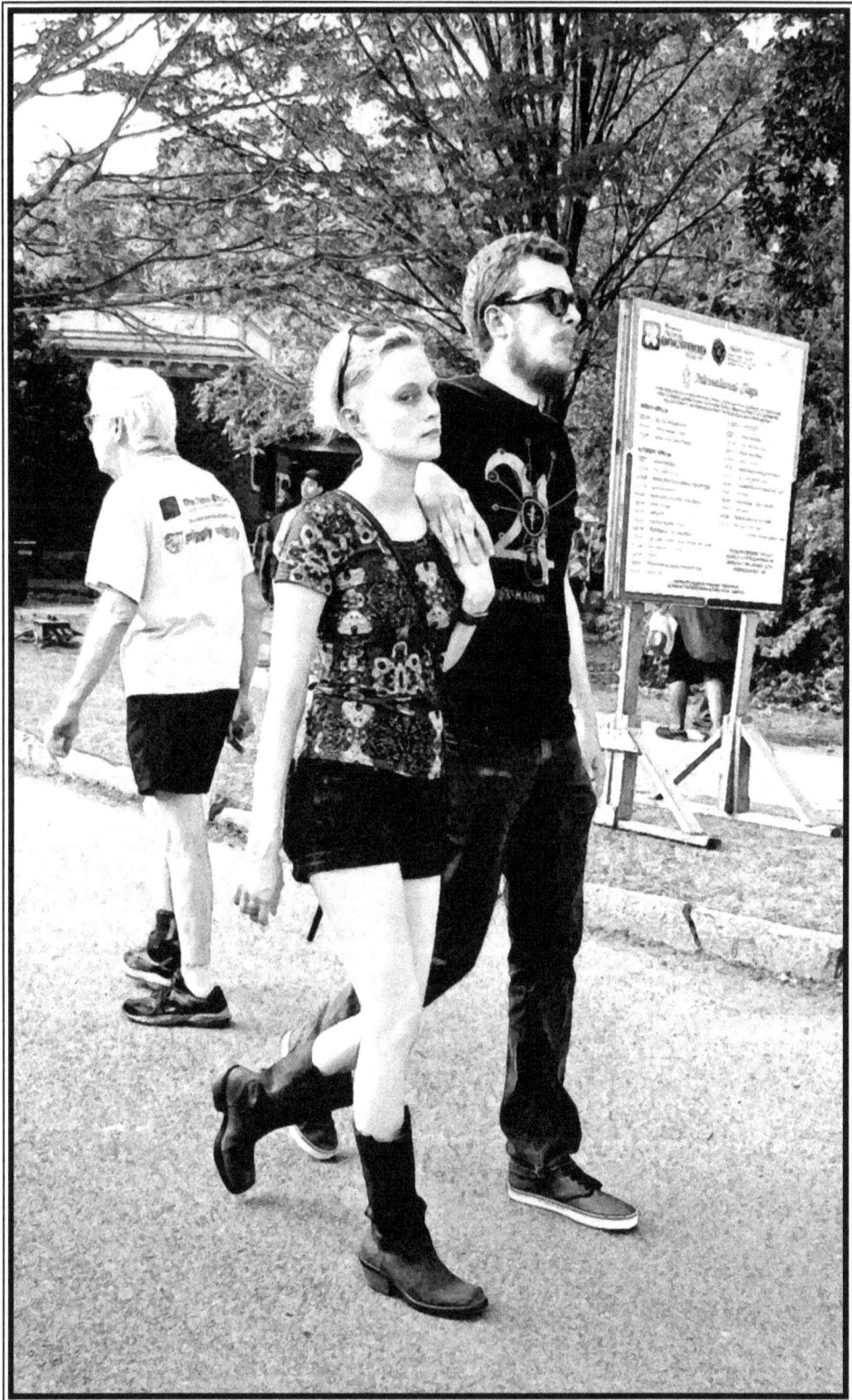

MIMI JENNINGS

TRUCE AT THE CARE CENTER

He looks up, golf cap askew
from the loveseat. Cloudy blue eyes focus slowly, "Go away."
Claws scratch at air.
"Move over, Dad," I shoulder and hip him upright
knock the hat off, worm next to him—
his arms folded, jaw set.
I reach for a hand, he swats the air between us.
I meet his palm with a smack. He points
at me, wrinkles his nose
in censure of my hairstyle—familiar provocation. I scowl
point back at his crown
see his skull.

Young, I feared him
wanted his favor.
Lore has it age fourteen, after his tyrant father's funeral
he taught himself to drive
and to inflict pain.
I made him sick / had a lot of crust / was not his.
Well before fourteen I began using my hurt, escalating hostilities—
insert here: decades enlisting allies,
boyfriends as buffers, changes of venue at Christmas.
I bear the marks
of his scars—
recoil at a glower like his, am given to disdain.

Today, opening gambits over, we sit, his sneer eroded
(blessed dementia),
his words soft, bemused,
my guard comfortably down,
both noses wrinkled, funny hair—
history very much present—on this loveseat.

MARIANNE PEEL

ACCUSATION

I don't recognize the crazed mother
I've become when they walk through the door.

No hugs or rushing to greet me.
Those hellos that used to knock me almost off my knees
with their giggling thrust into my arms are now so gone
and replaced with whispers between them confirming
it's all my fault
this monster who has rejected their father.

They know nothing of drowned passion
of rigid backs in the night of disembodied sex
drained of all intimacy. I left their father
because I couldn't pretend anymore
because behind the shut-tight eyes I was
floating in a foreign land, wandering,
further and farther away, wrapped in my
exotic scarves, a patchwork of a palette

And when they walk through the door now they drag
in such hatred, such acidic accusation.

As if I could remain false without my bones
fragmenting under my skin, splintering my marrow.
I cannot count the shards that swim and slug
beneath my skin.

They won't comply with the simplest
of requests like please wash your hands before dinner
or please place your clean laundry in your drawers
or please brush your teeth before going out into
the world becomes a battleground of feet
stomping up the stairs behind slammed doors.
Their disdain simmers beneath the surface of their skin
raw like uncooked meat boiled under the slab of sun.

Even when I squint my sore eyes at night
I no longer recognize my own daughters.

DONNA BANTA

COLLISIONS

On November 7, 1975, I broke my mother's heart. It wasn't picked up by the tabloids. I didn't need rehab, bail or an abortion. I was on the honor roll and active in church. Hell, I even registered Republican. (To please her.) Then on that day in 1975, I came home from school, kissed her hello, washed my hands at the sink, and while pouring a glass of milk, let slip that I would not be applying to Brigham Young University. The moment of impact was still a blur. White noise, milk sloshing over the lip of my glass. A string of reassuring lies. (I'll still go to church every Sunday, I promise.) Didn't matter. I was no longer Deanna Sutton, model Mormon girl. The girl who chose to leave California for humble BYU.

The clock read 6:15 a.m. Too late to go back to sleep. I felt across the bed for Paul. Not a stir.

According to my mother, it was all because of that Simon Post, my high school lab partner. Would that she could turn back time, and forbid me from seeing him socially. But how was she to know? He seemed like such a nice boy, for a non-member.

Simon's lesser church affiliation acted on me like an aphrodisiac. On date number three, at my urging, we pulled off en route to mini-golf, removed our glasses, and engaged in a delicious make-out session. It began in the front seat, progressed to the back and culminated in my first non-penetrating orgasm.

Our romance was short-lived. A dip in our midterm grades combined with a class seating rearrangement compelled us to put our glasses back on. (I've often wondered if Simon's mom was behind the lab partner shuffle, perhaps after treating the stain inside of his corduroys.)

But as I sat four tables away from Simon, who now refused to look at me, I was strangely at peace. Normal even. Nothing like what I was taught.

I was supposed to be miserable, guilt-ridden, eager to confess to my bishop. That would have been Ned Shirt, a pale chinless creature, like one of those aquarium floor dwellers that appeared all of the sudden, and startled you away from the glass. As I balanced chemical equations, my mind alternated between two scenarios. In one, I'm in Bishop Shirt's office, tearful and repentant. In the other, I'm looking into his lidless pop-eyes and announcing, "I came for the first time and it was fantastic!"

As the BYU application deadline drew closer, so did my discontent. For the better part of two decades, I had been stuffed inside a small dark room. Suddenly the door had flung open, and I was propelled into the sunshine. In the end, my decision had little to do with Simon Post. Nevertheless, the memory of our back seat coupling still tasted like a fresh-from-the-oven cookie. Moist, sweet, and molten, it scalded the roof of my mouth.

Again I reached for Paul. He rolled onto his back. I recognized the invitation, and climbed on top of him. I moved my lips over his chest, up his neck to the tiny mole behind his earlobe, then finally his mouth. We enjoyed kissing, as much now as in our early days. But as our breathing quickened, our urgency grew and we were soon shedding our nightclothes. I climaxed just after he entered, faster than usual, but with the same unmistakable coital moan. (I could never fake it with Paul; he knew the sound.) "Letting me off easy this time," he teased, when we were finished. After a few seconds he added, "Do you want me to shower first?"

For god's sake, for a brief moment I'd actually taken my mind off the funeral. I jumped from the bed and collected my strewn pajamas.

Hot water caressed my head and neck. A rain showerhead, one of our best investments. Right up there with the garage door opener and the window A/C unit in our bedroom. All newfangled gadgets my mother didn't need. (Are you too spoiled to get out and open your own door?) But then, that new Cadillac of hers was OK, as were her weekly wash and sets. "One must keep up appearances," she explained. Words I remembered whenever I hid my dirty hair under a scarf. In deference to Mom, I pumped out a generous portion of shampoo and worked it into a lather on my head.

My mother's rules were difficult to pin down. But then she came from a culture that not only forbade alcohol and tobacco, but also tea and coffee. Caffeinated soft drinks sparked endless debate, as did chocolate consumption. Was vanilla extract permissible? (Well then, why not just spike it with vodka?)

One summer morning Mom sent me to the garden to pick lettuce for

Dad's lunch box. As I'd been taught, I gingerly removed a couple of the outer leaves, without disturbing the head. When I returned, I expected to see meat on the cutting board. Instead she was slathering peanut butter onto the bread.

"Lettuce on a peanut butter sandwich?"

"And what's wrong with that? Your father loves peanut butter and lettuce, so did his father. It's a perfectly respectable combination. If you want to be a good wife, you need to be creative, try new things."

As I rinsed beneath my unnecessary and newfangled showerhead, I marveled at the irony of my mother's advice. In the first place peanut butter and lettuce, having been a favorite of my father and grandfather, could hardly be called a new thing. Rather, it was a respectable combination. Secondly, my mother could hardly be called creative, any more than I could be called respectable.

That evening Dad grilled burgers, Mom and I assembled a salad fresh from the garden, and Jimmy dangled from his favorite branch of our cherry tree. When we were seated for dinner, Dad called on my brother to ask the blessing. Jimmy, being Jimmy, assumed a mock sober expression and droned the prayer like Lurch on The Addams Family. Of course, because he was Jimmy, he was neither reprimanded nor required to do it over. Then during the competition over condiments, I took the jar of Bob's Blue Cheese Dressing, spooned some onto my salad, and, in a burst of creativity, dolloped it onto my burger as well.

"Why'd ya do that?" said Jimmy.

"I'm being creative. Mom suggested it."

I looked to her for confirmation, but instead received a cold stare.

"I'm sure I never meant anything so bizarre as blue cheese dressing on a hamburger."

Her words stuck like the thorns on her blackberries. Honestly, I thought she'd be pleased.

"You eat that whole thing, young lady." Then to my father, "Larry don't you make her another one until she finishes."

Dad sat with both elbows on the table, a privilege extended only to him. "Anyone wants more, let me know."

"Store bought dressing isn't cheap, Deanna Sutton," Mom continued, while I fought back tears. "You'd better find yourself a rich husband."

"I did, Mom," I said out loud, and then shut off the faucet.

I stood staring at the steamy marble, letting the anger drain. Sadness crept into its place. That was the summer of my tenth year. The summer we were Mimi and Deenie, when I was her little helper, and we grew the best garden ever. Baked the best pies, preserved the best jam. Late that August she took me shopping for school shoes, then on a lark, stopped at the jewelry counter in Penney's and bought us matching lockets. They were round, genuine gold-filled, and engraved with tiny roses. When we fastened them around each other's neck, we meant to wear them forever.

I toweled off, wondering what bothered me most. The constant fault-finding? That she never appreciated me? Or perhaps it was that my most vivid memory of our "best summer ever" was the time she went off on me over blue cheese dressing.

When the deadline passed, and the church members learned that Deanna Sutton wasn't going to BYU, my mother and I took off our genuine gold-filled lockets. My departure for college inspired little fanfare, my trips home were dismal and infrequent. When I graduated from UC Davis, my family failed to make the ninety-minute car trip. There was my father's work, Mom explained, and poor Jimmy. Of course, there was always poor Jimmy.

I owned two black dresses. A strapless number I wore to Paul's hospital galas, and a lumpy linen shift that fell almost to the floor. "When are you going to take up that hem?" I heard my mother ask as I slipped it over my head. Paul, meanwhile, monopolized the mirror. Redoing his tie, brushing his suit coat, still going the extra mile for my mom.

I remembered the day I brought him home. Tall, blue eyed, in his first year of medical school. He was impossible not to like. And she did like him, as much as she liked any non-member, as much as Simon Post, even.

At first Paul was on her side. (Dee, she's your mom for chrissakes.) But his allegiance shifted when my father died. I was not invited to speak at the funeral. Jimmy delivered the eulogy, and with his usual panache, captivated the congregation with hilarity and warmth. Also imagination, as his riotous description of our father had little in common with the man himself. Afterward Mom offered the closing prayer. In front of a packed congregation, she begged the Lord to "soften the heart of her only daughter, so that she might see her father again."

"You have my permission to hate her," Paul had said when we pulled away from the church.

I turned to him now. He was in the driver's seat, as he was then, and every bit as handsome. "You OK?" he asked. I told him yes.

When our daughter was born we called a truce, and planned a few visits a year. While uncomfortable, they served their purpose. On Paul's side of the family, Eleanor had Nonnie and Poppy who played dominoes, took her on trips, and visited her college dorm. On mine, she had Grandmother Sutton who offered her milk, cookies, and criticism. (Doesn't your mother ever comb your hair?)

)()()(

A few months ago I witnessed a head-on collision. Screeching tires, crunching metal, airbags, ambulance, police, fire truck, it blocked the entire road. Amazingly both drivers were fine, barely bruised. Used to be an accident like that left the cars intact but the people dead. Now the cars were totaled, but the passengers survived. Since life was a series of collisions, I figured it was best to choose a vehicle you could walk away from. Not my mother. She insisted on banging around in the same old jalopy.

When I earned my PhD she asked, "Who needs a degree to grow a tomato?" When I dedicated my book on sustainable farming to her, she responded with, "I hope people don't think I'm one of your tree huggers." (Once on a trip to the Redwoods, Mom wrapped her arms around one of the massive trunks and inhaled.) Would she have found reason to criticize if my degree had been from BYU? If my book had been about food storage ahead of the Apocalypse? Probably. But there would have been an absence of nastiness, some reward for having chosen the correct mode of transportation. When we ceased to have church in common, we no longer had anything.

God knows she always forgave Jimmy. Even when he wrecked her Cadillac, or got busted for drugs. When he was kicked out of Utah Tech, kicked off his Mormon mission, kicked out by his first, and then his second wife. He was still her prodigal, aching to do good but struggling with the execution. At least he went to Utah for school, at least he left on a mission, at least he married in the temple. (Twice.) My brother traveled through life in an outdated rattletrap of his own, its destination obvious to everyone except my mother. Until today.

Paul touched my knee. "We're a few minutes early, want me to drive around the block?"

I looked up, startled to see we were no longer on the freeway. "No, just go slow," I said, and rooted my handbag for lipstick.

I was struck by how old she sounded on the phone, and faint. I could barely hear her. Then her phrasing. "Our poor Jimmy is dead." In the past he'd been "my poor Jimmy" or "your brother," depending on the news. But never "ours." Also, we were to meet at the graveside, not the church, and there would be no eulogy, only a few words from our former bishop, Ned Shirt.

Our group was so small we almost drove past. Only a sprinkling of dark suits and modest church dresses. I recognized Merrilee Price, my old Sunday School teacher, and Amanda, Jimmy's second wife who'd meant well.

Mom wore a slim black dress with a cream bolero jacket. She eyed my hemline as I approached. Then she looked at me and said, "I'm glad you're here."

"Well . . . of course." Jesus, did she think I wouldn't be?

In the middle of my hello to Bishop Shirt it caught my eye. I parted her cream lapels to see. It was smaller than I remembered, and the genuine gold-filled veneer was not as shiny.

"Do you still have yours?" Mom asked me.

Ten years ago I would have been pleased to see her wear it, twenty years ago, delighted. But now it was just an old locket, something that belonged to the past. Only, she had saved it for all of these years. I had to acknowledge that. Its reappearance was like a green shoot on the stump of a dead tree. Even though you knew it would never grow back like it was, you watered it anyway, and hoped for the best.

"Of course I have it, Mom."

We hugged. Tight and close like Mimi and Deenie, only now I was the taller of us, and the stronger. Then, arm and arm, we approached the cherry casket, and signaled it was time for our Jimmy to be laid to rest.

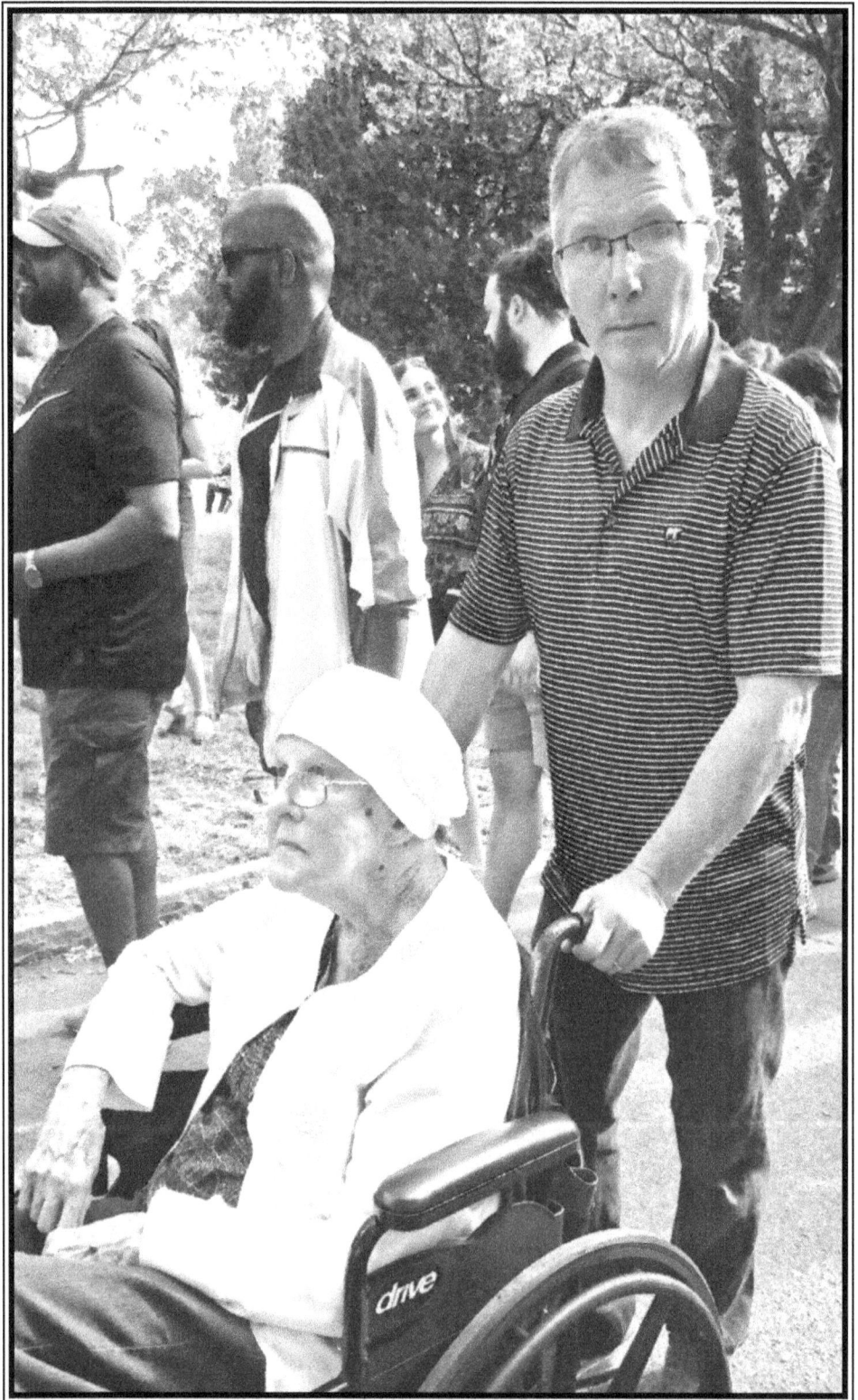

BETH MCKIM

PEACE AND POLITICS

I remember it well. Sitting on the porch of my grandparents' farmhouse in North Alabama on summer evenings. Listening to the crickets chirping, watching the lightning bugs shine, swatting at meddlesome flies that dared to crash the party. I was just a child, so I kept very quiet. Children were to be seen and not heard in those days. But it was worth it to me to hear the group of mostly men talk politics. My grandfather, my dad, various uncles, older cousins, and an occasional neighbor from down the road carried on lively discussions about the world around them. "Will Communism take us all over someday?" Some of the participants, like my grandfather, never left the area at all yet seemed to know an awful lot about what was going on. "Do y'all think a Catholic could be president?" They gave careful thought to all opinions and never raised their voices.

By the time I got to college, I was having the occasional intense political discussion with just my dad around our Lazy Susan dinner table. My two younger siblings had no interest in the subjects. Mom, who only believed and voted for whomever my dad endorsed, sometimes asked, "Beth, how did you get to be so opinionated?" But I also caught certain looks that let me know she silently agreed with some of the things I said, especially about "women's lib." My best memory of these talks was the respect that Dad role-modeled for me. He listened carefully to my point of view, took pauses, and then calmly stated his, even though it might be the opposite of mine. I felt intellectually stimulated by these exchanges and always felt heard. And many of his ideas I carry with me to this day because he calmly expressed them.

I remain today somewhat of a political junkie. I get together often with friends, and the talk turns to causes we believe in and support, government leaders, upcoming elections, and the various candidates. These discussions are usually lively with lots of humor and at times, fear. But the thing I find sad and somewhat alarming is that we only do this with like-minded people. If a member of the group expresses a different opinion, we quickly change the subject, making mental notes to continue at a later date. In other places and situations like gym locker rooms or family get-togethers when people don't change the subject and keep talking, tempers take over and personal insults start to fly.

The biggest challenge I've faced is at home, though. I married a man, who is also a political junkie. He is also one of the kindest, most generous, and intelligent people I know. He just happens to be misguided on some very important matters. Except for social issues, he and I are on the opposite sides of the political fence. In earlier days, he tried desperately to convert me to his conservative way of thinking. I secretly hoped my more liberal views were contagious and he would eventually move to my side. We pictured ourselves a "real life," gender-reversed Mary Matalin-James Carville duo, except we didn't get paid for our insightful commentary, and we actually got angry.

Having both failed miserably at our goals of becoming one politically, we grew weary of the pointless arguments that ensued, resulting in only bitter statements and hurt feelings. By mutual agreement, we now have a *Politics Free* home. Our friends know the rules too so the latest hot topics are carefully avoided in our combined presence. We are an intense couple so our political differences threaten our sense of unity. Instead, my husband and I intensely focus on and are deeply gratified by the things we have in common like exercise and nutrition, our devotion to family and travel, our Labradoodle, Lucy, and most important, our deep and abiding friendship, steady love, and a commitment to support each other through good times and bad.

But I still recall longingly at times the steady, honest ruminations of the men on the porch in Nauvoo, Alabama and later, Dad's pauses, and his careful, earnest tries for mutual understanding as we lingered over dessert at our kitchen table long after other family members had left to do something that interested them.

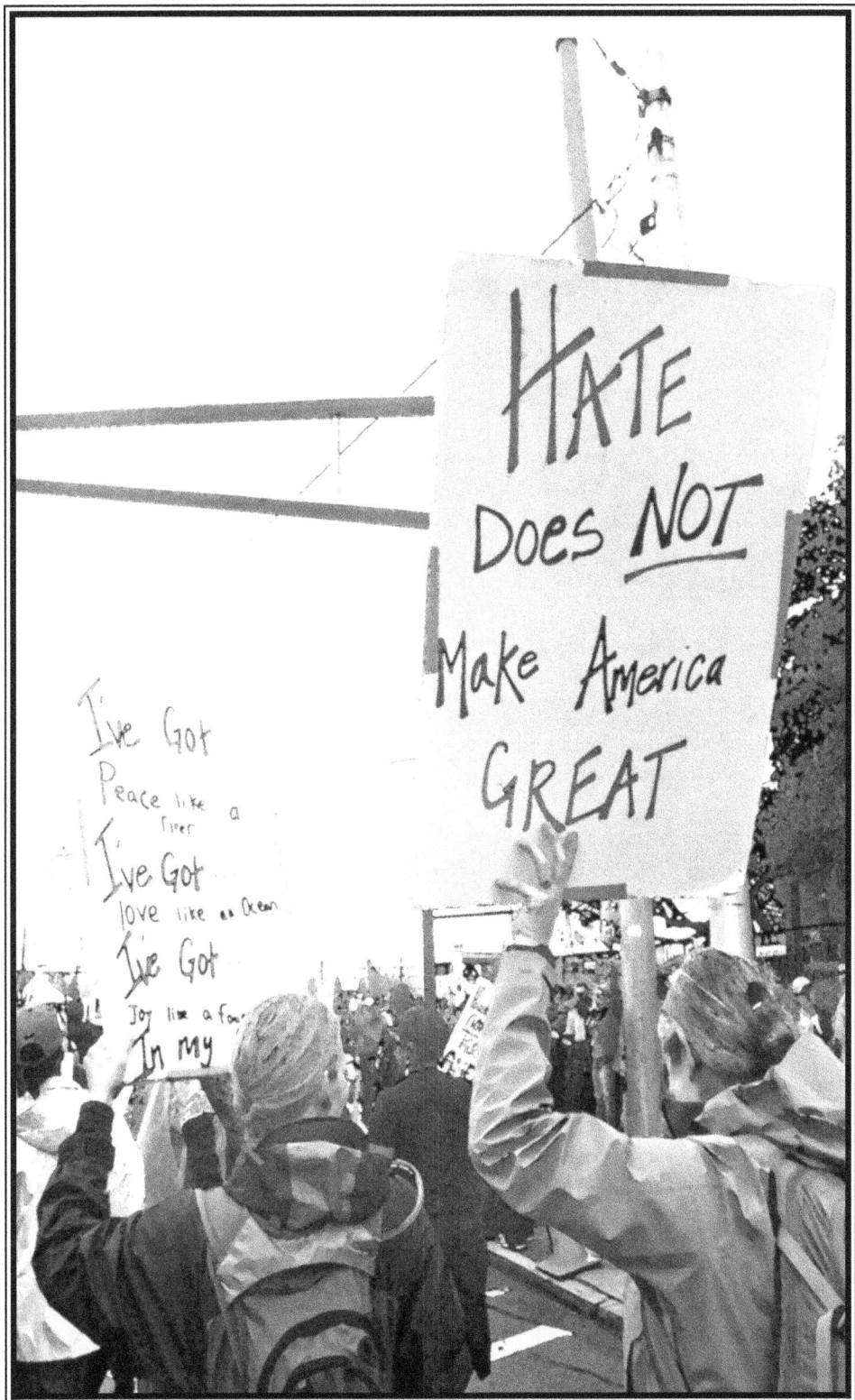

LORI LEVY

I'M RIGHT, YOU'RE WRONG,
BUT TALK TO ME PLEASE

Tight lines now where smiles used to be.
Words erupt, some so raw
they can't be spoken, only screamed.
On and on until neither can hear anything
but blame, like stones pounding a wall.
Both insist they're done with the marriage.

It's a game we all play, stabbing our certainty
in the other's chest, wounding with each thrust
of "I'm right, you're wrong." Still, in the middle of battle,
we find solace in a thread—the way it weaves through
and connects.
We gamble on uncertainty, peeling petals from a daisy:
"loves me, loves me not."

Now, too, we listen for doubt; for a "maybe,"
fresh as clear eyes—or tired as a sigh
hanging in the space between his truth and hers.
Or just a lull in the anger; something to call love
as we fumble for answers to what seems so simple:
"Can't he just . . . Can't she . . ."

The partners, as we watch, grow large as nations
locked in disagreement. Same haggling over terms,
same hope slinking off as blame swaggers in,
threatening to smother what struggles in both:
a child-adult, raising arms to be held,

reaching out.

WHEN ONE SAYS A AND THE OTHER HEARS B

Consider this: that *A* is *A*.
That when she asks, "Why did you do it?"
and he replies, "I don't know,"
hers is the simple "why" of childhood,
that lust to know why the world is as it is;
the insatiable need for answers to questions,
like how something works—or what went wrong
and made it break.
And his, an honest response,
like that of a child who can't remember
an historical date or has no clue
how to solve a problem—or why he jumped
from the top of the slide.

Now consider *B*: a nuance in tone.
Same "why" on her lips,
but he hears "damn you, how could you?"
Sharp and persistent as interrogation—
like peeling an onion, one "why"
leading to another.
And she hears secrets in "I don't know,"
as if it distorts what he's really saying:
"I know, but I won't tell you."

Consider it's neither, that under them both
is a trembling *C*, tender and bruised:
"I need a hug."
"Me too."

So much at stake in the barest words.
A war could erupt on a syllable
or love explode in a pause.

PATRICIA BARONE

THE WIDOW REGRETS

She has secrets.
And so does he,
even though he's dead.
Call it the subtext of love—
the deliberate kiss,
the thoughtful repair
of a wedding ring.

She thinks he has "passed on"
but doesn't like the phrase.
It sounds like he took a test.
On the other side,
surely he sees
her gray heart.

Oh the ways she failed him!
Does he recognize her feigned sleep now?
The way she hid the money for the cradle?
Will she ever stop grieving the times
he wouldn't let her in?

What should she have asked
to elicit more than "okay"
to the hopeless question,
"How are you?"
Was the answer
(a) in hell, or
(b) suffering a day on earth?
He didn't deny he was brave.

She didn't make him promise to visit her
or expect his spirit in a cyclone
of whirling dust or a spout of water.

Maybe he had something to do
with the eclipse, the moon
silencing the birds
and blotting out the sun just long enough
for her to burn the book of shame.

Come back, Stan, come back!
All is forgiven. Am I?

ELEANOR ELLIS

MY CHÁVEZ

When I first saw Hugo Chávez Frías on our tiny TV screen in the evening of November 4, 1992, I was secretly impressed by his dashing appearance. He was impeccable, in a crisp uniform that belied the exertion of the military coup he had just attempted, starting early that morning, and the red beret that later became his signature fashion statement. He took responsibility for the defeat his forces had just experienced, famously declaring to the Venezuelan nation that, *por ahora* (for now) his forces had to stand down. *Por ahora*, of course, turned out to be prescient, because he did indeed return, again and again.

After that night, Chávez was, presumably, sent off to jail, where he remained a folk hero to many Venezuelans, mostly, but not only, the poor, and to me, until he was, controversially, exonerated by then-president Rafael Caldera, on March 26, 1994. After that, he won two presidential elections, rewrote the country's constitution, renamed the country, survived a coup attempt and a general strike, started numerous social programs, created strong ties with left-leaning countries in South and Central America and the Caribbean, confiscated numerous ranches or *fincas*, nationalized several industries, established firm price and currency controls (which led to unbridled corruption), set the country onto a path of destitution, and, finally, died of cancer in 2013. But this is my story, not a brief history of Venezuela, or a biography of Hugo Chávez.

In our living room in a small town in an area called the Alto Mirandinos, located near the capital of Venezuela, Caracas, where we lived for many years, watching the young Colonel Chávez with my Venezuelan husband, fifteen-year-old daughter and eight-year-old son, I felt no premonition about the cataclysmic and finally catastrophic changes this man was going to make in our lives or in the lives of the millions of Venezuelans watching him. No tingle, no warning, and, strangely, no sense of alarm affected me during the long day preceding this television appearance, during which tanks had gone up the stairs to the presidential palace in Caracas and the president had, reportedly, escaped just in time. Rather, I was fascinated by Chávez's charisma and focused on finding food because, as had happened several times before in my long experience living in Venezuela, there was a run on grocery stores, and the shelves were empty.

҉҉҉

Twenty-one years later, I attended Hugo Chávez's funeral. At the edge of the enormous crowd, we stood behind the motorcyclists dressed in their red shirts, as was my husband. *Hasta siempre, Comandante!,* the crowd roared, many with tears rolling down their cheeks. I felt a deep sadness for this forceful, charismatic man who was only a year older than me. My sadness at that point was not due to any admiration for his politics or even because I thought he was a great man or leader, because, by then, I did not. Chávez's overwhelming presence had been a part of my life and the lives of most of the people I knew, since that evening in 1992. A human life, with huge appetites, with hopes and dreams, plans, compassion, rage, fear, and laughter, was over, as were the hopes of the people who believed so passionately in him and in his vision, although most did not realize that.

I felt like an imposter in that crowd. Years before President Chávez's illness and death, my initial excitement about him had been replaced by distrust, fear, and even repugnance. My husband, however, took another trajectory. He found in Chávez the answer to his youthful idealism and deep desire for social equality. He once explained to me that Chávez's hours-long televised speeches, where he danced, and sang, and made jokes and public policy, while his ministers, family members, and general sycophants sat silently admiring him (or at least, not sleeping) were directed towards the president's people, the poor, the dispossessed, the alienated, not the middle class. My daughter shared this passion for social justice and during her young adulthood worked in many social projects initiated by the government.

However, during those first years before the 2002 coup attempt, I was still mystified and a bit enchanted by Hugo Chávez. Although I distrusted and feared his populism, his huge crowds and passionate followers decked out in red T-shirts, I was impressed by his social programs and simply the force of his personality. He won two presidential elections and the country, including our family, entered into a phase of optimism and abundance. The polarization of the country, however, was increasingly evident. I remember, for example, a little boy who I encountered near our country home asking me if I was a *Chavista* or an *Escualida* (literally, a squalid one, a term popularized and oft repeated by the president to refer to those who opposed him).

I was working in an international school, surrounded by colleagues who despised Chávez and his government. I was appalled by the overtly racist and frankly incoherent comments of some of these people and angered by the behavior of the opposition, who were always disrupting traffic and daily life with protests, encouraging violence. As time went on, however, my feelings changed. Following the general strike, the president seemed to radicalize. I felt frightened when names of countries like Iran showed up in speeches, and Venezuela, led by Chávez, seemed to take a clear anti-American stance, and I began to stop myself from speaking English in public. Chávez's speeches seemed more violent and offensive. I watched with misgiving as he took on more and more power, extending indefinitely the presidential term limit.

Looking back, it is astonishing and frightening how much one man (or woman) can affect the lives of millions of people. Of course, Chávez is not the only charismatic leader who has shaped national and international events, but I lived through Chávez's meteoric rise to power and am still experiencing the consequences of his actions, decisions, and policies. Obviously, Chávez did not act alone. His 1992 coup attempt was preceded by numerous events and he was supported by millions of Venezuelans and people from other countries. His appeal was massive—and he found fertile ground because of many factors, which erudite historians and political scientists have written about and will continue to write about for decades and maybe centuries to come. The extremes of poverty and wealth, for example, led people like my husband to desperately want a change in the years preceding Chávez's appearance in the public awareness. I am convinced, because I lived and witnessed this particular moment of history, however, that Chávez was a uniquely powerful voice that captured the imaginations and hearts of many and initiated a process in Venezuela and the region that would not have happened without him.

The years of Chávez's presidency were good years for us, economically. I started a small business in addition to my work at the school, and I was paid in dollars, as the dollar steadily grew in value to the Venezuelan currency (which changed names and value several times). Ultimately, however, the process cost my family dearly in many ways, which my husband still refuses to acknowledge. Due to the rampant inflation and currency controls, both of our retirement incomes and savings accounts were reduced to nothing. We had to sell that beautiful country house in 2013 because of the increased insecurity in the area. The school I worked in gradually became smaller due to the lack of international families moving to Venezuela and, eventually, I left the school and worked in another school in a smaller city in Venezuela, believing mistakenly that our lives would be easier there. Due to the extensive layoffs in the petroleum industry, my husband lost all the contacts he had and could not continue the contract work he had done after his early retirement.

From 2013-2015, we witnessed longer and longer lines in the supermarkets and finally no longer shopped in the city where we lived, rather returned regularly to Caracas, where we could, at that time, more easily find food and other necessities. After those two years, we finally left Venezuela, not because of the situation in the country but because I found an interesting job overseas. Again, I felt no premonitions. We left behind most of our belongings, thinking, like many others, that the shortages would soon be resolved. We lived in Europe for two years, but, finally, after more than forty years, I returned to my native country with my son and husband, and here we are.

Despite this odyssey, I count us lucky. As I sit in our patio on a rare cool and stormy day in Florida, watching a red-headed woodpecker hop up and down the trunk of a palm tree, I think of those millions of Venezuelans who are scavenging for a life in foreign, and often hostile, countries. I also see a strength and resilience in myself that I did not know I possessed. I have developed a flexibility and willingness to compromise for my single-minded purpose: to keep my family together. I am not sure that this is necessarily a laudable goal, nor is it a goal I consciously defined for myself, but it is, looking back, the mission that has guided my actions, particularly over the six years since Chávez died.

My husband continues to believe in the Chávez revolution and to support Chávez's hand-picked, and, to my mind, disastrous successor, Nicolas Maduro. When our diverging opinions first became evident, we had many passionate arguments. One ended with my getting out of the car and angrily stomping up the hill on the side of a busy and dangerous road. There was a moment, because of these and other conflicts, that he went to live in the country home before we sold it. When he was gone, I realized how much I missed the sound of his voice. He returned, and these arguments have all but ceased. He now listens to his biased news on his phone and I listen to mine on my phone, and we avoid the subject as much as possible. The Venezuelan situation is the elephant in the room, one that we have all made an unspoken agreement not to talk about in order to avoid arguments that will rupture our uneasy peace. My husband does his part by maintaining a stolid silence when he encounters anti-Maduro and Chávez opinions, as he often does. We focus on daily living and on what we can agree on.

Of course, these widely divergent opinions have taken a toll and are a constant reminder of how politics can divide rather than unite people. Through my desire to maintain the unity of my family, I learned how much I demonize people because of their opinions and have come to understand how radically different opinions can result in similar actions. Violence is violence and kindness is kindness, regardless of the beliefs that motivate the actions. When I think of the human and political situation in Venezuela, I am infuriated by the infant mortality, the universal extreme poverty, the massive emigration, the political persecutions: all the human suffering caused by the callous, corrupt, and self-serving actions of Maduro and his regime, as well as the governments that support him. From the little that we speak about this, I know, however, that my husband sees in Maduro a courageous warrior who is fighting valiantly and so far victoriously for the survival of Chávez's dreams, his government, and social justice against the powerful attacks of the United States. I will never convince him to think differently, and he will never change my mind, either. We concur, however, in our desire to help individual Venezuelans as much as we can and in our search for peaceful coexistence. Like all families, perhaps, we are a small boat that remains almost miraculously afloat in the stormy waters of political and social turmoil.

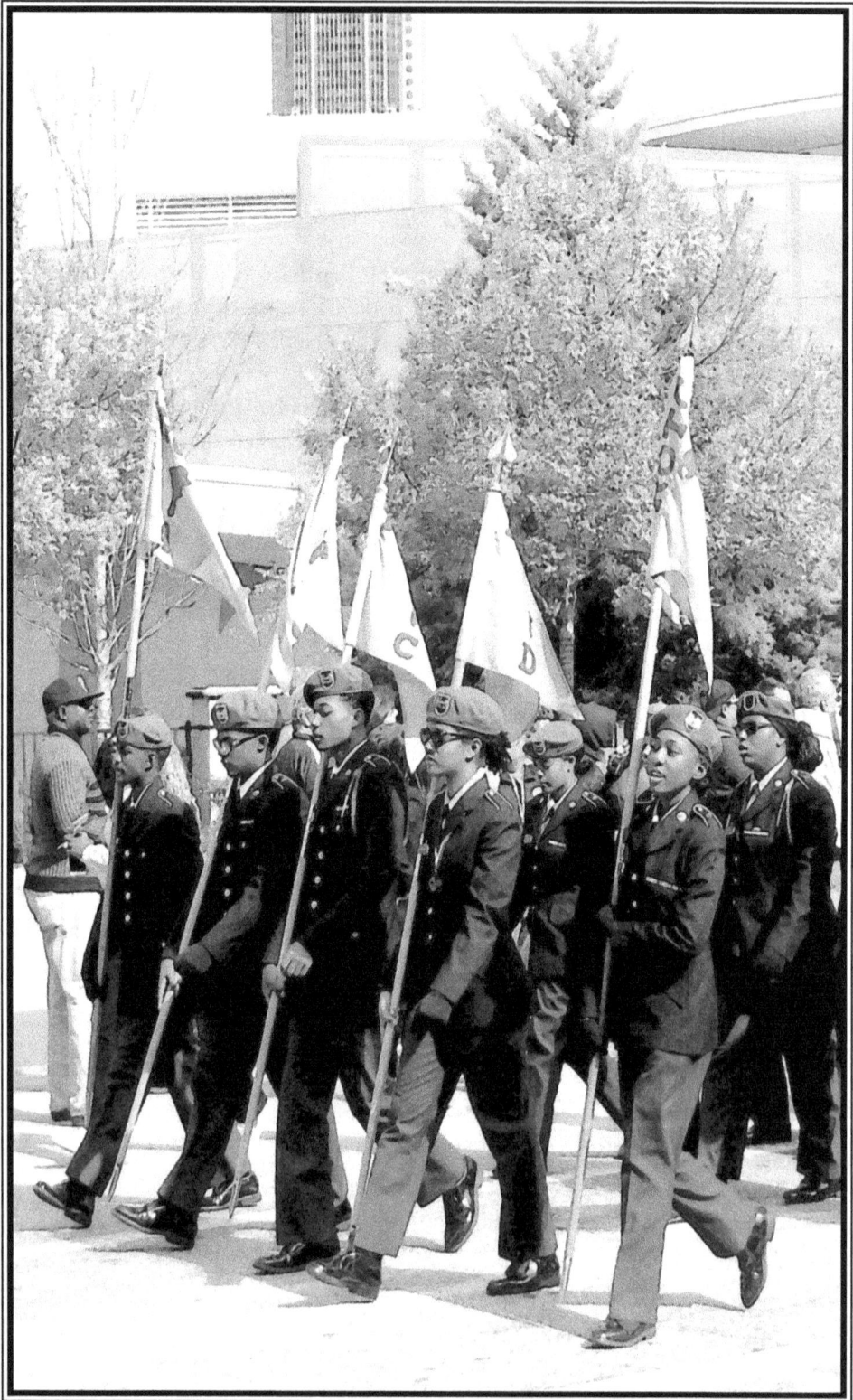

VIII. COMMON CHORD

ELIZABETH BRULÉ FARRELL

TO BUILD A DRIVEWAY

They gesture back and forth in animated
conversation I cannot hear from the window.

Since the trees were cut down to build
a driveway they are finally meeting

as though for the first time, stopping
when taking out the trash, or clipping

the bushes at the edge of the curb.
There is always something to discuss.

To see them stand together in the space
we thought would be just for cars is beautiful.

LORETTA DIANE WALKER

A SUDDEN BLAZE
(After Tony Hoagland)

Love is not a victory march
it's a cold and it's a broken hallelujah—Leonard Cohen

Meet me where the sun loiters on hinge of sky,
where light has licked away layers of bushy darkness.

Meet me between the cold-faced house
with broken hallelujahs spilling out the windows,
between the hungry boy's bony bare shoulders,
between the memories of my ancestors' chained ankles.

Meet me between Kobani and Bodrum's beach,
between anonymous faces floating in a fruitless channel
where the wings of twelve wounded birds stop flapping
in a dark wet limb of space.

Meet me between the slashed syllables
of in/ex/plic/a/ble

where shirts have no bones or flesh
to lift them from muddied water,
where refugees are treated like bombs.

Meet me under the fruitless mulberry
where the neon 7-11 sign sings its electronic song,
where the blue-eyed lady with the torn velvet coat
rants about kisses with violence, poverty, vigilance
between the flame and feather inked on her thigh.

MONICA MISCHE

ON THE PATH TO TOTALITY

When I was six, I saw an astronomy show at the Hayden Plan-etarium. I watched in amazement as the sun dipped below the horizon, the room darkened, and across the domed ceiling appeared a multitude of stars, first faint, then glimmering, then bright. Finally, sweeping and lu-minous against this wondrous all, emerged a magnificent cloud of light— the Milky Way. My heart froze, and with wavering breath, I whispered to my sister, "Is this really true?" As if to answer, a voice reverberated: "These stars surround us, even during the day. We cannot see them because our sun blocks them out. At night, our city lights do the same. But the stars are there—always—whether we see them or not."

Forty-four years later, I'm sitting cross-legged on a bench in the grand hall of Washington DC's Union Station. It's late August. I'm wearing faded jeans and a sleeveless blouse, searching through my backpack crammed with almonds, apples, power bars, an extra pair of shoes, looking for a folded slip of paper, my ticket to Charleston. High above me, in windowed recesses of the gold-leaf vaulted ceiling, stand statues of Roman Legionnaires. Adorned with capes and crested helmets, bare legs apart, muscular arms balancing em-blazoned shields, these concrete figures stare unfaltering ahead, safeguarding travelers for over a century. Legend says the shields were not part of the sculp-tor's original design. Included for modesty's sake, they conceal any semblance of the soldiers' manhood, protecting the eyes of passengers below.

A man approaches, offering me a brochure. He invites me in his soft West African accent to attend Bible study at his church. He asks if I know Jesus, if I believe. The man's intense gaze impels me to reply. Jumbling my words, I attempt to relay some undefined spiritual sensibility—respect for Christianity, reverence for the mysteries of the universe. The man nods, but my own speech falters. I stare at my shoes. Thanking him for his time, I zip up my pack and head for the trains.

I join a crowd at the departures display and discover my train will be late. I have time for coffee. Behind me is Starbucks, and positioned unexpectedly against the shop's exterior is a statue of A. Philip Randolph, civil rights organizer and leader of the Brotherhood of Sleeping Car Porters. I touch the celebratory plaque and see Randolph arising from the black granite slab, his carved face ennobled, his left arm reaching out, imploring the passing throng, who seem unmindful of his presence.

I order my coffee and sit down to read. A friend has given me this copy of the *Post* for its coverage of tomorrow's celestial event. Called the Great American Eclipse, it will be the first time in a century that an eclipse will be visible from all forty-eight states. The band of totality will stretch from Oregon to South Carolina. Millions of people are travelling to experience two minutes of darkness. I am one of them. That is why I am here.

> *As my sisters and I were growing up, my mom displayed in our apartment images of the earth as seen from space. She taped one poster to our pantry door: the iconic photo taken by the Apollo 11 astronauts after lift-off. I'd contemplate our planet emerging from darkness—white clouds whirling over the red brown deserts of the Arabian Peninsula, over the green jungles of central Africa, over the deep blues of the Atlantic. I'd imagine how it must feel to encounter that view, what bodily sensations, what primal stirring of the spirit and heart.*

I fold my newspaper and walk to the gate. Next to me stands a woman of about my age, dressed crisply in white. "Are you going to see the eclipse?" she asks. A doctor from Charleston, she has spent her birthday weekend in DC with her best friend from London. They had visited the new Museum of African American History. She describes her journey from the dusky cellar to the airier upper floors, from the Middle Passage to the present day. "Of course, I've studied history" she confides, "But actually seeing it—that makes an impact." She converses with her friend, then turns back to me. "Where will you be staying in Charleston?" I explain, shyly, that I don't have a place, or a plan either; I'll be there for just one day, arriving pre-dawn tomorrow and departing on the night train. I have not thought beyond that. "Well, it will be an adventure anyway," she smiles reassuringly and pats my arm.

The loudspeaker announces our boarding and the crowd is ushered down a lengthy platform. As I board, a dark hand touches my shoulder, and I turn to face the friendly doctor. "Here's my number. Call me if you run into trouble in Charleston, if you get lost or hungry or need a place to sleep. Anything." I thank her. She turns left, I turn right, as directed. I cross the threshold and enter the dimly-lit car.

The passenger by the window is lean and balding, with a trim grey beard and shining eyes. His face is beaming: "Are you going to see the eclipse?" I nod and smile and sit beside him. He tells me his name is Henry. In DC for a chemistry convention, he is, like me, escaping academic duties for a thirty-six-hour celestial tour. With a lurch, the train leaves the station. It trudges through the shadowlands of industrial DC then picks up speed and heads south into the deepening night. Passengers settle in for the journey, headphones positioned, seats reclined, jackets draped as blankets. Henry, though, enjoys conversation, and I soon discover that he teaches at the small midwestern college that my parents attended. For thirty years, he has lived in the town my father was raised in, near the farmlands and quarries where my immigrant ancestors labored, where my great-grandfather was killed in a mining explosion, where my sisters and I visited relatives every year. Henry's town is my lineage, my blood.

We share other commonalities too: children passionately engaged in instrumental music; favorite radio programs; long distance running. In fact, Henry met his wife while running. He explains how he had observed her for several days, beautiful, jogging around his same lake-path, following his same orbit. Ever the scientist, he calculated his morning entrance to the lake to match her circuit. It turns out they ran naturally at the same pace! Some months later, Henry proposed to his wife—in darkness—during an eclipse. Henry describes the experience of totality, how when the moon rises to meet the sun and begins to shield her face, the air changes, the temperature drops, breezes pick up, shadows change shape. When the sun is fully covered, a red glow appears around the horizon. Then a hush, sometimes a rush of birds. A golden halo surrounds the now-black moon and then just before totality, a diamond bursts from one side. Henry explains the science of these phenomena; I just retain the feeling.

Our conversation slows, then ceases. Henry joins the other passengers in sleep. I watch the passing shadows and listen to the rumble, the low, mournful whistle of the train. Another passenger is awake, a young man dressed in a skull-cap and a white dress shirt; the fringes of his prayer shawl hang below his waist. He walks to the front of our car, which is the front of the train. There is nothing beyond but the engine. He presses his hands against the door's dark pane, and gazes into the night. He stands there for some minutes, arms raised, bearing his weight, eyes fixed forward, contemplating—something.

> *When the sun is shining on the surface at a very shallow angle, the craters cast long shadows and the Moon's surface seems very inhospitable, forbidding, almost. I did not sense any great invitation on the part of the Moon for us to come into its domain. I sensed more almost a hostile place, a scary place.*—Michael Collins, on his Apollo 11 voyage into space (In the Shadow of the Moon (2007))

When I awaken, it's almost 5 a.m. Passengers are stirring. Henry has been tracking the weather. He's worried about a batch of storms due to hit Charleston mid-afternoon, the time of the eclipse. What an upset that would be. Henry decides to drive from Charleston to Columbia, where the skies are predicted to be clear. He had reserved a car just in case. Would I like to travel with him? As I have no plans beyond stepping off this train, as I am feeling less certain about exploring an unfamiliar city on my own, and as I feel that Henry and I have made some connection, I accept his offer.

5:45 a.m. North Charleston depot is pulsating. Most eclipsers are heading south, down to the harbor, or east to the ocean, to watch the event in the presence of water, in the presence of a multitude. Some arrange to share Ubers or to breakfast at the same cafe. But Henry and I must travel north to rent the car. As we climb into our Uber, I see the kind doctor and her British friend across the lot. They call to me, inquiring. I smile and tell them that I'm going to Columbia with a scientist. They laugh and shake their heads, speeding us on our journey.

Our driver's name is Kairi. His dreadlocks reach the middle of his back and his brilliant smile covers half his face. Only twenty-three, he's lived in Charleston all his life. He loves it, but lots of people moving in, he says. It's getting expensive. Hard to make rent. He'd love to travel the world someday. For now, though, he's content driving Uber. He meets lots of interesting people, some of them crazy. If only he had a video camera, he grins. We ask if he plans to see the eclipse. Definitely. He wouldn't miss it. He'll stop the car if needed and watch it from the road. Henry asks about a diner near the car rental. Oh, that's a good place, Kairi affirms, great chicken and waffles. We pull into the restaurant lot, dark and empty, save for the towering, orange signpost: Early Bird Diner. And under that an illuminated message: Happy Solar Eclipse! Kairi wishes us luck, flashes a million-dollar smile, and drives off to greet his next customer. The diner won't open for another forty minutes, but there's a bench outside the door. Henry and I put down our packs. We stand for some moments in the darkness. Then we sit and watch the sun rise.

Some things attract while they blind us. And some things are too beautiful, too powerful, too devastating to see, except in rarefied moments of light: the soul of another; the suffering of another; and the fragile connectors that lie in between.

Inside, we delight in the aroma of coffee and pancakes, in the chalkboard menu, the colorful countertops and stools. This seems like the real thing. We decide to order in a Southern vein, but even so, Henry stays on the healthy side, with grits and fresh fruit. I go full-throttle: bacon, fried eggs, home fries, melted cheese on thick slices of buttered toast. We discuss our teaching, our students, our academic interests. Henry tells about bringing environmental issues into his chemistry classes. He describes a video clip that shows ordinarily invisible carbon emissions as purple smoke, that when people see, they believe. A soft voice filters across our booth's partition. Just two feet away, a woman gazes at us, her golden eyes majestic against her deep bronze skin. She is slender, wears her greying hair in a bun, and dons a wrinkled blue cardigan. Melodically, she whispers: "Might you spare a dollar please for a coke?" Henry glances at me and then asks: "How would you like a real breakfast? Something warm?" She smiles fully and reveals a missing tooth. The woman nods, accepts our offering, then slips to the counter, where she sits, hands clasped, head down, waiting to be served.

Outside the diner, Henry confirms our Uber pickup. Eyes a-twinkle, he whispers: "Our driver's name is Ulysses!" We wonder what this cool-headed, long-enduring, man of craft will be like. The car arrives, its windows tinted dark. Inside, we encounter the rhythms of electric blues guitar and the scent of cedar. A gravelly voice welcomes us, and as we settle into the plush seats, we see a heavy-set man with a close-shaven head. He asks if we are ready for the eclipse, if we have our protective glasses. He points to his pair, strapped to his dashboard. We assure him that we are set, but he cautions, "Are you sure yours are real? They're out there selling fake ones. Can you believe it? Fake ones! What people do for money. The lies they tell! They don't care if someone gets hurt. They don't care if children get blinded. Criminal conscience. Criminal." We arrive at the car rental. As we disembark, his deep voice carries: "Be careful. Don't trust everyone. Watch out for your eyes."

Our sun is 93 million miles away. Its light spreads to earth in just eight minutes. We can see the sun's radiation in the photosphere, but we cannot see its outermost layers. The cooler light of the chromosphere and the intense heat of the corona are visible only during a total eclipse, the former as a scarlet rim, the latter as beams of light shooting royally outward. When the moon shields the sun, we can safely view this majestic display. But when the photospheric light pierces through again, it threatens blindness; we must don shades. And we miss the beauty, the power, of what lies beyond.

We are driving west on I-26, blue skies with just a few white clouds. Neither of us has visited Columbia. Most of what I know is from middle-school American history—that it is the capital of South Carolina, that it was a backdrop to the secession, that at the war's end, large swaths burned to the ground. But I also recall two summers ago Governor Nikki Haley standing on the Statehouse steps announcing the removal of the confederate flag after nine church-goers were murdered by a white supremacist. This is what I remember. This is what sticks. Yet something in me yearns for a brighter vision. From my phone, I read aloud to Henry: Columbia sits on the confluence of three rivers. It has beautiful bridges, an award-winning library, a renaissance of artists . . . it is nicknamed the City of Dreams.

Passing Orangeburg, the terrain is less flat—long stretches of hills, embraced by red earth and pines, the sun higher in the sky. Henry tells me about his kids, about how, now, in their late-twenties, they are carving their paths in the world. I tell him about my three oldest, now in college. We reflect how this stage of parenthood requires a different type of nurturing, a different type of care. We watch our children journey from afar. They may look to us for guidance, and we assure them as we can, but they are now their own captains, and we know in our hearts that there is no safe roadway. Everyone travels in darkness. The best we can do is to shine what light we have and help our loved-ones do the same. Maybe, together, that is enough.

Last fall, I went camping with my ten-year-old son in the foothills of the Shenandoah. It was just he and I in our small orange tent, and it was raining. He'd brought a toad into his sleeping bag and we read aloud by flashlight. When the rain stopped, we let the toad free. Above us, through the dark dripping branches, the misty moon shone, startlingly bright. My son commented that his brother and his sisters, away in other states, might also be looking at the moon, and that it was the same moon, and that their separate gazes were like gossamer threads, connected by the moon to each other.

We pass highway signs for Cayce. Henry tells me about an op-ed he published in his city's paper—about climate change and how for democracy to work, citizens must not blind themselves to science, how we must look truth squarely in the eye. Indeed, Henry plans to meet with his congressman tomorrow in DC; they'll discuss this face-to-face. He will skip part of his conference to do so because this is imperative. I think about how I've lived near DC for twenty-six years and never have I done such a thing. What must it be like to have that vision, that strength of purpose, that courage to come out of the shadows and show you are here.

We are entering Columbia. It is beautiful indeed. We drive through the red-bricked downtown, and park on a side street. The sun is almost overhead. Our walk to the visitor's center leaves us red-faced and parched. Inside, we are greeted by two boys, ages nine or ten, faces aglow, exuberantly jumping. Are we here for the eclipse? Do we want a free poster? Do we need a pair of glasses? We can have one for free! They escort us into an office, dancing all the way. We meet a woman with sparkling eyes and caramel colored skin, her hair gathered loosely atop her head—as in a Boticelli portrait. The mother of one of the boys, she wears, like them, a powder blue T-shirt: "Total Eclipse Weekend, Columbia, SC." She offers cold water and gives us parking passes to a secret lot, better than the meters. We ask what we might see in the hours before the eclipse. "Oh, most people enjoy the Statehouse, the grounds are gorgeous. You can stay cool inside and even take a tour." On a map, she marks the path to follow. For eclipse viewing afterwards, she suggests Finlay Park. There's a lake and places to sit in the shade. Before we depart, Henry and I each buy a T-shirt from the spirited boys. They jump higher than ever.

I remember another portrait from my childhood apartment—a photo taken by the Apollo 8 astronauts. The grey lunar surface looms in the foreground, and arising farther back is the brilliant earth, illuminated like a fragile glass globe. When the astronauts saw that vision, instinctively, in veneration, they read aloud over the NASA airwaves the opening lines from the book of Genesis.

The Statehouse grounds are picturesque, with towering palmettos and lush magnolias. Flowerbeds are stationed throughout, as are dozens of memo-rials. We stroll past a Revolutionary War gravestone, past monuments for the Mexican and Spanish American Wars, past the site of the original Statehouse, which burned to the ground in 1865. Greeting visitors at the main entrance is a statue of George Washington. He stands serene, gazing toward the sky. The bottom of his walking cane is missing—destroyed, the plaque recounts, by retreating Union soldiers. Behind him, the edifice rises: white granite steps, soaring Corinthian columns, a great bronze dome that glitters in the sun. We walk east, past the African American memorial—past the iron-gated slave ship packed with bodies, past the twelve sculpted panels of suffering and strength. We find an open entrance. Inside, the air is cool. I touch the marble walls and gaze at the arched ceiling. White columns melt into clouds. I join Henry by the staircase where a small crowd has gathered for a tour, ready to hear the voices of history.

> *I was thirteen the year the first Cosmos series came out. My family watched it every Sunday on our black and white TV. The knob was bro-ken, so we used pliers to turn it. We'd lie on our braided rug with popcorn and apples and watch Carl Sagan in his turtleneck and corduroy blazer speak about lofty astronomical concepts in words we could understand. He relayed the mysteries of time dilation, supernovas, cosmic rays, the multiverse, black holes, the potentialities for extra-terrestrial life. I felt entranced by his ebullience, by his unabashed awe of the universe. One segment, especially, seized my imagination: the cosmic calendar. If the fif-teen billion-years since the Big Bang were condensed into twelve months, our sun and earth would not appear until September, and the whole of human existence would flicker forth in just the last seconds of the last minute of December 31. I found it soul shuddering—this glimpse into the catacombs of time.*

The Senate chambers are blue and gold, with ornate carvings. Paintings of revered South Carolinians cover the walls; the newest is State Senator Clem-enta Pinckney, one of the nine murdered in Charleston's Emanuel Church. Our guide speaks in a honeyed voice. Her auburn hair casts a warm glow. She explains the legislative process, the old-fashioned voice voting system, and the ceremony in which a white-gloved sergeant-of-arms lays the state swords across a massive mahogany desk. Asked about the gender breakdown of the Senate, our guide laments that only four members are women. Henry's eyes gleam, then he whispers: "What if most were women? Would they still have the sword ceremony? Maybe they would think of a different tradition for honoring democracy."

Henry takes a call about his congressional meeting tomorrow. I follow the tour to the library conference room. Books line the wall, and an ancient chandelier hangs in the center, encircled by an iron balcony and black spiral stairs. Next, comes the House chamber. Portraits of Jefferson, Reagan, FDR, and Robert E Lee gaze at each other from interfacing walls. Our tour ends in the lobby, surrounded by plush chairs, marble statuary, oil paintings, and stained glass. Light pours in from a breathtaking dome. As our guide shares Statehouse stories, I stare at the concentric circles radiating light—blue, grey, cream, and gold. Henry rejoins the gathering: "What did I miss?" I whisper that apparently this dome is fake. It is not the one visible from the outside. Housed within a larger dome, it's offset, to appear more symmetrical, more pleasing from within. There must be a grander view outside of it that no one ever sees.

> *The biggest joy was on the way home. In my cockpit window, every two minutes: The Earth, the Moon, the Sun, and the whole 360-degree panorama of the heavens. And that was a powerful, overwhelming experience. And suddenly I realized that the molecules of my body, and the molecules of the spacecraft, the molecules in the body of my partners, were prototyped, manufactured in some ancient generation of stars. And that was an overwhelming sense of oneness.*—Edgar D. Mitchell, Apollo 14 Astronaut (In the Shadow of the Moon (2007))

Shielding our eyes, we cross the street to Finlay Park, where a silver lake dances with sequins of light. Seeking refuge from the heat on the shaded steps of a stone amphitheater, we can still see the sky amid the trees, the moon just inches now from the beating sun. Henry weaves among other eclipsers, chatting with a physicist from a local university. I sit and take mental pictures—of the sun and moon, but mainly of the people. To my left, three students from India set up a tripod camera. With upward glances, they debate apertures and focal points. Behind me, an elderly couple sits knee-to-knee, heads tilted to the same degree, silently gazing at the sky. To my right, a family with children tests their home-spun pinhole camera, made from a Cheerios box; the youngest, in beaded braids, dances on one foot. Immediately below me a yellow-haired, sunburned woman holds hands with a shirtless African-American man. Both are gaunt. She appears older than he, and when she smiles at him,

I see she is missing most of her teeth.

> *I remember in college learning about the Pythagorean "music of the spheres," the idea that our planets, perfectly aligned in their orbits, create heavenly tunes, beautiful melodies inaudible on earth. Perhaps humans, in the presence of an eclipse, become likewise perfectly aligned, and the music released can be felt, if not heard—experienced as either a laud or a lament.*

The moon is now encroaching the sun, the overlap forming a small black jewel. Far below me, against the lake, a man in a Rastafarian hat forms a striking silhouette. He gazes at the sun, leaning backward, his arms outstretched in a welcoming "Y." Henry and I descend the amphitheater steps. The black jewel covers nearly half the sun, altering the shapes of shadows below. Leaves appear on the sidewalk as hundreds of miniature crescent moons.

We make our way to the lawn and find our place amid a sea of dark glasses. Two college students sit behind us. Henry explains to them the physics of the moment, and they stare from under their baseball caps at the splendor in the sky. In front of us, younger boys toss a football. Laughing, jostling, familiar, their soft tackles seem tender, like passing embraces. Near the lake, a man dances, loose limbed, in slow-motion, turning, spinning, one arm overhead; his yellow shirt is unbuttoned and floats in the breeze. He sings as he dances, his voice low and mournful, then higher, more piercing, transmuting finally into a primeval cry.

Just a sliver of sunlight remains. The temperature drops. The light begins to fade. I lie on the cool grass and extend my arms, palms to the ground. I feel like I am hugging the earth. Henry lies down too. The sky is a deepening violet, and the horizon glows like gold. I don't hear birds, but I feel in my bones a reverberation, perhaps the collective rising of our breath.

Moments away from totality, the sun is covered by a near-perfect disc. Now, darkness. The boys stop playing football. They fall to the ground. They do not speak.

A ring of yellow erupts from behind the black jewel, and then the flash of light, the diamond ring! There is a communal gasp, an involuntary voicing, a bodily response. "Take off your glasses!" Henry exclaims. We face with naked eyes the force of the sun (which is our past), the starkness of the moon (which is our future), and we stare into the fleeting juncture of the two.

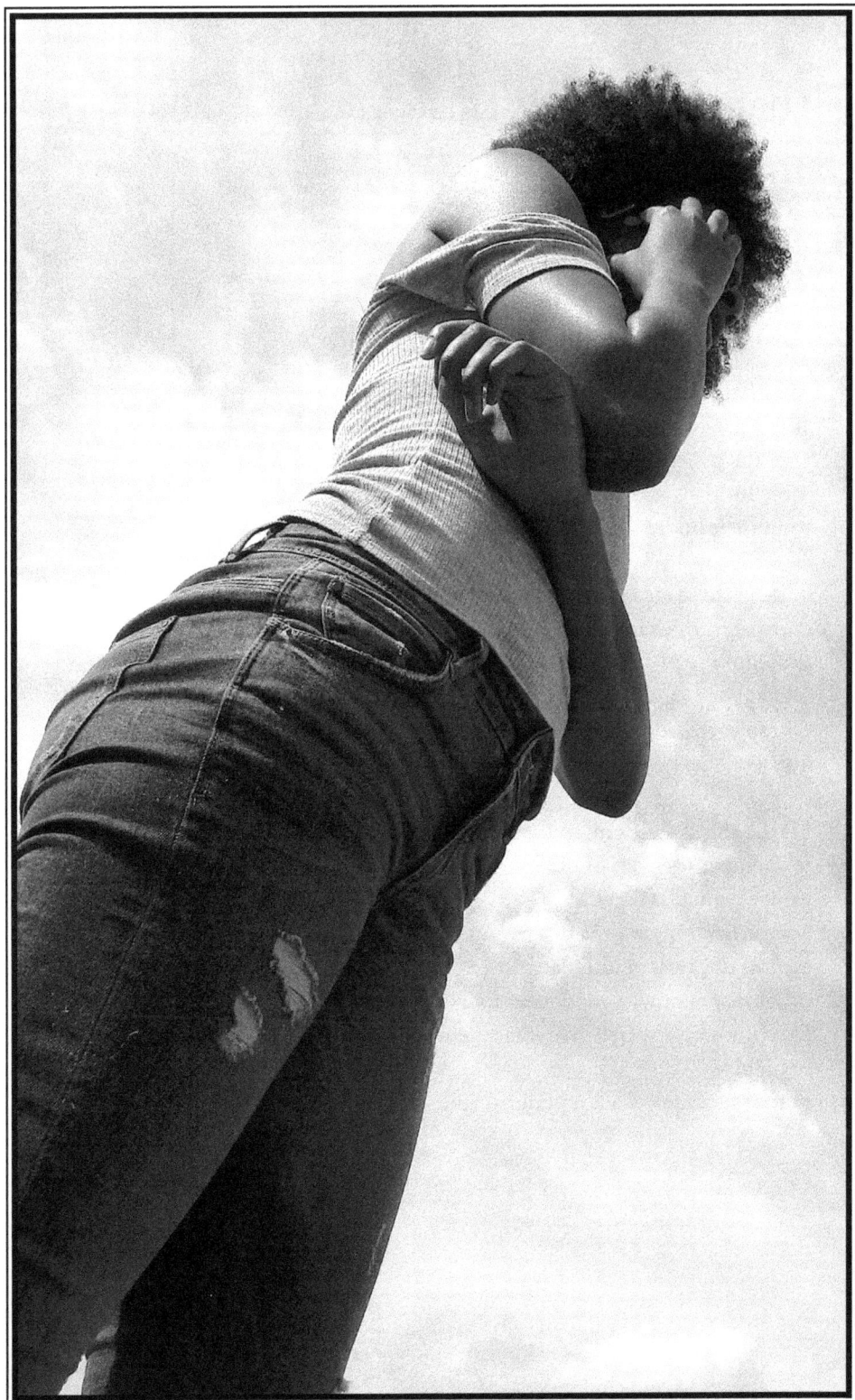

LORETTA DIANE WALKER

THE FIRST JUNETEENTH

After freedom rose from the fire,
after the news rolled onto Galveston beach,
after the winding plantation exodus,
some freed slaves sloughed their tattered clothes
from their bodies like dead skin.

Tossing those rags into the Gulf of Mexico,
they paced the banks, witnessed their past
sink into the swamp of the unknown.
Did anyone salvage a cuff, a pocket, a yoke?
Oh, to eavesdrop on gossiping gar
overshadowed by cotton.

Maybe this is freedom—
to shoulder the pain of others,
gather remnants together.
Maybe freedom is a river
each of us can step into daily,
rid ourselves of what no longer fits.
Maybe water is to sacrifice what silence is
to dignity—
so the vulnerable walk without shame.

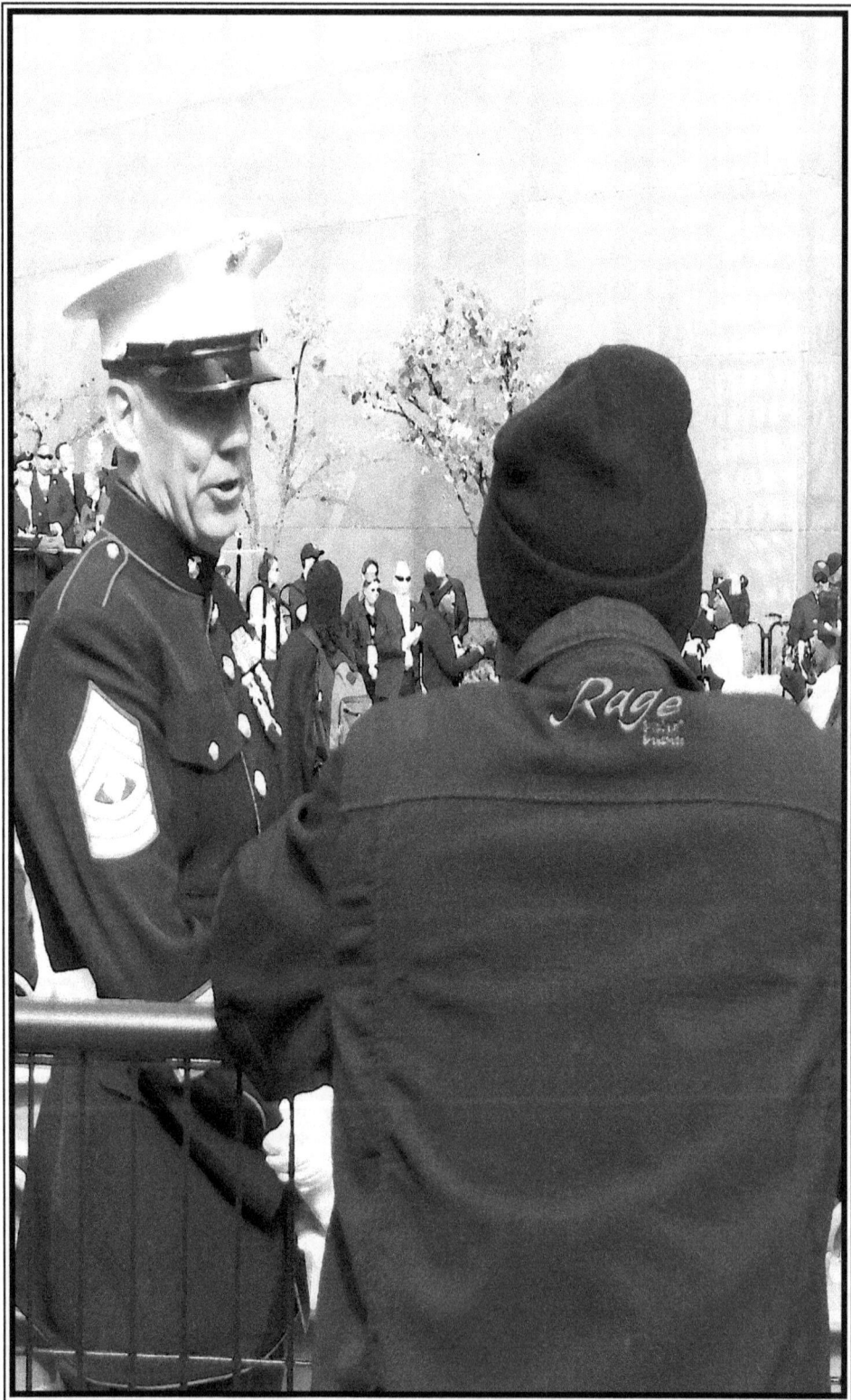

CODA

CHARLES D. BROCKETT

CENTRIFUGAL FORCES: SHARING RESPONSIBILITY

Many of us worry about the increasing polarization that is fraying our social fabric, that is overwhelming our common chord. Few examples make the basis of this concern more vivid than the following three:

Back in 1960 about five percent of Democrats and Republicans when surveyed objected to the idea of their children marrying across partisan lines. By 2010 the percentage soared to 33 for Democrats and 46 for Republicans (Illing 2017).

Chart 1 shows the increasing percentage of people across the decades viewing the other party "very unfavorably." And remember that the starting point of 1994 was no year of warm fuzzy feelings about the opposition—that was the year when Newt Gingrich's Contract with America swept Republicans into control of the House of Representatives. Note too that in 2014 respondents were also queried about seeing the other party "as a threat to the nation's well-being."

Chart 1. Viewing the Other Party Very Unfavorably & as a Threat (%)

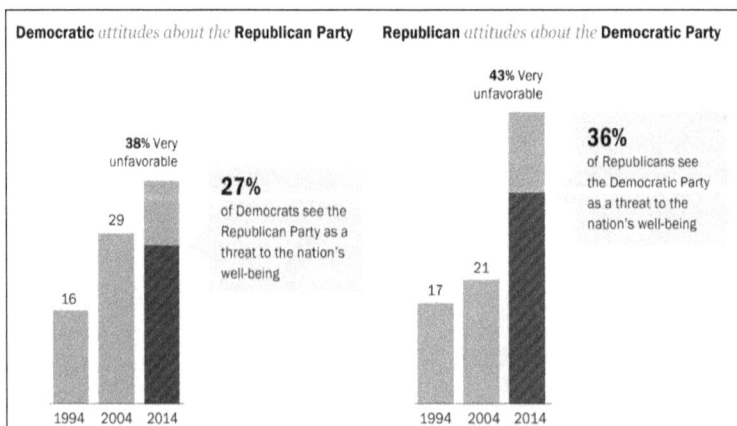

Source: Dimock et al., 2014: 7 (Pew Research Center).

Finally, and most astonishing to me, a recent survey found around 42 percent of both Democrats and Republicans viewing the adherents of the other party as "downright evil" (Edsall 2019).

Presented with such alarming findings it is easy to lose sight of the many important areas where broad consensus remains. A good set of questions relevant to recreating our common chord from one of the most respected research organizations asks, "What is important in being American?" and then presents respondents with eight possible characteristics. We still are united on the following dimensions (Sides 2017):

    respect American political institutions & laws (94% agree);
    have American citizenship (92% agree);
    be of European heritage or descent (only 20% agree).

For two other characteristics broad agreement remains among the general public but differences between the parties are more notable (15% and 20% partisan differences):

    accept diverse racial & religious backgrounds (88% agree);
    be able to speak English (85% agree).

For the final three characteristics there is significant disagreement between us (although the partisan differences are no greater than with the set above except for the last of the three for which the gap between the parties is 26%):

    live in America for most on one's life (58%);
    born in America (56% agree);
    be Christian (42% agree).

A similar mix of consensus and disagreement was found in another recent study comparing voters in the 2012 and 2016 presidential elections on twelve different issues and attitudes (Drutman 2017). On some there were virtually no differences between people who voted Democrat in both elections and those who voted Republican in both:

politics is a rigged game	3% partisan difference
importance of Social Security/Medicare	4%
foreign trade	7%

But on other important issues and attitudes there were major disagreements between the two sets of voters:

government intervention	46% difference
economic inequality	39%
moral issues	35%
immigration	32%
Muslims	31%
black people	30%

Our polarization even extends to the kind of communities in which we prefer to live. As Chart 2 shows, 77% of consistently liberal respondents in a 2014 survey prefer smaller houses where you can walk to schools, stores, and restaurants. However, 75% of consistently conservative respondents would rather have larger houses several miles away from such amenities.

Chart 2. Community Type Preference by Ideology (%)

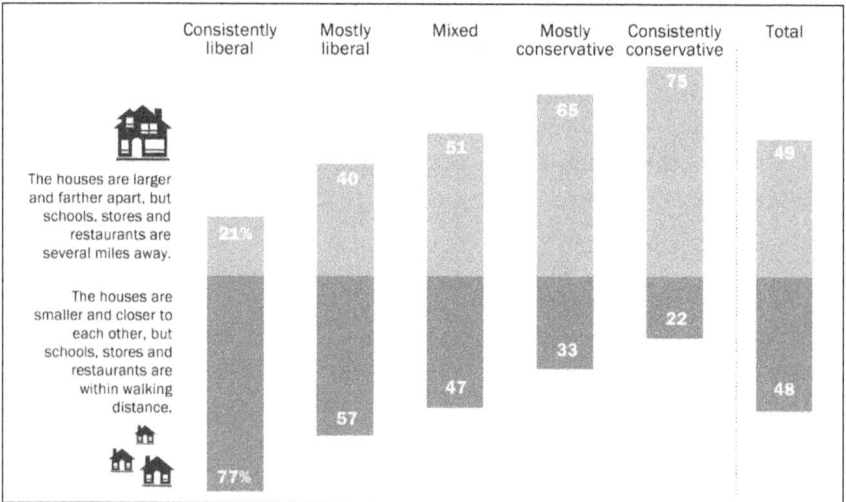

Source: Dimock et al., 2014: 13 (Pew Research Center).

What To Do

Many concerned people have been offering solutions to this pernicious polarization—many are good remedies for re-creating our common chord. My own contribution will be in three areas: first, the *direction of attitude change*; second, the deep *personality basis* for many of our attitudes; and third, *structural sources* of polarization. Awareness of these, I believe, calls all of us to be more understanding and tolerant of those with whom we disagree.

To be clear, to call for more understanding and tolerance of those with whom we disagree is not a call for us to back away from advocating and acting on our own commitments. It is unlikely that the people on the other side are going to stop. After all, intense polarization is most pronounced among those who are most interested, best informed, and most politically active (Abramowitz 2013). The point is, we can disagree without demonizing.

It is also important to acknowledge the situation undoubtedly feels different if you are a member of a minority that has been historically oppressed. Even so, if you are, then you have probably also participated in many discussions about the pragmatic imperatives inherent in being a member of an outnumbered group.

The Direction of Attitude Change

When it looks like social norms and public policy over time have been moving *away* from our core beliefs and attitudes, we are in a different situation than if that change has been *in* our preferred direction. In the second situation our struggle over political differences presents the *possibility* of loss but in the first situation we *are losing*. Shouldn't the person benefitting from the direction of change be more understanding than the one who is losing?

For issues and attitudes where polarization has been increasing, it is also important to identify the underlying dynamics. If the significance of an issue is increasing for one or both sides then polarization increases as well. This dynamic is undoubtedly important to our current situation but is difficult to measure and will not be further addressed here.

A second dynamic is opinion change, the major subject of the rest of this section. Are both sides changing but in opposing directions or is the polarization largely caused by changes from just one side? If change is largely one-sided, is it not reasonable to expect the changing side to make more effort to be understanding of the more constant side?

Let's be more concrete. Take the issue of homosexuality. Back in 1973 we were polarized on whether homosexuals should be allowed to teach—an even 48%/48% split. This was not a partisan divide as Democrats and Republicans had essentially the same scores in 1973—as they still did in 2018 when now 88% agreed. [The change was too late, though, for my brother who was fired from his teaching position in Southern California in the mid-1980s for precisely this reason when he made the mistake of confiding to his principal (and friend up to then) about his sexuality.]

On this issue the more relevant source of division in attitudes has been education. As Chart 3 shows, the gap between the highest and lowest education categories was immense. Though it has closed over time, still in 2018 there was a 27% spread between people with college educations and those who have not completed high school. Age has been another important source of division, though, not as strongly (and not shown on this chart). The difference between 18-34 year olds and people 65+ was cut in half from 1973 to 2018 down to 17%.

Chart 3. Should Homosexuals Be Allowed to Teach by Education (% yes)

Source: Tom W. Smith, et al. *General Social Surveys, 1972-2018* [machine readable data file]. Sponsored by National Science Foundation. Chicago: NORC, 2018. GSS Data Explorer output created by Charles Brockett July 2019.

The more pressing issue in recent years concerning homosexuality has been the right to marry. Here the pattern has been different. Originally there was only a minor partisan difference. Indeed, as recently as 2008 there was only a 12 point split among those who strongly agreed [see Chart 4]. However, by 2018 that had grown to a 26% difference. It is important to note that the strongly agree sentiment has been increasing among Republicans, but just not as fast as among Democrats—strong agreement for Republicans in 2018 had reached essentially the same level as among Democrats just eight years before.

Chart 4. Gay Marriage by Party (% strongly agree)

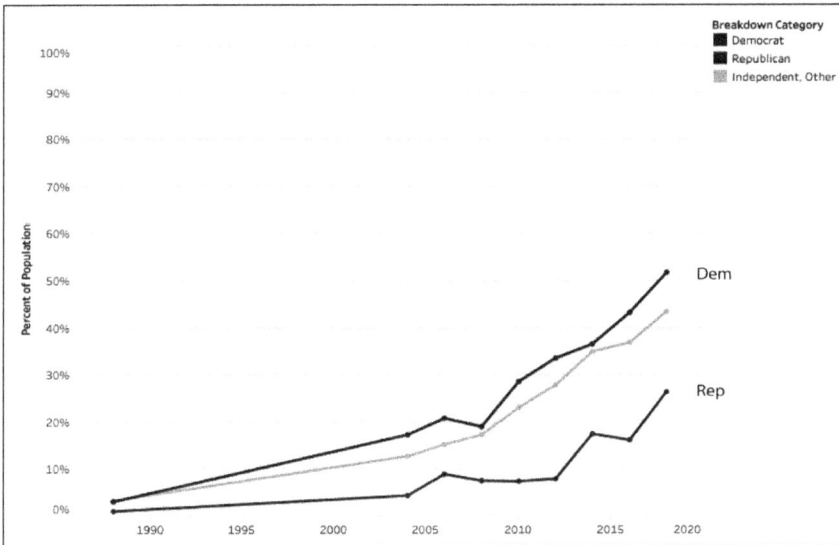

Source: Tom W. Smith, et al. *General Social Surveys, 1972-2018* [machine readable data file]. Sponsored by National Science Foundation. Chicago: NORC, 2018. GSS Data Explorer output created by Charles Brockett July 2019.

One of the most contentious issues of the past half-century has been access to abortion. It is hard to read the trends for Chart 5 through 1990 but that is the point: there were no meaningful differences between the two parties up until then on agreement that abortion should be available to women for any reason. Since then a partisan divide has opened and grown, especially in the most recent years. The 35% difference in 2018 resulted from changes for both parties, but especially by Democrats.

Chart 5. Abortion for any Reason by Political Party (% yes)

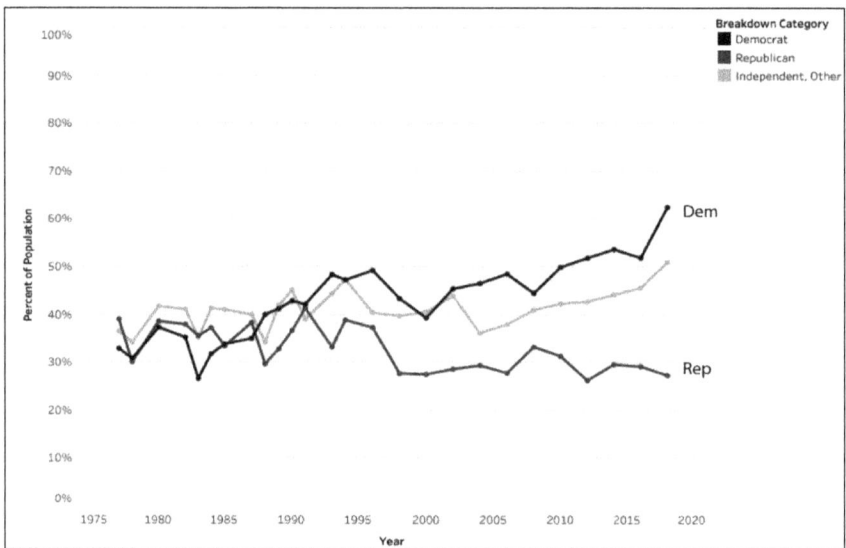

Source: Tom W. Smith, et al. *General Social Surveys, 1972-2018* [machine readable data file]. Sponsored by National Science Foundation. Chicago: NORC, 2018. GSS Data Explorer output created by Charles Brockett July 2019.

For many who oppose abortion it is fundamentally a religious issue. A relevant question concerns confidence in the existence of God [Chart 6]. As recently as 2000, Republicans and Democrats were indistinguishable on the question with a little over two-thirds expressing no doubts about God's existence. In 2018, Republicans had not changed but Democrat's belief had dropped 20 points, half of that decline over just the prior four years.

Chart 6. Confidence in Existence of God by Political Party (% yes)

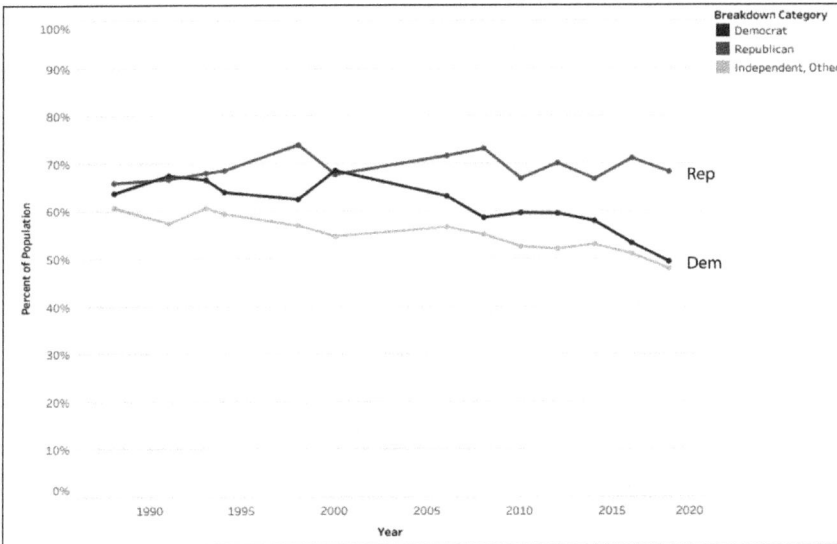

Source: Tom W. Smith, et al. *General Social Surveys, 1972-2018* [machine readable data file]. Sponsored by National Science Foundation. Chicago: NORC, 2018. GSS Data Explorer output created by Charles Brockett July 2019.

Another area of increasing polarization is environmental policy. When the issue is the Greenhouse Effect (that is climate change or global warming), we find again most change on the part of Democrats [Chart 7]. The percentage of Democrats agreeing that the "Greenhouse Effect is extremely dangerous" more than doubled from 2000 to 2018 while there was little change for Republicans. Consequently, what had been a 2 to 1 difference between them doubled to 4 to 1.

Chart 7. Greenhouse Effect Is Extremely Dangerous by Political Party (%)

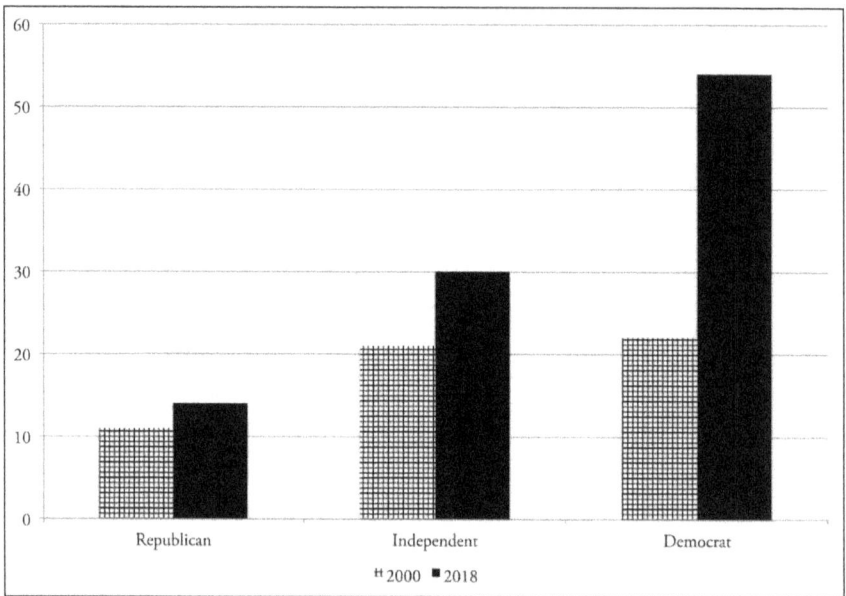

Source: Tom W. Smith, et al. *General Social Surveys, 1972-2018* [machine readable data file]. Sponsored by National Science Foundation. Chicago: NORC, 2018. GSS Data Explorer output created by Charles Brockett July 2019.

A different pattern appears for national spending on improving and protecting the environment for which we have data over a longer period. As Chart 8 illustrates, back in 1990 there was essentially no difference between the two parties among those believing too little was spent on the environment. This was the year of bipartisan support for renewal and expansion of the landmark Clean Air Act during the presidency of George H. W. Bush. Democrat agreement that too little is spent has since climbed up to the present but not as much as Republican agreement has dropped, accounting for the preponderance of the current 36 point partisan split.

Chart 8. Spending on Environmental Protection Too Little by Party (%)

Source: Tom W. Smith, et al. *General Social Surveys, 1972-2018* [machine readable data file]. Sponsored by National Science Foundation. Chicago: NORC, 2018. GSS Data Explorer output created by Charles Brockett July 2019.

Some of our most significant polarization is around race-related issues and in at least some aspects it is increasing. For example, on the question of "national spending on improving the conditions of blacks," as Chart 9 shows, there has always been a split between partisans (although in 1976 only of 4%). In 2018, 33% of Republicans agreed that this spending was too little, only 10 points less than what Democrats had said in 2012 but a substantial 40 point difference with the Democrats' high point across the chart in 2018 at 73% agreement.

Chart 9. Spending on Improving Condition of Blacks Too Little by Party (5)

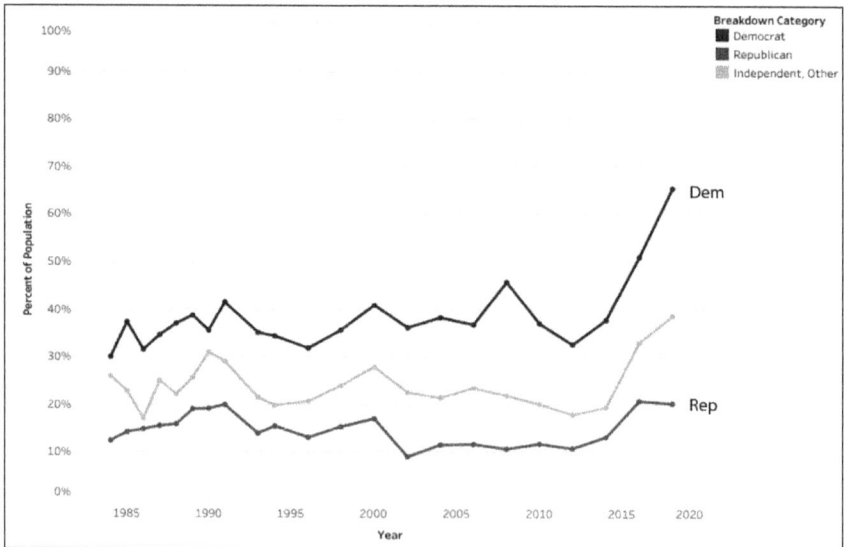

Source: Tom W. Smith, et al. *General Social Surveys, 1972-2018* [machine readable data file]. Sponsored by National Science Foundation. Chicago: NORC, 2018. GSS Data Explorer output created by Charles Brockett July 2019.

This polarization between the parties in 2018 was even greater than that between the races. Not shown on the chart, white agreement that there was too little spending was 46%, for blacks it was 79%. Hispanic respondents usually have not varied too much from whites on this question, in fact in 2018 their scores were the same. This is also one issue where the amount of education has not made much difference.

Our two major political parties, of course, are very broad umbrellas. A recent study breaks us down further into seven "tribes" from the way we cluster together based on a variety of different characteristics. Chart 10 shows the substantial differences between these groups on two race-related questions. While 64% of whites agree that "many people nowadays are too sensitive about things to do with race," for Devoted Conservatives agreement jumps all the way to 94%. Similarly, while 67% of African Americans agree that "many people nowadays don't take racism seriously enough," for Progressive Activists (who are largely white) that agreement jumps to 92%.

Chart 10. Sensitivity to Racism by "Tribe" and by Race (%)

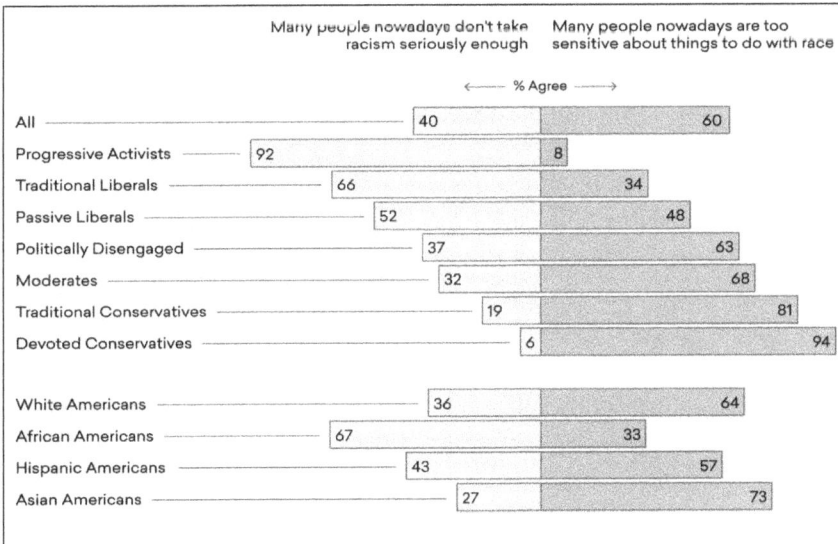

	Many people nowadays don't take racism seriously enough	Many people nowadays are too sensitive about things to do with race
	←——— % Agree ———→	
All	40	60
Progressive Activists	92	8
Traditional Liberals	66	34
Passive Liberals	52	48
Politically Disengaged	37	63
Moderates	32	68
Traditional Conservatives	19	81
Devoted Conservatives	6	94
White Americans	36	64
African Americans	67	33
Hispanic Americans	43	57
Asian Americans	27	73

Source: Hawkins 2018: 97.

The identification of these seven different tribes comes from a 2018 study titled *Hidden Tribes: A Study of America's Polarized Landscape*. What the report shows is that acute polarization in area after area is driven by the extremes (who also tend to be the most politically active). It is the middle groups, what the report calls "the exhausted majority," that are more likely to support more listening and compromising, to believe that we all have "more in common" (which is the name of the sponsoring organization).

David Brooks nicely summarized the difference between the two extreme tribes in his *New York Times* column. The Devoted Conservatives (6% of the total), he wrote, have a Hobbesian narrative. For them, "It's a dangerous world. Life is nasty, brutish and short. We need strict values and strong authority to keep us safe." In contrast, the Progressive Activists (8% of the total) have a Rousseauian worldview. To them, "People may be inherently good, but the hierarchical structures of society are awful. The structures of inequality and oppression have to be dismantled" (Brooks 2018).

Attitudes and Personality

Increasingly researchers are discovering that in many cases our attitudes are less a result of our intentional thinking issues through and more a product of our inherent personality. And, increasingly these differences are related to the divisions between our two major political parties, at least for non-Hispanic whites.

Think back, for example, to Chart 2 about your preferred community type. How could there be such vast difference between conservatives and liberals? Researchers have keyed in on "openness" as an especially relevant core dimension of our personalities. People who score high on this dimension value independence, self-direction, and novelty; accordingly, for them diversity is a core value. People who score low on this dimension instead value social cohesion, certainty, and security; accordingly they are more likely to adhere to traditional values and norms (Edsall 2018).

Other researchers have focused on the related dimension of "authoritarianism," which is best measured by answers to questions related to child-rearing attitudes. People scoring high on this dimension are more likely to feel society is fragile and under attack. They support authorities who will defend the traditional order. People scoring low on this dimension, in contrast, are more likely to value personal autonomy, fairness, and diversity over social conformity (Hetherington and Weiler 2009). [More recently, the same authors in their cleverly titled book *Prius or Pickup?* (2018) have switched the labels to "fixed" and "fluid".]

So here is our dilemma. Increasingly our political divisions are aligning with these core personality differences (and there are others too identified by other researchers). This intensifies the feeling of these differences because they cut so deeply into us, making tolerance and compromise all the more difficult. Yet, because they do emanate from who we are, shouldn't all of us be more understanding of those with whom we differ?

Structural Sources—Inequality

Whether we are Republican or Democrat, black or white, female or male, poor or rich, young or old, or well educated or not, in significant ways our polarization is often driven by deeper forces for which we are ultimately responsible collectively but seldom individually. Of these, two in particular stand out to me.

The first is profit-driven polarization. The point is simple. It is often made, but seldom better than this: "Tribal outrage works as a business model for social media, cable television and talk radio" (Hawkins 2018: 136). We have come a long way from the days when media discourse was dominated by three middle-of-the-road television networks. The changes have been fast, they have been substantial, and we have yet to find our way.

During the same time that profit-motivated narrowcasting based on fear and anger has been pushing polarization, the United States also has been growing more unequal by measure after measure. I will not attempt to document that here [see my essay in our prior anthology, *Crossing Class*]. Rather, it is the connection between inequality and polarization that needs to be addressed.

Polarization in the U.S. House of Representative has been growing, responding to many forces both internal to Congress as well as those operating throughout society. One of those has been inequality in society at large—notice the tight correlation between the two in Chart 11 on the next page. Why might polarization and inequality be connected?

Substantial evidence from around the world clearly establishes the strong links between inequality and all types of adverse social consequences. The most unequal of the industrial democracies, the United States performs the worst among its cohort on indices both of child well-being and of health and social problems. Compared to our peer countries, we have higher rates of mental illness, homicide, and incarceration, and lower rates of social mobility (Wilkinson and Pickett 2019: 242).

What researchers are finding goes beyond the obvious conclusion that the least advantaged in the United States are worse off than their counterparts in the other industrial democracies. They are finding that we all are worse off on measures important to the health of our society. There is a direct connection between greater inequality and people being less willing to help others, be that neighbors, the elderly, immigrants, or the sick and disabled (p. 65).

While that finding applies to both the poor and the rich, other studies are finding more anti-social behavior on the part of the better off—that is, the better off in the most unequal countries but not in the most equal. For example, drivers of expensive cars in the United States are less likely to yield to pedestrians than are drivers of cheaper cars and are less likely to wait their turn at intersections (p. 89).

Chart 11. Polarization in House of Representatives & U.S. Income Inequality

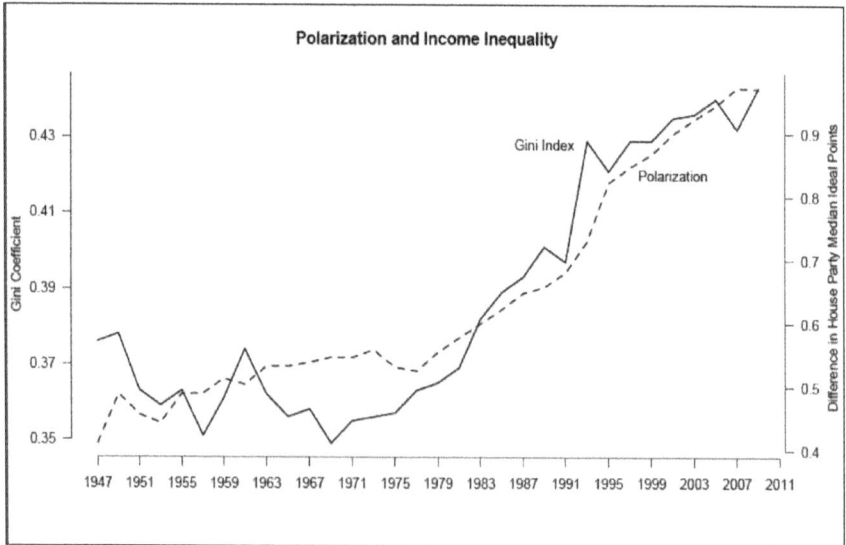

Source: Nolan McCarty, Keith Poole, and Howard Rosenthal, reprinted in Payne 2017: 111.

In an experimental money-making game where all players actually perform equally well, some are told that they had performed better than the rest. In a subsequent discussion when there were disagreements, these supposed higher performers were the most likely to see the other players as more biased, more incompetent and less rational. Given the opportunity to set the rules for subsequent players of the game, those who thought they had performed less well wanted everyone to have an equal vote but the "higher performers" wanted to eliminate the votes of those who disagreed with them (Payne 2017: 109-110).

Inequality contributes to social segmentation and creates greater distance between people. It contributes to declining social cohesion, social trust, and understanding across group lines. It fosters a sense of entitlement on the part of higher status people. Inequality promotes polarization. Inequality is increasing in the United States.

Conclusion

Re-creating our common chord is the responsibility of all of us. But I hope that those of us who have benefitted more from our societal divisions are comfortable taking on more of that responsibility than we would expect from those who have benefitted less. I am thinking first of those divisions that have been long-lasting, reinforced by power imbalances, with race being the most salient. I am thinking too of issues that matter deeply to us where the direction of change has clearly been in the direction favored by some, but away from that held by others.

Finally, and to conclude on a positive note . . . even if it does come from the world of . . . rats. White rats raised only with rats of their color will try to help a trapped white rat but not a black rat (and the same for black rats). A black rat raised with white rats will try to help a trapped white rat but not a black rat (and conversely). A rat raised with both black and white rats will try to help rats of either color. To make the conclusion explicit, "it is not the rat's color that determines which type of rat it will show empathy for, but the social context in which it was raised" (Garrett 2018).

References

Alan Abramowitz. 2013. *The Polarized Public? Why Our Government Is So Dysfunctional.* New York: Pearson.

David Brooks, "The Rich White Civil War," *The New York Times*, October 15, 2018. Web. Web.

Michael Dimock, et al. *Political Polarization in the American Public*, Pew Research Center, June 12, 2014. Web.

Lee Drutman, *Political Divisions in 2016 and Beyond.* Democracy Fund Voter Study Group Report, 2017. Web.

Thomas B. Edsall, "No Hate Left Behind," *The New York Times,* March 13, 2019).

Thomas B. Edsall, "The Contract With Authoritarianism," *The New York Times,* April 5, 2018.

Henry James Garrett, "The Kernel of Human (or Rodent) Kindness," *The New York Times*, December 28, 2018. Web.

Stephen Hawkins, et al., *Hidden Tribes: A Study of America's Polarized Landscape.* New York: More in Common, 2018. Web.

Marc J. Hetherington and Jonathan Daniel Weiler. *Authoritarianism and Polarization in American Politics.* New York: Cambridge University Press, 2009.

Marc J. Hetherington and Jonathan Weiler. *Prius or Pickup?: How the Answers to Four Simple Questions Explain America's Great Divide.* Boston: Houghton Mifflin Harcourt, 2018.

Sean Illing, "20 of America's top political scientists gathered to discuss our democracy. They're scared," *Vox*, October 13, 2017. Web.

Keith Payne. *The Broken Ladder: How Inequality Affects the Way We Think, Live, and Die.* New York: Viking Press, 2017.

John Sides, Race, *Religion, and Immigration in 2016.* Democracy Fund Voter Study Group Report, 2017. Web.

Richard Wilkinson and Kate Pickett. *The Inner Level: How More Equal Societies Reduce Stress, Restore Sanity and Improve Everyone's Well-Being.* New York: Penguin Press, 2019.

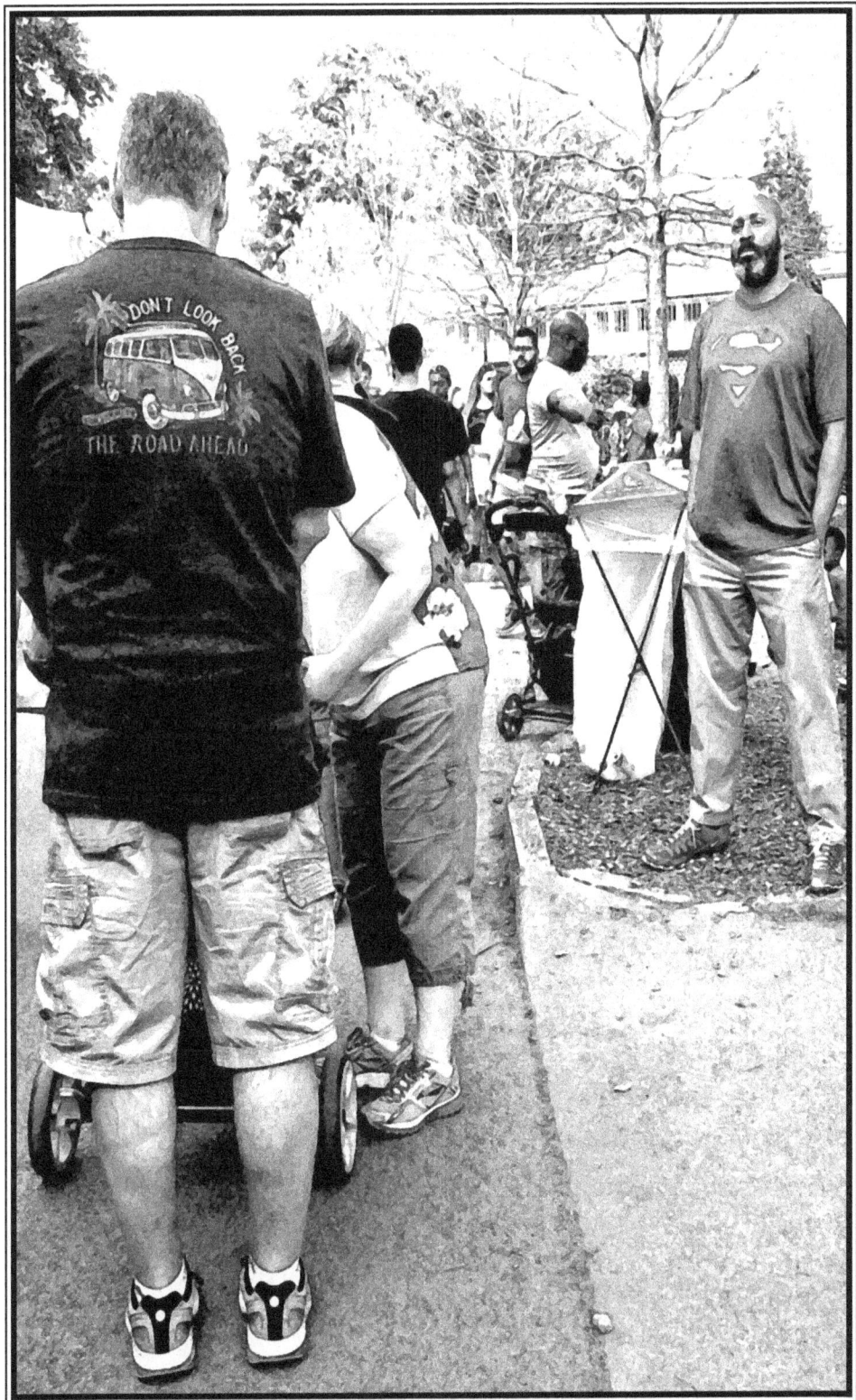

ACKNOWLEDGMENTS

Patricia Barone's "The Widow Regrets" previously appeared in her collection, *Your Funny, Funny Face* (Blue Light Press, 2018).

Maryah Converse's "The Peace of Iraq's Mothers" was first published in *New Madrid* (Winter 2017) and reprinted in *DoveTales* (May 2017).

Gaye D. Holman's "Power, Respect, and the Convict Code" is from her book *Decades Behind Bars: A 20-Year Conversation with Men in America's Prisons* © 2017, used by permission of McFarland & Company, Inc., Box 611, Jefferson NC 28640.

Daniel M. Jaffe's "A Blessing on Your Head" has been previously published in *The Forward* as well as in his *The Genealogy of Understanding* (Lethe Press).

Laurie Klein previously published "Eucharist" in *Relief* (2008) and "Hunger's Plate of Secrets" in *Ancient Paths* (2015) and *Where The Sky Opens* (2015).

Murali Kamma's "The Visitor and the Neighbor" previously appeared in a different version ("A Welcome Guest") in *AIM: America's Intercultural Magazine* and in his recent short story collection, *Not Native* (Wising Up Press).

Marianne Peel previously published "Accusation" in *Apricity Magazine* (January 2017).

Ada Jill Schneider's "Near the Nancy A. Messinger Trail" appeared earlier in her collection *This Once-Only World* (Pear Tree Press, 2015).

Patty Somlo has previously published "A Nightly Interruption" in *The Sand Hill Review* and *Wilderness House Literary,* as well as in her collection, *From Here to There and Other Stories* (Paraguas Books, 2010; Adelaide Books, 2019).

J. J. Steinfeld's "The Chess Master" has appeared in slightly different form in his collections *The Apostate's Tattoo* (1983) and *Dancing at the Club Holocaust* (1993), both by Ragweed Press.

Loretta Diane Walker has previously published "Black History Month" in *Voices de la Luna*, "A Sudden Blaze" in *Red Review Review,* "First Juneteenth" in *WordFest Anthology*, and "Stiletto" in her collection *Word Ghetto* (2011).

A special acknowledgement to Ms. Julia Blair who wrote us so movingly about how, sharing this re-creating our common chord journey with Heather in small conversations over several years, she was able to find reconciliation with a close friend of thirty years even in these polarizing times. The benefit has been mutual. Special thanks as well to Geanie Jones and Joy Pope-Alandete for the several long honest and heartfelt discussions we had in the spring of 2017 that helped shaped this Common Chord listening project.

We could not do what we do without the able, loyal, and amazingly generous assistance of the Wising Up Press editorial group: Kerry Langan, Michele Markarian, Kathleen Housley, and Murali Kamma.

Photographs by Heather Tosteson. One is based on a photo generously shared by Bonni Chalkin.

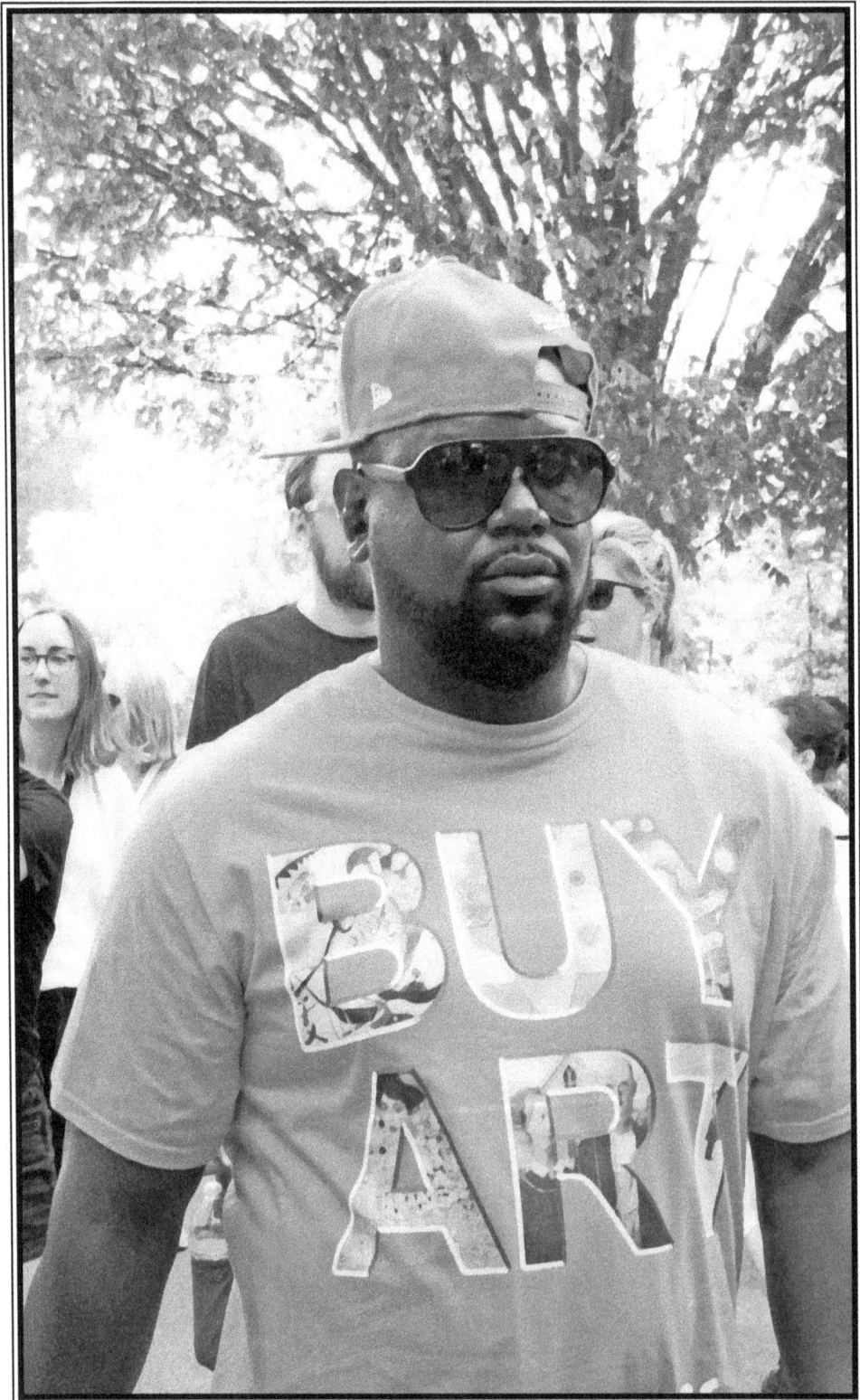

CONTRIBUTORS

Thomas Abakah is student at Montgomery College, where he is pursuing a degree in Building Trades. He also works, previously at UPS, and now as an Uber driver. In his spare time, he likes to read books and hang out with his friends. He has been published in the *Washington Post Sunday Magazine*. This is his first full-length essay publication.

Eve Mills Allen (also published under Eve Mills Nash) is a mental health therapist in Moncton, New Brunswick, Canada. She worked in the field of journalism for more than thirty years. In 2002, her memoir, *Little White Squaw: A White Woman's Story of Abuse, Addiction and Reconciliation*, coauthored by Kenneth J. Harvey, was published by Beech Holme Publishing in Vancouver.

David Arango-Dimitrijevic (pseudonym) was born and raised in the Midwest, the son of Colombian and Serbian immigrant parents. He has taught high school English for over twenty years, taking occasional leaves of absence to live and work in South America, East Africa, and the UK.

Donna Banta has published three novels. Her short fiction has appeared in various literary journals and story collections including, *Latter-Gay Saints: An Anthology of Gay Mormon Fiction* (Lethe Press). She lives with her husband in San Francisco where they tend a small, unwieldy garden.

Patricia Barone's fourth book, *Your Funny, Funny Face,* was published by Blue Light Press, as was *The Scent of Water.* New Rivers Press released *The Wind* and *Handmade Paper.* She has received a Loft-McKnight Award of Distinction, a Lake Superior Contemporary Writers Award, and a Minnesota State Arts Board Career Opportunity Grant, a workshop with the Irish poet Eavan Boland.

Judy Catterton is a retired lawyer who currently teaches memoir and essay writing for the Rehoboth Beach Writers' Guild. She was named the 2015 Emerging Artist Fellow for non-fiction by the Delaware Division of the Arts. Her essays have appeared in literary journals, including: *Alligator/Juniper* (contest finalist); *Noise* (Grand Prize); *Chatter House Press* (third prize) and *The Ravens' Perch*.

Bonni Chalkin is a Reiki master, intuitive healer, possibility coach, artist, and writer. Her writing has been published in *And Then* magazine, and her paintings have been sold around the world. She is passionate about helping people embrace their own power and follow their intuition.

Susan K. Chernilo writes stories and novels about social change and the people who make it happen, and has published excerpts in previous Wising Up anthologies. She holds degrees in English and Psychology but feels she's learned more from the communities of people she's worked with. She's taught ESL to adult immigrants in the Boston area for almost twenty years.

Maryah Converse was a Peace Corps educator in Jordan, 2004-2006. Her publications include *From Sac, Silk Road Review, Newfound, The Matador Review*, and *Michigan Quarterly Review*. Maryah teaches Arabic. She is currently working on an essay collection, *Lessons from the Desert*, and her Peace Corps memoir, *Trusted With Their Children*.

Eleanor Ellis lived in Venezuela for forty years. During that time, she raised a family, learned Spanish, obtained a master's degree in a Venezuelan university and worked as an educator. She lived through Hugo Chávez's rise to power, his presidency, and his funeral, as well as the first two years of his hand-picked successor, Nicolas Maduro.

S. J. Engstrom teaches Humanities and Creative Writing at College of Lake County in Illinois. She writes essays focusing on her life experience. She also wrote and produced a one-act play, *Pieces,* based on the history of women pioneer quilters. Her work has appeared in *The Willow Review* and *Ethics & Action* (Unitarian Universalist Association).

Elizabeth Brulé Farrell has published poems in *The Awakenings Review, The Healing Muse, Watch My Rising, Earth's Daughters, Common Ground Review, Paterson Literary Review, Poetry East, Spillway, The Perch,* and more. Forthcoming work will appear in *Comstock Review* and *Except for Love.* She believes the greatest gift we can offer is the ability to listen to each other.

Judith Gille's essays have appeared in *The New York Times* Modern Love column, in anthologies, magazines and online literary journals. Her memoir *The View from Casa Chepitos: A Journey Beyond the Border* won Writer's Digest's Grand Prize. Her second book, *Todavía México,* will be forthcoming in early 2020. Judith divides her time between Seattle and San Miguel de Allende.

Stephanie Hart is the author of *Mirror Mirror: A Collection of Memoirs and Stories* (And Then Press, 2012). Her essays and short stories have appeared in anthologies, including *The Kindness of Strangers* (Wishing Up Press, 2016) and literary magazines, *The Sun,* and *Jewish Currents.* She is currently at work on a novel about the McCarthy era.

J.O. Haselhoef is a social artist who writes and travels. She spent the last twenty years developing communities in multi-cultural environments. Whether a population of two or two hundred, she is compelled to document their interactions. Her work is published by *Surprised by Joy* (Wising Up Press), *Fiction Southeast, Evening Street Review,* and *HerStry, Milwaukee Journal Sentinel.*

Sharon Hilberer grew up in Pittsburgh, Pennsylvania and lived in Ohio, California, and North Dakota before taking up residence in Minnesota to teach English as a Second Language in the Minneapolis Public Schools. A language geek from the get-go, her poems grow out of current events, overheard and remembered conversations, and from listening to the natural world.

Gaye D. Holman, a retired sociology professor, taught in Louisville-area prisons where she coordinated her school's prison program. Her book, *Decades Behind Bars: A Twenty-Year Conversation with Men in America's Prisons* (McFarland, 2017), is a result of her work with long-term incarcerated men. Her prison writings have been featured in *LEO Weekly* and *Motif: Seeking Its Own Level* (Motes Books).

Susan Martell Huebner's poetry has appeared in print anthologies and journals as well as in online venues. Finishing Line Press published *Reality Changes With the Willy-Nilly Wind*. Both the poetry chapbook as well as her literary fiction novel, *She Thought the Door Was Locked*, are available on Amazon.

Daniel M. Jaffe is an award-winning fiction writer whose short stories and personal essays have appeared in dozens of literary journals and anthologies. He is author of the novels *Yeled Tov*, *The Genealogy of Understanding*, and *The Limits of Pleasure*, as well as the collection, *Jewish Gentle and Other Stories of Gay-Jewish Living*.

Mimi Jennings taught French in Detroit and Saint Paul, English in France, dharma in prisons. She has received both Fulbright and NEH (2) grants as well as first place awards (*Bugle* 2019, Banfill-Locke 2018, Saint Catherine University 2012). Publications include *Martin Lake, Negative Capability, Persimmon Tree, Red Bird, Silkworm11, Sleet*. She circulates semi-assiduously her two poetry collections; favors rap, sonnets, family, enigma; gets that all are kin.

Murali Kamma's debut collection, *Not Native: Short Stories of Immigrant Life in an In-Between World*, was recently published by Wising Up Press. His stories have appeared in numerous publications, including *Rosebud, South Asian Review* and prior Wising Up anthologies. As the managing editor of Atlanta-based *Khabar* magazine, he has interviewed Salman Rushdie, Anita Desai and William Dalrymple, among others. He did his studies at Loyola College in India and the State University of New York at Buffalo.

Laurie Klein is the author of *Where the Sky Opens* and *Bodies of Water, Bodies of Flesh*. A Pushcart nominee and winner of the Thomas Merton Prize, her work has been heard on NPR and has appeared in *The Southern Review, New Letters, MAR, Barrow Street, The Pedestal*, and *River of Earth and Sky: Poems for the 21ˢᵗ Century*.

Lori Levy's poems have appeared in *Rattle, Nimrod International Journal, Paterson Literary Review*, and numerous other literary journals in the U.S., the U.K., and Israel, where she lived for sixteen years. Her work has also been published in medical humanities journals, including a hybrid (poetry/prose) piece she co-authored with her father, a physician. She lives in Los Angeles.

Chuck Madansky is the grandfather of six and lives by a pond in Brewster, Massachusetts. His poetry has been published in *The Cape Cod Poetry Review*, *Pure Slush* and several anthologies. Chuck has also been featured on Poetry Sunday, a production of the local NPR station. He lives with his wife, poet and playwright Wilderness Sarchild, and their dog Ruby.

Beth McKim grew up in Alabama and now lives in Houston with her husband and their Labradoodle, Lucy. Beth is an actress as well as a writer. Her poems, essays, and short stories appear regularly in niche publications and anthologies, including *Siblings* (Wising Up Press). Beth longingly remembers times when politics could be discussed civilly and with love and respect for different points of view.

Monica Mische teaches literature and writing at Montgomery College. She lives with her family in Greenbelt, Maryland where she has been active in social justice and youth outreach programs. She has essays forthcoming in *JAEPL*, *Pedagogy*, and the anthology *Deep Beauty*.

Sharon Lask Munson grew up in Detroit, Michigan. She taught school in England, Germany, Okinawa, and Puerto Rico before driving her blue Oldsmobile to Anchorage, Alaska where she taught for the next twenty years. She is the author of two chapbooks, *Stillness Settles Down the Lane* and *Braiding Lives,* a finalist in the Poetica Publishing chapbook contest. She has two full-length books, *That Certain Blue* and *The Weight of Snow*. She lives and writes in Eugene, Oregon.

Marianne Peel is now nurturing her own creative spirit after having taught middle and high school English for thirty-two years. She has spent three summers in Guizhou Province, teaching best practices to teachers in China. She received Fulbright-Hays Awards to Nepal (2003) and Turkey (2009). Marianne participated in Marge Piercy's Juried Intensive Poetry Workshop (2016). Her poetry appears in *Muddy River Poetry Review, Belle Reve Literary Journal, Jelly Bucket Journal,* among others. She has a collection of poetry forthcoming in 2020 from Shadelandhouse Modern Press.

Ada Jill Schneider, winner of the National Galway Kinnell Poetry Prize, is the author of four volumes of poetry including her most recent, *This Once-Only World*. She directs "The Pleasure of Poetry," a program she founded, at the Somerset Public Library in Massachusetts. Ada has an MFA in Writing from Vermont College.

Patty Somlo's books, *Hairway to Heaven Stories* (Cherry Castle Publishing), *The First to Disappear* (Spuyten Duyvil) and *Even When Trapped Behind Clouds: A Memoir of Quiet Grace* (WiDo Publishing), have been finalists in the International Book, Best Book, National Indie Excellence, American Fiction and Reader Views Literary Awards. *From Here to There* is forthcoming from Adelaide Books in August 2019.

J. J. Steinfeld is a Canadian fiction writer/poet/playwright living on Prince Edward Island. He has published nineteen books, including *Identity Dreams and Memory Sounds* (poetry, Ekstasis Editions, 2014), *Madhouses in Heaven, Castles in Hell* (stories, Ekstasis Editions, 2015), *An Unauthorized Biography of Being* (stories, Ekstasis Editions, 2016), *Absurdity, Woe Is Me, Glory Be* (poetry, Guernica Editions, 2017), and *A Visit to the Kafka Café* (poetry, Ekstasis Editions, 2018).

Kelly Talbot has edited books and other content for more than twenty years for John Wiley and Sons, Macmillan, Pearson Education, Oxford, and other publishers. His writing has appeared in dozens of magazines and anthologies. He divides his time between Indianapolis, Indiana, and Timisoara, Romania.

Lucia Talenti is a quiet writer in a noisy world. Parent, spouse, caregiver, educator, she believes that every person has the power to make a positive difference in the world.

Loretta Diane Walker, a multiple Pushcart nominee, and Best of the Net nominee, won the 2016 Phyllis Wheatley Book Award for poetry for her collection, *In This House* (Bluelight Press). She has published four collections of poetry. Her fifth collection, *Ode to My Mother's Voice and Other Poems,* is forthcoming in 2019 from Lamar University Literary Press.

Tyree Wilson lives in Ohio.

EDITORS/PUBLISHERS

HEATHER TOSTESON is the author of seven books of fiction, poetry and non-fiction, including most recently the novel *The Philosophical Transactions of Maria van Leeuwenhoek, Antoni's Dochter*. She has worked in health communications with a focus on communication across disciplines, racism, social trust, and how belief systems develop and change. She has an MFA (UNC-Greensboro) and PhD in English and Creative Writing (Ohio University).

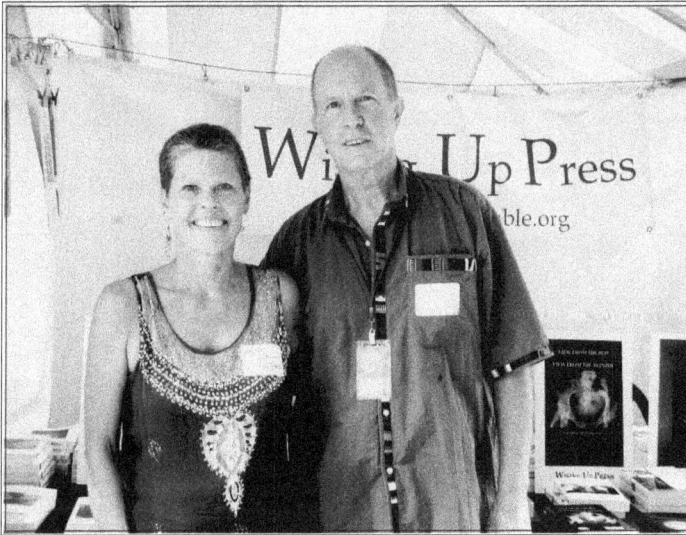

CHARLES BROCKETT has a PhD from UNC-Chapel Hill and is a recipient of several Fulbright and National Endowment for the Humanities awards. A retired political science professor, he has written two well-received books on Central America and numerous social science journal articles and book chapters. With Heather Tosteson, he is co-founder of Universal Table and Wising Up Press and co-editor of the Wising Up Anthologies.

Visit our website and learn about our other publications,
our readers guides, and calls for submissions.

www.universaltable.org
wisingup@universaltable.org

P.O. Box 2122
Decatur, GA 30031-2122

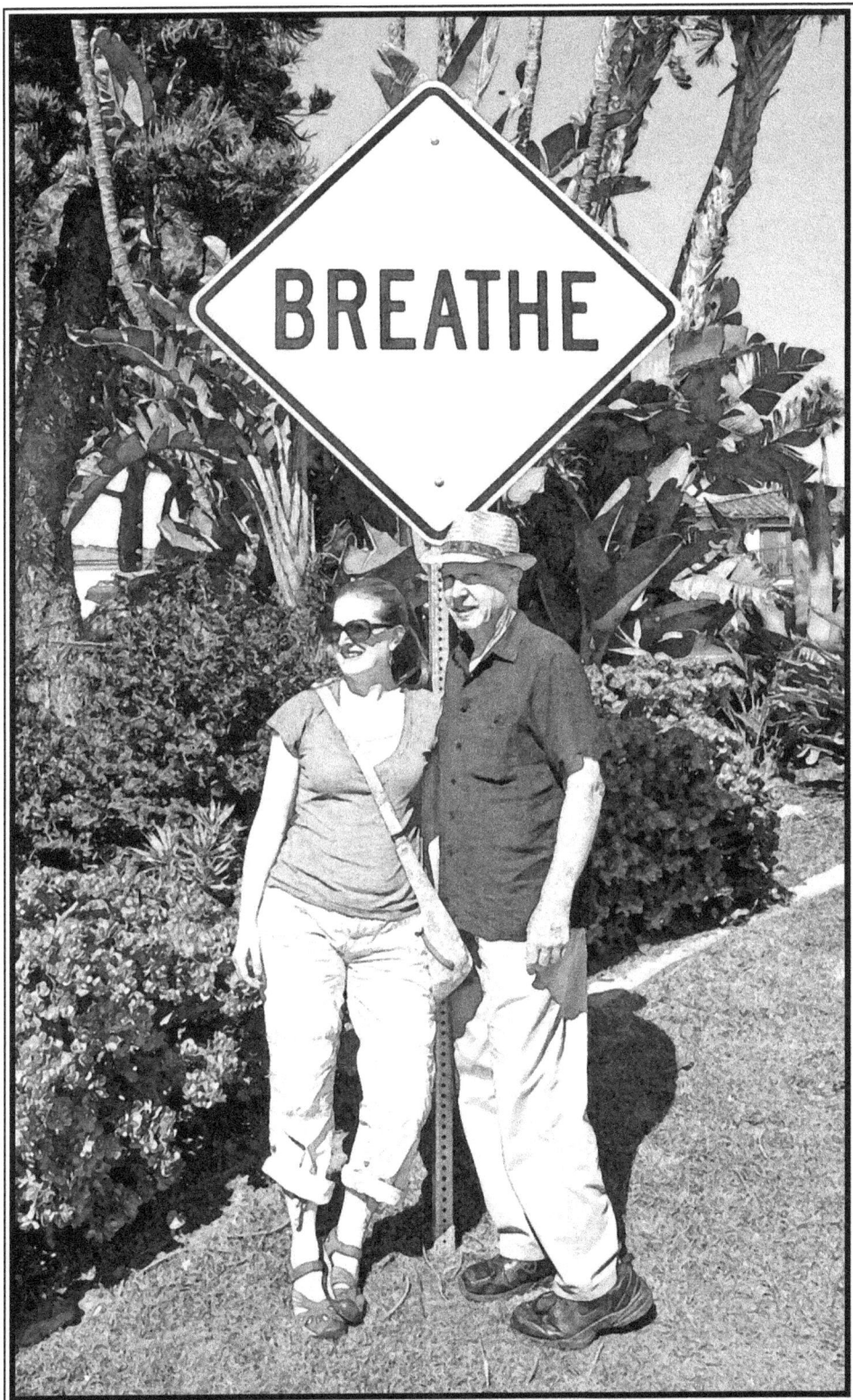

www.ingramcontent.com/pod-product-compliance
Lightning Source LLC
Chambersburg PA
CBHW031425270326
41930CB00007B/580